The 8 GREAT DEBATES of BIBLE PROPHECY

RON RHODES

HARVEST HOUSE PUBLISHERS
EUGENE, OREGON

Except where noted, Scripture quotations are from The ESV® Bible (The Holy Bible, English Standard Version®), copyright © 2001 by Crossway, a publishing ministry of Good News Publishers. Used by permission. All rights reserved.

Verses marked NASB are taken from the New American Standard Bible®, © 1960, 1962, 1963, 1968, 1971, 1972, 1973, 1975, 1977, 1995 by The Lockman Foundation. Used by permission. (www.Lockman.org)

Verses marked NKJV are taken from the New King James Version®. Copyright © 1982 by Thomas Nelson, Inc. Used by permission. All rights reserved.

Verses marked KJV are taken from the King James Version of the Bible.

Cover by Dugan Design Group, Bloomington, Minnesota

Cover photo © dell / Fotolia

THE 8 GREAT DEBATES OF BIBLE PROPHECY
Copyright © 2014 by Ron Rhodes
Published by Harvest House Publishers
Eugene, Oregon 97402
www.harvesthousepublishers.com

Library of Congress Cataloging-in-Publication Data
Rhodes, Ron.
The 8 great debates of Bible prophecy / Ron Rhodes.
    pages cm
Includes bibliographical references.
ISBN 978-0-7369-4426-7 (pbk.)
ISBN 978-0-7369-4427-4 (eBook)
1. Eschatology. 2. Bible—Prophecies. I. Title. II. Title: Eight great debates of Bible prophecy.
BT821.3.R46 2014
236'.9—dc23
                                                            2013045508

All rights reserved. No part of this publication may be reproduced, stored in a retrieval system, or transmitted in any form or by any means—electronic, mechanical, digital, photocopy, recording, or any other—except for brief quotations in printed reviews, without the prior permission of the publisher.

Printed in the United States of America

14 15 16 17 18 19 20 21 22 / VP-CD / 10 9 8 7 6 5 4 3 2 1

In loving memory of Tom, Alpha, and Paul—
"Away from the body and at home with the Lord"
2 Corinthians 5:8

Acknowledgments

Few books are solo efforts. As any author will tell you, most books involve a lot of work not only by the author but also by countless other individuals. A book is shaped by the author's personal interactions with his family, friends, and professional colleagues, as well as by folks at church, readers, conference attendees, and of course, the many members of the publishing team. The more books I write, the more I sense my indebtedness to countless individuals in all these areas and more.

My desire is to thank everyone I can think of, but space limitations allow me to single out only a few. I remain forever thankful for my family—my wife, Kerri, and my two grown children, David and Kylie. I am grateful to Harvest House Publishers, whose staff is brimming with committed Christians who are true professionals at what they do. Most of all, I express profound thanks and appreciation to our Lord Jesus Christ, who Himself is the heart and center of biblical prophecy. May He be glorified in this book!

Contents

Introduction

Debating Bible Prophecy

Bible prophecy enthusiasts come in many varieties. Regarding the millennial kingdom, there are premillennialists, amillennialists, and postmillennialists. On the issue of the rapture, there are pretribulationists, midtribulationists, and posttribulationists. Other Christians hold to the partial-rapture theory, and still others hold to the pre-wrath view. Some Christians are dispensationalists while others are in the covenant theology camp. Even within the dispensational camp, we have traditional dispensationalists, revised dispensationalists, and progressive dispensationalists. Likewise, within the covenant theology camp are those who subscribe to the classical covenant view and those who subscribe to the modified covenant view. No wonder many Christians are more than a little confused about some of the finer points of Bible prophecy.

We Christians have our own unique terminology (appropriately called *Christianeze*), and we love to debate and sometimes argue about our various prophetic views. Honesty compels us to admit that in many cases we tend to generate more heat than light when discussing our prophetic differences.

I wrote this book to help Christians understand the biblical backdrop to these various views on prophecy. A book like this provides a number of benefits.

- After reading it, you will no doubt better understand why you believe what you believe about Bible prophecy. You will strengthen your personal convictions about Bible prophecy.

- You will likely come to appreciate the fact that those who hold to a different position than you do still believe the Bible, just as you do. They just interpret it differently.

- On each of the eight great debates of Bible prophecy, I'll tell you what my personal position is and why. If you end up agreeing with me, great. If you end up disagreeing with me, that's okay too. My only exhortation is that you prioritize "rightly handling the word of truth" (2 Timothy 2:15). After all, our commitment is to the Bible, not to a man-made system of theology.

- Through the process, I hope we will all learn to agree to disagree in an agreeable way on issues where we differ. Perhaps we will become skilled at generating more light than heat!

In Nonessentials, Liberty

I believe that Bible prophecy is an important component in the broader field of biblical studies. Of the 23,210 verses in the Old Testament, 6,641 are prophetic. (That's about 28.5 percent.) And of the 7,914 verses in the New Testament, 1,711 are prophetic. (About 21.5 percent.) Merging the Old and New Testaments together, 8,352 of its 31,124 verses are prophetic. That means prophecy makes up 27 percent of the Bible—more than one-fourth. That alone should motivate us to study prophecy and form some conclusions, always treating each other in a Christlike way when we disagree.

I love the way my late colleague Walter Martin handled this. He hired me in the 1990s to work at the Christian Research Institute. He interviewed me for more than an hour. We talked about areas of agreement (of which there were many) as well as areas of disagreement. The timing of the rapture was one of those areas of disagreement.

Once the interview was over, Walter came around from the desk and gave me a big bear hug (he was famous for doing that). He hired me despite the fact that he was a posttrib and I was a pretrib. We treated each other in a Christ-honoring way despite minor differences in our prophetic views. Of course, we agreed on all the big issues—the nature of God, the deity of Christ, the gospel of salvation, and the like. So in the scheme of things, our difference on the timing of the rapture was a relatively minor issue.

Both Walter and I had long been proponents of the venerable dictum "In essentials, unity; in nonessentials, liberty; in all things, charity." This is a great dictum to keep in mind as we explore the various Christian views of Bible prophecy.

How This Book Is Organized

This book deals with eight great debates in Bible prophecy. Each part of this book focuses on one debate and contains a few concise chapters that describe the various views Christians have held on that issue.

You will notice that there are 27 chapters divided among the eight primary debate topics. This means that some of the debates involve discussions on a number of subtopics. As you might expect, a book with 27 chapters must necessarily be selective regarding the content of each chapter. Brevity is the rule. Because of space constraints, I paint in broad strokes so you can see the big picture of each issue without getting buried in unnecessary details. My prayerful goal is for this book to be concise and user friendly, brimming with helpful information while avoiding tedious theological details that are more appropriate for the seminary classroom.

So if you're ready, strap on your seatbelt, and let's begin our prophetic journey. We have a lot to explore.

> *Father, we pray that You would enlighten the eyes of our understanding as we study the important issue of Bible prophecy. Help us to gain clarity on the various views, and enable us to anchor ourselves in what we believe to be the correct position. Teach us to rightly handle the word of truth.*

We ask also that You would help us to respond to those who hold to different views in Christ-honoring ways. Help us to understand that we can personally come to rock-solid conclusions on issues related to Bible prophecy while flavoring our words with grace and charity toward those who disagree. Through it all, Lord, help us to have humble and teachable spirits. In Jesus's name, amen.

Should Prophecy Be Interpreted Literally or Allegorically?

The Hermeneutics of Bible Prophecy: Literal or Allegorical?

Should prophetic verses be interpreted allegorically or literally? This is a foundational question. Obviously one's response will affect one's entire eschatology, so this is the place to consider this question.

Viewpoint 1: Prophecy Should Be Interpreted Allegorically

Early in the history of the Christian church (around AD 190), an allegorical school of prophetic interpretation arose in Alexandria, Egypt. In this school, Scripture was consistently interpreted in a nonliteral sense. Hidden, symbolic meanings were sought. The emergence of this allegorical school of interpretation led to the rise of amillennialism in the early church. According to this view, the prophecy in Revelation 20 regarding the millennial kingdom should not be interpreted as a literal 1000-year reign of Christ on earth. Rather, it refers to Christ's present spiritual rule over the church from heaven.

The grammatical-historical (literal) approach to Scripture was largely regained by the Church Fathers in the second and third centuries. Nevertheless, premillennialism, which is based on a literal interpretation of prophecy and holds to a literal 1000-year reign of Christ on earth, eventually fell by the wayside. North Africa, in particular, emerged as a hotbed of Alexandrian allegorization.[1]

This early emergence of the allegorical method had enormous influence on subsequent generations. The great theologian Augustine adopted the point of view that Scripture, with the exception of prophecy, should be interpreted naturally and literally. Even regarding prophecy, however, Augustine was inconsistent. He accepted a literal second coming of Christ as well as a literal heaven and hell, but he concluded that prophecies of a future millennial kingdom would not be literally fulfilled. He believed that to take these passages literally, one would have to conclude that people in the millennial kingdom would regularly engage in excessive feasting, which he viewed as carnal and unworthy of believers. He concluded that the church was already living in the millennium as part of the spiritual kingdom of God. Indeed, he believed that Christ is even now reigning in the hearts of Christians.

Augustine's view became the dominant view of the Roman Catholic Church. Reformation luminaries, such as Martin Luther and John Calvin, also adopted his view. Because such well-known theologians in church history interpreted millennial prophecies allegorically, many today have adopted the same view. In fact, some today apply the allegorical method not only to the millennium but also to other aspects of biblical prophecy.

Whether one interprets prophecy allegorically or literally will determine how one answers many questions related to biblical prophecy.

- Will the millennial kingdom be a literal 1000-year reign of Jesus Christ on earth, or does this refer to the present spiritual reign of Christ from heaven?

- Will the covenant promises made to Israel in Old Testament times (the Abrahamic and Davidic covenants) be literally fulfilled in Israel, or will they be spiritually and allegorically fulfilled in the church?

- Are the various judgments referred to in prophetic Scripture (such as the judgment seat of Christ for Christians, the judgment of the nations following Christ's return, and the great white throne judgment for unbelievers following the millennium) separate and distinct judgments (as a literal interpretation would indicate), or do these various terms describe one general judgment at the end of the age (as per an allegorical interpretation)?

- Are the various resurrections in prophetic Scripture (the rapture, the first resurrection, the second resurrection, and the like) distinct resurrections (the literal view), or do these various terms refer to one general resurrection at the end of the age (the allegorical view)?

Amillennialists, who use the allegorical method, concede that if one interprets Bible prophecy literally, one will indeed end up believing in distinct judgments, distinct resurrections, a fulfillment of the Abrahamic and Davidic covenants for Israel, and a literal 1000-year reign of Christ on earth. For example, amillennialist Floyd Hamilton affirms that "we must frankly admit that a literal interpretation of the Old Testament prophecies gives us just such a picture of an earthly reign of the Messiah as the premillennialist pictures."[2]

Obviously one's choice of an interpretive method is of enormous importance. One should therefore weigh this debate very carefully. I will present the case for a literal interpretation of prophecy, which I believe to be the correct view.

Viewpoint 2: Prophecy Should Be Interpreted Literally

The word *literal* as used in hermeneutics (the science of interpretation) comes from the Latin *sensus literalis*, which refers to seeking a literal sense of the text as opposed to a nonliteral or allegorical sense of it. It refers to the understanding of a text that any person of normal intelligence would get without using any special keys or codes.

Another way to describe the literal approach to Scripture is that it embraces the normal, everyday, common understanding of words. Words are given the meaning they normally have in common communication. It is the basic normal or plain way of interpreting a passage.

Having said this, I want to briefly address three key qualifications.

The literal method does not eliminate figures of speech. When the Bible speaks of the eye, arms, or wings of God (Psalm 34:15; Isaiah 51:9; Psalm 91:4), these should not be taken literally. God does not really have these physical features—He is pure spirit (John 4:24). Likewise, He cannot literally be a rock (Psalm 42:9), which is material. But we would not know what is *not* literally true of God unless we first know what *is* literally true.

For example, if it were not literally true that God is pure spirit and infinite, we would not be able to say that certain things attributed to God elsewhere in the Bible are not literally true—such as materiality and finitude. When Jesus said "I am the true vine" (John 15:1), the literal method of interpretation does not take this as physically true. Rather, we understand this as a figure of speech, telling us that believers derive their spiritual life from Christ, our spiritual vine. Understanding this is important because prophetic apocalyptic literature—such as the books of Daniel and Revelation—make heavy use of figures of speech.

Determining when a passage should and should not be taken literally may sometimes be difficult. But certain guidelines help us make this determination. Briefly, a text should be taken figuratively when…

- it is obviously figurative, as when Jesus said He is the door (John 10:9);
- the text itself authorizes the figurative sense, as when Paul said he was interpreting Scripture allegorically (Galatians 4:24); or
- when a literal interpretation would contradict other truths inside or outside the Bible, such as when the Bible speaks of the "four corners of the earth" (Revelation 7:1).

Bible expositor David Cooper suggests that we ought to "take every word at its primary, ordinary, usual, literal meaning, unless the facts of the immediate context, studied in the light of related passages and axiomatic and fundamental truths, indicate clearly otherwise."[3]

The literal method does not eliminate the use of symbols. The Bible is filled with symbols. But each symbol is emblematic of something literal. For example, the book of Revelation contains many symbols that represent literal things. John said the seven stars in Christ's right hand were "the angels of [messengers to] the seven churches," and the seven lampstands were the seven churches (Revelation 1:20). He saw the prayers of the saints as bowls full of incense (5:8), and the "peoples and multitudes and nations and languages" appeared as waters (17:15). Clearly then, each symbol represents something literal. Textual clues often point us to the literal truth found in a symbol—either in the immediate context or in the broader context of the whole of Scripture.

The literal method does not eliminate the use of parables. Jesus often used parables that are not to be taken literally. Yet parables always convey a literal point. Jesus wanted His parables to be clear to those who were receptive—He carefully interpreted the parables of the sower (Matthew 13:3-9) and the tares (verses 24-30) for the disciples. He did this not only so their correct meaning would be clear but also to teach believers how to properly interpret the other parables. Christ did not interpret His subsequent parables because He fully expected believers to follow the method He demonstrated and understand the parables' literal truths.

Six Good Reasons to Take a Literal Approach

I can think of at least six good reasons for adopting a literal interpretation of Scripture, including biblical prophecy.

1. A literal interpretation is the normal approach in all languages.
2. The greater part of the Bible makes good sense when taken literally.
3. A literal approach allows for allegorical or symbolic meanings when indicated in the context, as is often the case

in such apocalyptic literature as the books of Daniel and Revelation.

4. As noted previously, all allegorical or symbolic meanings actually depend on the literal meaning. In other words, we would not know what is *not* literally true unless we first know what *is* literally true.

5. The literal method is the only sane and safe check on our subjective imaginations.

6. The literal method is the only approach that is consistently in line with the nature of inspiration—the idea that the very words of Scripture are God-breathed. By contrast, "The system of spiritualizing Scripture is a tacit denial of the doctrine of the verbal, plenary inspiration of the Scriptures."[4]

A Literal Approach Is Confirmed in the Biblical Text

The biblical text provides a number of confirmations of the literal hermeneutic. For example, later biblical texts interpret earlier ones literally, as when the creation events in Genesis 1–2 are taken literally by later books (see Exodus 20:10-11). This is likewise the case regarding the creation of Adam and Eve (Matthew 19:6; 1 Timothy 2:13), the fall of Adam and his resulting death (Romans 5:12-14), Noah's flood (Matthew 24:38), and the accounts of Jonah (Matthew 12:40-42), Moses (1 Corinthians 10:2-4,11), and numerous other historical figures.

Further, more than a hundred predictions about the Messiah were literally fulfilled in Jesus's first coming, including that He would be...

> from the seed of a woman (Genesis 3:15)
> from the line of Seth (Genesis 4:25)
> a descendent of Shem (Genesis 9:26)
> the offspring of Abraham (Genesis 12:3)
> from the tribe of Judah (Genesis 49:10)
> the Son of David (Jeremiah 23:5-6)
> conceived of a virgin (Isaiah 7:14)

born in Bethlehem (Micah 5:2)
heralded as the Messiah (Isaiah 40:3)
the coming King (Zechariah 9:9)
the sacrificial offering for our sins (Isaiah 53)
pierced in His side at the cross (Zechariah 12:10)
killed about AD 33 (Daniel 9:24-25)
resurrected from the dead (Psalm 16:11)

Theologian Charles C. Ryrie is spot-on in his assessment:

> In the interpretation of unfulfilled prophecy, fulfilled prophecy forms the pattern…The logical way to discover how God will fulfill prophecy in the future is to discover how He fulfilled it in the past. If the hundreds of prophecies concerning Christ's first coming were fulfilled literally, how can anyone reject the literal fulfillment of the numerous prophecies concerning His second coming and reign on the earth?[5]

We may therefore expect that the prophecies of the end times will be fulfilled just as literally as the prophecies of the first coming of Christ. Theologian Charles Feinberg summarizes the point this way:

> Take the words of Gabriel in the first chapter of Luke where he foretells of the birth of Christ. According to the angel's words Mary literally conceived in her womb; literally brought forth a son; His name was literally called Jesus; He was literally great; and He was literally called the Son of the Highest. Will it not be as literally fulfilled that God will yet give to Christ the throne of His father David, that He will reign over the house of Jacob forever, and that of His glorious kingdom there shall be no end?[6]

I want to briefly make a few other observations before closing. First, by specifically indicating in the text the presence of parables (see Matthew 13:3) or an allegory (Galatians 4:24), the Bible thereby indicates that the ordinary meaning is a literal one. And by interpreting a parable,

Jesus revealed that parables have a literal meaning behind them (Matthew 13:18-23).

Second, notice that by rebuking those who did not interpret the resurrection literally, Jesus indicated that the literal interpretation of the Old Testament was the correct one (Matthew 22:29-32). We might say that Jesus's use of Scripture constitutes one of the most convincing evidences that Scripture ought to be interpreted literally.

Clearly then, our best approach in understanding God's prophetic revelation is to use a literal approach. This is the only approach that yields the intended meaning of the biblical author, which is the only true meaning.

Conclusion

Those who hold to an allegorical method of Bible interpretation come up with different meanings of a passage of Scripture. They end up disagreeing not only with premillennialists (who take a literal approach) but also with each other. Of course, this is what one would expect of an allegorical method. We cannot expect objective consistency among those who use a subjective methodology.

2

Covenant Theology Versus Dispensationalism

In chapter 1, I addressed the debate over literal versus allegorical interpretation of Bible prophecy. Various interpretive schools of thought have emerged along a spectrum that spans from literalism to allegory. I will very briefly address five primary schools of thought:

> traditional dispensationalism,
> revised dispensationalism,
> progressive dispensationalism,
> classical covenantalism, and
> modified covenantalism.

These terms may sound strange, but hang with me. We will focus on the big picture, and it will all make sense to you soon.

These approaches agree in many of the major areas of biblical doctrine. The reason for this is that all five use a rather literal hermeneutic when it comes to such doctrines as God, Jesus, the Holy Spirit, the Trinity, salvation by grace through faith, and the like. When it comes to biblical prophecy, however, some take a literal approach, and others take more figurative approaches.

All five groups participate in the debate over literal versus allegorical interpretation. As well, they all debate over whether Israel is distinct from the church. This book has separate chapters on both of these issues, so in this chapter I will address them only briefly as I describe the five schools of thought.

Traditional Dispensationalism

Dispensationalism is a system of theology that is characterized by (1) a consistent literal method of interpreting the Bible, (2) a clear distinction between Israel and the church, and (3) the glory of God as God's ultimate purpose in the world. The word *dispensation*—from the Greek *oikonomia* (meaning "stewardship")—refers to a distinguishable economy in the outworking of God's purpose.

This system of theology views the world as a household run by God. In this household, God delegates duties and assigns humankind certain responsibilities. If people obey God during that dispensation, God promises blessing. If people disobey, He promises judgment. In each dispensation, we generally see the testing of humankind, the failure of humankind, and judgment as a consequence. As things unfold, God provides progressive revelation of His plan for history.

Traditional dispensationalism identifies seven dispensations.

1. *The dispensation of innocence (Genesis 1:28–3:6).* This dispensation relates to Adam and Eve up until the time they fell into sin at the Fall.

2. *The dispensation of conscience (Genesis 3:7–8:14).* This dispensation includes the time between the Fall and the flood (see Romans 2:15).

3. *The dispensation of human government (Genesis 8:15–11:9).* Following the flood, God began a new dispensation when He instituted human government to mediate and restrain evil on the earth.

4. *The dispensation of promise (Genesis 11:10–Exodus 18:27).* This dispensation relates to God's call of Abraham and the specific promises God made to him and his descendants, both physical and spiritual.

5. *The dispensation of law (Israel) (Exodus 19–John 14:30).* This dispensation is characterized by God's giving of the law to Israel as a guide to live by, governing every aspect of their lives. Note that the law was not presented as a means of salvation. Note also that the law was temporary, lasting only until Christ came and fulfilled it.

6. *The dispensation of grace (the church) (Acts 2:1–Revelation 19:21).* In this dispensation, the rule of life in the church is grace.

7. *The dispensation of the kingdom (Revelation 20:1-16).* This dispensation relates to Christ's future millennial kingdom, over which He will rule for 1000 years on the throne of David. The church will rule with Christ as His bride.

Traditional dispensationalism is represented in the writings of John Nelson Darby (1800–1882) and C.I. Scofield (1843–1921).[1] This system utilizes a literal hermeneutic in interpreting Bible prophecy, and it distinguishes between the church and Israel, so it espouses a literal fulfillment of the various covenants for Israel (the Abrahamic, Davidic, and new covenants). A distinguishing characteristic of this viewpoint is that it recognizes two new covenants—one for Israel (yet to be fulfilled) and one for the church (presently being fulfilled). Some Bible verses are viewed as referring to a new covenant for the church (such as Hebrews 8:6; 9:15; 10:29; 13:20), and other Bible verses are viewed as referring to a new covenant for Israel (for example, Hebrews 8:7-13; 10:16). In this view, Israel and the church are seen as two separate peoples with different destinies—one in heaven (the church) and the other on earth (Israel).

Revised Dispensationalism

Revised dispensationalism, represented in the writings of John F. Walvoord (1910–2002) and Charles C. Ryrie (born 1925), also utilizes a literal hermeneutic in interpreting Bible prophecy.[2] It thus espouses a literal fulfillment of the Old Testament covenants for Israel. Unlike traditional dispensationalism, however, this view holds that there is only one new covenant, which has a present application to the church and a later literal fulfillment in national Israel.

Even though revised dispensationalism recognizes distinctions between Israel and the church, both are viewed as collectively composing one people of God who share in the spiritual redemption wrought by Christ. Traditional and revised dispensationalism have much in common, but these finer points about Israel and the church are important components in the growth of dispensationalism. This revised dispensationalism has been taught in many dispensational seminaries, though some more recently have opted for progressive dispensationalism.

Progressive Dispensationalism

Progressive dispensationalism—represented in the writings of Robert Saucy (born 1930), Craig Blaising (born 1949), and Darrell Bock (born 1953)—is open to some figurative interpretation of Bible prophecy.[3] This form of dispensationalism takes a step in the direction of covenant theology (discussed later in this chapter) by rejecting the idea of a fixed objective meaning of the biblical text. Rather, it holds that there are many meanings in a biblical text and that we ought to seek a deeper understanding than the author's expressed meaning. Craig Blaising and Darrell Bock espouse what they call a "complementary hermeneutic." As prophecy expert Thomas Ice explains it, "Complementary hermeneutics appears to be a synthesis of the two older approaches which have battled each other for years—the spiritual and literal approaches—in their handling of how the New Testament uses the Old Testament."[4]

This view suggests that there will be a literal fulfillment of the Abrahamic, Davidic, and new covenants in ethnic Israel, but it also finds a present inaugural fulfillment of these various covenants in the church. It holds that the fulfillment of the Davidic covenant began when Christ ascended to God's right hand. Robert Saucy, as a case in point, interprets Psalm 110 to say that the Son of David reigns on two thrones—one in heaven (now) and one on earth (later, during the millennium).[5] Likewise, Darrel Bock believes the kingdom is both present and future at the same time. Thus, the current church age is not entirely distinct from the future kingdom. Instead, our current age involves the invisible kingdom rule of Jesus.

This is where the word *progressive* comes into the picture. Progressive dispensationalists "are using the word 'progressive' to refer to a progressive fulfillment of God's plan in history. They see a progressive relationship of past and present dispensations as well as between the present and future dispensations."[6]

Like covenant theologians, progressive dispensationalists stress that there is one people of God, and they embrace a hermeneutic that reads the Old Testament promises to Israel in the light of their inaugural fulfillment in Christ and His church. This represents quite a departure from both traditional and revised dispensationalism.

Here are a few of the more significant criticisms of progressive dispensationalism.

- Those who approach prophecy with an openness to figurative interpretations are being inconsistent, for they approach the rest of Scripture literally. This explains why traditional and revised dispensationalists agree with progressive dispensationalists on other aspects of doctrine but disagree on prophecy. Approaching the whole of Scripture with one literal hermeneutic makes more sense.

- Traditional and revised dispensationalists note that there are no objective criteria by which one can determine an alleged figurative meaning. Allegory is far too subjective. Five different people might come up with five different figurative interpretations of the same passage of Scripture. A literal approach is much more objective and consistent.

- The prophecies of the first coming of Jesus Christ set a precedent for interpreting all Bible prophecy. On pages 18-19 I listed several of the more than 100 messianic prophecies that

Christ fulfilled literally in His first coming. Likewise, the prophecies relating to His second coming (and the events before and after it) will be fulfilled literally as well.

- The multileveled approach that progressive dispensationalists use—for example, interpreting Psalm 110 to say that Christ rules from heaven now and will rule on the earth during the millennial kingdom—is untenable. This represents an alteration of the psalmist's intended textual meaning and constitutes a form of eisegesis (reading a meaning into the text).

- Because of its obvious close connections with covenant theology, one wonders if progressive dispensationalists will soon join the covenant camp. This is something of great concern to traditional and revised dispensationalists.

The Classical Covenantal View

In the classical covenantal view—represented in the writings of Johannes Cocceius (1603–1669), Charles Hodge (1797–1878), Oswald Allis (1880–1973), and many in the Reformed camp—a strict literal interpretation of prophetic Scripture is rejected.[7] This means that dispensational interpretations (with the possible exception of some aspects of progressive dispensationalism) are outright rejected.

Covenant theology is built on two primary features—the covenant of works and the covenant of grace. According to covenant theologians, God entered into a covenant of works with Adam before the Fall. God promised eternal life for obedience. However, Adam failed, and in Adam, all humanity failed.

After the Fall, God entered into another covenant with Adam—the covenant of grace. In this covenant, God promised eternal life to all who would believe in Jesus Christ.

All of this is said to be based on the more foundational covenant of redemption, made in eternity past by the triune God, in which "the Father delegated the Son, who agreed to provide salvation for the world through His atoning death. The covenant of grace is understood as the application of the covenant of redemption and is thereby restricted to the elect."[8]

According to this school of thought, the Old Testament covenants made with Israel are fulfilled in the New Testament church, God's "spiritual Israel," rather than being literally fulfilled in national Israel. The millennium, instead of being a literal 1000-year reign of Christ on earth, is symbolic of the church age.

> Just as Christ is the fulfillment of Israel's sacrificial system, even so He is said to be the fulfillment of the Abrahamic and Davidic land- and throne-promises through which Messiah will have a political reign. Hence, believers should see the Old Testament promises to Israel through this spiritual lens, and they will thereby observe that the New Testament church is the spiritual Israel, a continuation of the Old Testament ethnic Israel. No future literal fulfillment of these Old Testament prophecies can be expected.[9]

Traditional and revised dispensationalists view this position as engaging in eisegesis (reading a meaning into the text) rather than exegesis (deriving the meaning out of the text). They charge that this position is not consistent in using the historical-grammatical method but rather interprets prophetic portions of Scripture figuratively. In other words, classical covenantalists use a literal historical-grammatical method to interpret the rest of Scripture (which is why they agree with dispensationalists on nonprophetic doctrines), but they interpret prophecy figuratively. Moreover, in this theological schema, the Old Testament is not interpreted in its own Old Testament context. Rather, the New Testament (and New Testament eschatology) is read back into these Old Testament texts. This is not a proper interpretive methodology.

The Modified Covenantal View

Like classical covenantalism, modified covenantalism, which is represented in the writings of Anthony Hoekema (1913–1988) and Vern

Poythress (born 1944), rejects a strict literal interpretation of biblical prophecy.[10] However, this viewpoint modifies things a bit by allowing for a future literal fulfillment of land and throne promises made to Israel (Genesis 12:7; 13:15; 15:18-21; 2 Samuel 7:12-16). These promises are initially fulfilled spiritually in the church, but Israel and the church will share in a more fully realized and literal fulfillment in the future. Most modified covenantalists believe the promises to Israel in the covenants will be fulfilled not in a literal 1000-year reign of Christ (the millennium) but rather in the new heaven and new earth.

Traditional and revised dispensationalists rebut that while modified covenantalists have taken a step in the right direction, ultimately their view is no less problematic, for it is constructed on the foundation of the same faulty hermeneutic. Instead of attempting to have a foot in both camps (covenantalism and dispensationalism), proponents of modified covenantalism would have been better off to have made a full transition into dispensationalism. At least then they would be using a consistent hermeneutic. A consistent use of the historical-grammatical method requires that the unconditional land and throne promises be literally fulfilled in Israel.

Even from the perspective of Jesus Christ Himself, the church was in no sense a continuation of Old Testament Israel but rather was viewed as an entity that was yet future from the time He spoke. He said "I *will* build my church" (Matthew 16:18; see also Ephesians 3:1-10). The church was inaugurated at the advent of the Holy Spirit on the day of Pentecost (Acts 2:1-12; 1 Corinthians 12:13). This is why Paul continued to distinguish the church from Israel in 1 Corinthians 10:32. This is also why the church was categorized as a new creation of God (2 Corinthians 5:17). In keeping with this distinction, the apostle Paul was clear that national Israel will be restored before Christ returns (Romans 11:1-2,29). Both classical and modified covenantalism fail to take account the whole teaching of Scripture on the church and Israel.

Conclusion

Certainly much more could be said in describing and critiquing these various schools of thought. The above is sufficient, however, to illustrate their similarities and differences. Having examined all the data, I find myself in strong agreement with revised dispensationalism. This viewpoint consistently interprets biblical prophecy literally, it distinguishes between the church and Israel, and it recognizes a single new covenant that is for both the church and Israel.

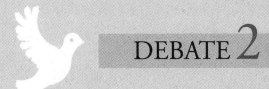

DEBATE 2

Are Israel and the Church Distinct in Bible Prophecy?

The Case for the Church Replacing Israel

Will God's promises to Israel in the Old Testament covenants be fulfilled literally by Israel or figuratively by the church? As we saw in the previous chapter, some interpreters—such as mainstream dispensationalists—believe that all the promises made to Israel will be fulfilled by Israel. Others, such as covenantalists, believe that the church is the new Israel and therefore all Old Testament promises made to Israel will be fulfilled in the church. This latter view is appropriately called replacement theology. I will summarize the primary supportive evidence for this view.

Replacement Theology

Those who subscribe to replacement theology believe the church replaces Israel as the recipient of God's promises and blessings. This view is also known as supersessionism because the Christian church is said to have superseded Israel in God's plan.

European scholar Ronald Diprose defines this system of theology this way: "The Church completely and permanently replaced ethnic Israel in the working out of God's plan and as the recipient of Old Testament promises addressed to Israel."[1] Diprose does not support replacement theology, but Kenneth Gentry does. He asserts, "We believe that the international Church has superseded for all times national Israel as the institution for the administration of divine blessing to the world."[2] Gentry is convinced that "in the unfolding of the plan of God in history, the Christian Church is the very fruition of the redemptive purpose of God. As such, the multi-racial, international Church of Jesus Christ supersedes racial, national Israel as the focus of the kingdom of God."[3]

Gentry, like others in his theological camp, appeals to certain verses in the New Testament that he believes establish that the church is the new Israel. For example, he points to Galatians 6:16, where the church is called "the Israel of God." He notes that the church is called "Abraham's offspring" in Galatians 3:29. The church is likewise called "the circumcision" in Philippians 3:3. All these are Jewish terms. As well, both Jew and Gentile are now viewed as "one new man" (Ephesians 2:15).[4] Hans LaRondelle, in his book *The Israel of God in Prophecy*, reasoned that since the church is the seed of Abraham, and Israel is the seed of Abraham, the two entities—the church and Israel—must be one and the same.[5] In view of such New Testament statements, it seems clear that the church has replaced Israel as the recipient of God's promises and blessings.

Replacement proponents also point to Old Testament passages. Perhaps the most oft-cited is Joshua 21:43-45.

> Thus the LORD gave to Israel all the land that he swore to give to their fathers. And they took possession of it, and they settled there. And the LORD gave them rest on every side just as he had sworn to their fathers. Not one of all their enemies had withstood them, for the LORD had given all their enemies into their hands. Not one word of all the good promises that the LORD had made to the house of Israel had failed; all came to pass.

Replacement proponents reason that because this passage says God gave the Israelites the land, His obligation regarding the land promises to Israel have been completely fulfilled, and no future promises are yet to be fulfilled on the matter. After all, the text tells us that "not one word of all the good promises that the Lord had made to the house of Israel had failed; all came to pass." In view of this, replacement proponents assert that Israel's present possession of the land is not a fulfillment of biblical prophecy. After all, God's land promises to Israel were fulfilled in the past. Therefore, there is no such thing as "Israel in prophecy." Our focus today is solely on the church.

Christians throughout church history subscribed to this idea. For example, among the early church fathers, Justin Martyr (AD 100–165) commented that "the true spiritual Israel...are we who have been led to God through this crucified Christ."[6] Others include Hippolytus of Rome (died AD 235) and Tertullian (AD 160–220). Among the early commentators, Chrysostom identified the church with Israel.[7] During Reformation times, both John Calvin and Martin Luther supported this theology. More recently, well-known commentators such as William Hendriksen, R.C.H. Lenski, J.B. Lightfoot, Herman Ridderbox, and John R.W. Stott have supported this theological claim.

The Catholic Church has long taught that the promises made to Israel concerning its future blessings have been inherited by the church. When Zionism emerged more than 100 years ago, Pope Pius X indicated his feelings on the matter. "We [the Roman Catholic Church] are unable to favor this movement [Zionism]. We cannot prevent the Jews from going to Jerusalem—but we could never sanction it. As the head of the Church I cannot answer you otherwise."[8]

An increasing number of recent Protestant scholars have also voiced support for this theological view. In his book *The Latter Days*, Russell Jones made this comment about the establishment of the State of Israel:

> Many accept this as proof that the Jews are still God's Chosen People with a definite mission to be performed in the future. This cannot be true...The new Jewish state may or may not succeed politically. But to restore them to a primary place in the future outworking of God's redemptive purpose is to ignore the clear teaching of the New Testament and do violence to the cross of the Lord Jesus Christ... Jews collectively can have no such hope.[9]

Conclusion

Replacement theology is now firmly entrenched in both Catholic and Protestant circles. A number of replacement scholars are so convinced of their view that they consider the issue unworthy of debate. For them, replacement theology is a settled fact. But is it really a settled fact? We will consider the other side of the debate in the next chapter.

4

The Case for the Church and Israel Remaining Distinct

Contrary to those who hold that the church is the new Israel, many Christians believe that in biblical prophecy, the church is the church and Israel is Israel. They are distinct entities. This means that promises made to Israel in the Old Testament covenants will, in fact, be fulfilled by Israel and not the church.

A number of theological arguments support this position. First, let's deal with the key verses cited by replacement enthusiasts—that is, the verses that call the church "the Israel of God" (Galatians 6:16), "Abraham's offspring" (Galatians 3:29), and "the circumcision" (Philippians 3:3).

It is true that Galatians 3:29 tells us that "if you are Christ's, then you are Abraham's offspring, heirs according to promise." However, this does not mean that distinctions between the church and Israel are thereby obliterated. Thomas Constable, a former professor of Bible exposition at Dallas Theological Seminary, explains it this way:

> Those joined to Christ by faith become spiritual descendants of Abraham and beneficiaries of some of God's promises to him. This does not mean Christians become Jews. Christians are Christians; we are in Christ, the Seed of Abraham (cf. v. 16). God promised some things to all the physical descendants of Abraham (e.g., Gen. 12:1-3,7). He

> promised other things to the believers within that group
> (e.g., Rom. 9:6,8). He promised still other things to the
> spiritual seed of Abraham who are not Jews (e.g., Gal. 3:6-
> 9). Failure to distinguish these groups and the promises
> given to each has resulted in much confusion.[1]

Therefore, though believers in Christ are indeed Abraham's spiritual offspring, they remain distinct from Israel. One must not forget the pivotal teaching of the apostle Paul in Romans 9–11 that God still has a plan for ethnic Israel as distinct from the church.

Regarding Paul's reference to followers of Christ as "the circumcision" in Philippians 3:3, Paul was pointedly referring to the circumcision of the heart that occurs the moment a person trusts in Jesus Christ for salvation. It is a huge leap in logic to say that this verse proves that the church becomes the new Israel.

What then of Paul's reference to "the Israel of God" in Galatians 6:16? Paul is here referring to saved Jews—that is, Jews who have trusted in Jesus Christ for salvation. It is important to note that the term Israel refers to physical Jews everywhere else in the New Testament (some 65 times). Galatians 6:16 gives no indication that the term is to be taken any differently. In Paul's writings, the church and Israel remain distinct (see Romans 9–11; 1 Corinthians 10:32). New Testament scholar F.F. Bruce commented that "for all his demoting of the law and the customs, Paul held good hope of the ultimate blessing of Israel."[2] In view of this, Galatians 6:16 cannot be cited in support of the idea that the church is the new Israel.

Neither can the statement in Ephesians 2:15 that Jews and Gentiles are "one new man" be claimed in support. This verse simply indicates that the former barrier that existed between Jews and Gentiles is obliterated in Christ, for Christ at the cross effectively disposed of the old law with its meticulous sanctions and decrees. By no stretch of the imagination does the verse say the church replaces Israel.

What about Joshua 21:43-45, which says "the LORD gave to Israel all the land he swore to give to their fathers?" God did indeed fulfill His part in giving the Israelites the Promised Land. Israel, however, failed to take full possession of what God had promised to the nation. They failed to dispossess all the Canaanites despite the fact that God had given them the gift of land. It was there for the taking.

God had faithfully done for Israel what He promised. Israel, by contrast, was not completely faithful. The Lord had not failed to keep His promise, but Israel had failed by faith to fully conquer all the land.

Now, here is the important point. The idea that there are no further land promises to be fulfilled for Israel is false because many prophecies written far after the time of Joshua speak of Israel possessing the land in the future. This point is so critically important that I will cite a number of proof texts that support it.

- "Your people shall all be righteous; they shall possess the land forever" (Isaiah 60:21).
- "I will bring them back to this land. I will build them up, and not tear them down" (Jeremiah 24:6).
- "Thus says the LORD: Behold, I will restore the fortunes of the tents of Jacob and have compassion on his dwellings; the city shall be rebuilt on its mound, and the palace shall stand where it used to be" (Jeremiah 30:18).
- "Behold, I will gather them from all the countries to which I drove them in my anger and my wrath and in great indignation. I will bring them back to this place, and I will make them dwell in safety. And they shall be my people, and I will be their God. I will give them one heart and one way, that they may fear me forever, for their own good and the good of their children after them. I will make with them an everlasting covenant, that I will not turn away from doing good to them. And I will put the fear of me in their hearts, that they may not turn from me" (Jeremiah 32:37-40).
- "I will bring to it [the city] health and healing, and I will heal them and reveal to them abundance of prosperity and security. I will restore the fortunes of Judah and the fortunes of Israel, and rebuild them as they were at first. I will cleanse

them from all the guilt of their sin against me, and I will forgive all the guilt of their sin and rebellion against me. And this city shall be to me a name of joy, a praise and a glory before all the nations of the earth who shall hear of all the good that I do for them. They shall fear and tremble because of all the good and all the prosperity I provide for it" (Jeremiah 33:6-9).

- "Thus says the Lord GOD: When I gather the house of Israel from the peoples among whom they are scattered, and manifest my holiness in them in the sight of the nations, then they shall dwell in their own land that I gave to my servant Jacob. And they shall dwell securely in it, and they shall build houses and plant vineyards. They shall dwell securely, when I execute judgments upon all their neighbors who have treated them with contempt. Then they will know that I am the LORD their God" (Ezekiel 28:25-26).

- "For thus says the Lord GOD: Behold, I, I myself will search for my sheep and will seek them out. As a shepherd seeks out his flock when he is among his sheep that have been scattered, so will I seek out my sheep, and I will rescue them from all places where they have been scattered on a day of clouds and thick darkness" (Ezekiel 34:11-12).

- "I will take you from the nations and gather you from all the countries and bring you into your own land. I will sprinkle clean water on you, and you shall be clean from all your uncleannesses, and from all your idols I will cleanse you. And I will give you a new heart, and a new spirit I will put within you. And I will remove the heart of stone from your flesh and give you a heart of flesh" (Ezekiel 36:24-26).

- "Then they shall know that I am the LORD their God, because I sent them into exile among the nations and then assembled them into their own land. I will leave none of them remaining among the nations anymore" (Ezekiel 39:28).

- "For the children of Israel shall dwell many days without king or prince, without sacrifice or pillar, without ephod or household gods. Afterward the children of Israel shall return and seek the LORD their God, and David their king, and they shall come in fear to the LORD and to his goodness in the latter days" (Hosea 3:4-5).

- "I will surely assemble all of you, O Jacob; I will gather the remnant of Israel; I will set them together like sheep in a fold, like a flock in its pasture, a noisy multitude of men" (Micah 2:12).

- "In that day, declares the LORD, I will assemble the lame and gather those who have been driven away and those whom I have afflicted; and the lame I will make the remnant, and those who were cast off, a strong nation; and the LORD will reign over them in Mount Zion from this time forth and forevermore" (Micah 4:6-7).

- "I will restore the fortunes of my people Israel, and they shall rebuild the ruined cities and inhabit them; they shall plant vineyards and drink their wine, and they shall make gardens and eat their fruit. I will plant them on their land, and they shall never again be uprooted out of the land that I have given them, says the LORD your God" (Amos 9:14-15).

- "I will bring you in, at the time when I gather you together; for I will make you renowned and praised among all the peoples of the earth, when I restore your fortunes before your eyes, says the LORD" (Zephaniah 3:20).

- "Thus says the LORD of hosts: Behold, I will save my people from the east country and from the west country, and I will bring them to dwell in the midst of Jerusalem. And they shall be my people, and I will be their God, in faithfulness and in righteousness" (Zechariah 8:7-8).

Every Old Testament prophet except Jonah speaks of a permanent return to the land of Israel by the Jews.

Israel partially possessed the land at the time of Joshua, but it was later dispossessed. Contrary to this, the Abrahamic covenant promised Israel that she would possess the land forever (Genesis 17:8).

Another problem with replacement theology is the fact that the church and Israel are distinct throughout the New Testament. For example, we are instructed in 1 Corinthians 10:32, "Give no offense to Jews or to Greeks [Gentiles] or to the church of God." Israel and the church are viewed as distinct throughout the book of Acts, where the word *Israel* is used 20 times and the word *church* 19 times. New Testament scholar S. Lewis Johnson noted that "the usage of the terms Israel and the church in the early chapters of the book of Acts is in complete harmony, for Israel exists there alongside the newly formed church, and the two entities are kept separate in terminology."[3]

Remember that the prophecies that have already been fulfilled in Scripture—such as the Old Testament messianic prophecies that refer to the first coming of Jesus Christ—have been fulfilled literally. From the book of Genesis to the book of Malachi, the Old Testament abounds with anticipations of the coming Messiah. Numerous predictions fulfilled to the "crossing of the *T* and the dotting of the *I*" in the New Testament relate to His birth, life, ministry, death, resurrection, and glory (see pages 18-19). The prophecies that have been fulfilled completely have been fulfilled literally. This gives us strong confidence to expect that the prophecies not yet fulfilled will also be fulfilled literally—including the covenant land promises to Israel.

Scripture reveals that Israel will one day finally and wonderfully come to recognize Jesus as the divine Messiah and come into full possession of the promised land. The fullness of this possession will be in the future millennial kingdom. At present, however, Israel's regathering to the land is only partial, and Israel is yet in unbelief. This partial regathering in unbelief is setting the stage for Israel (also called Jacob) to eventually go through the tribulation period—the "time of distress for Jacob" (Jeremiah 30:7)—when a remnant of Israel will be saved. The apostle Paul refers to this in Romans 9–11. Israel will then come into full possession of her promised land in the millennial kingdom.

As for the Church Fathers' support of replacement theology, let us note that the early Church Fathers held to a number of views that most in the modern church no longer accept. For example, for the first five centuries of church history, Christians believed that a person becomes born again when baptized in water. Certainly most Christians today prefer the more biblical view that one becomes born again when trusting in Christ for salvation.

Scholar Peter Richardson is spot-on in his assertion that there is no historical evidence that the term *Israel* was identified with the church before AD 160.[4] This means that for more than a century after the time of the apostle Paul, such an identification was completely unheard of.

As I close, I can only express sorrow that replacement theology has done much damage to the cause of Israel. Because of this theology, many Christians are abandoning support for Israel and her right to stay in the land. Based on the Abrahamic covenant—an unconditional covenant—I believe the land unconditionally belongs to Israel, and I pray the United States will remain committed to protecting Israel against her many enemies.

I would be remiss not to mention that replacement theology has been a motivation to at least some people to engage in anti-Semitism. Prophecy expert Thomas Ice notes that "wherever replacement theology has flourished, the Jews have had to run for cover."[5] Christians therefore ought to give very careful consideration to this debate.

Conclusion

In my studied assessment, I believe that…

- God made unconditional covenants with the Jews in Old Testament times that have yet to be fully fulfilled,

- the church and Israel continue to be distinct entities in the pages of the New Testament, and

- the apostle Paul affirmed that God still has a plan for Israel (Romans 9–11).

All things considered, then, I reject in the strongest possible terms the idea that the church replaces Israel as the recipient of God's covenant blessings and promises. To be sure, God will indeed bless the church, but God will also fulfill His covenant promises to Israel.

What Can We Know About the Signs of the Times?

5

Do Current Signs Point to Prophetic Fulfillment?

A sign of the times is an event of prophetic significance that points to the end times. In a way, the signs of the times found in the pages of Scripture constitute God's "advance intel" regarding what the world will look like in the end times. Scripture specifies quite a few signs (for example, see Matthew 24–25; 1 Timothy 4:1-2; 2 Timothy 4:3-4).

This is always a favorite topic of discussion at the prophecy conferences at which I speak. As I dialogue with people at conferences, two extreme views often crop up. Some people view just about everything going on in the world as a sign of the times. Other people dismiss the significance of the signs of the times. The better policy is to seek balance.

Sign, Sign, Everywhere a Sign

Those who see signs of the times just about everywhere are often sensationalistic. To be sure, the second coming of Jesus Christ will be sensational. But that is different from having a sensationalistic mindset as we await the unfolding of the end times.

Some sensationalists give seemingly relentless consideration as to who in the world might be the antichrist (US presidents are often candidates). Every time a major earthquake or tsunami or other natural disaster occurs, they are strongly inclined to think these events portend the end. They speculate that radio preachers who set specific dates for the rapture may be correct.

Prophecy expert Mark Hitchcock offers this helpful warning: "The problem is that when everything becomes a sign, then nothing is a sign."[1] People can categorize so many things in the world as signs, the real signs lose their significance.

We must ever be cautious about falling prey to newspaper exegesis. Prophecy expert Arnold Fruchtenbaum, in his helpful book *The Footsteps of the Messiah*, commented that "current events must never be the means of interpreting the Scriptures, but the Scriptures must interpret current events."[2] Indeed, "when considering signs of the times, we must make sure that we view current events in light of the Bible and not the other way around."[3]

When we say that the Scriptures must interpret current events, we mean that our first goal is to study the Scriptures to find out what God has revealed about the future. Then, to accurately discern the times—something Christ clearly desires us to do (Matthew 16:1-3; Luke 21:29-33)—we measure current events against the Bible in order to thoughtfully consider whether there is a legitimate correlation. If we conclude there is, we can rejoice in God's sovereign control of human history while resisting the temptation to set dates, recognizing that this is something God forbids (Acts 1:7). All the while, we avoid sensationalism because Christ calls His followers to live soberly and alertly as they await His second coming (Mark 13:32-37).

Scoffing at the Signs of the Times

At the other extreme, some people tend to scoff at the signs of the times. One Christian author I know (a partial preterist—he believes that most of the prophecies in the book of Revelation have already been fulfilled) said he was getting sick and tired of how some Christians think they see a sign of the times whenever anyone burps in the Middle East. He and others in his camp seem to think it's not only unwarranted but even foolish to give consideration to the signs of the end times.

I am convinced that such a negative outlook is scripturally short-sighted. Consider Jesus's words in Matthew 16:1-3:

> The Pharisees and Sadducees came, and to test him they asked him to show them a sign from heaven. He answered them, "When it is evening, you say, 'It will be fair weather, for the sky is red.' And in the morning, 'It will be stormy today, for the sky is red and threatening.' You know how to interpret the appearance of the sky, but you cannot interpret the signs of the times."

This was quite a rebuke to these religious leaders! These guys—the religious elite of the time—were supposed to know the teachings of Scripture, yet they were completely unable to properly discern the times. The Pharisees and Sadducees had been surrounded by spiritual signs relating to the person of Jesus Christ and had missed them all. They were blinded to the reality that the Messiah was in their midst. Jesus's miracles (the blind seeing, the deaf hearing, the lame walking...) were clear signs to His divine identity, just as dark clouds in the sky are signs of impending rain. These miracles had been prophesied of the Messiah in the Old Testament (Isaiah 35:5-6), and the Pharisees and Sadducees—experts in the Old Testament—should have seen that Jesus fulfilled these messianic verses. But in their blindness, they could not "interpret the signs of the times." If we ignore the signs of the end times today, we will be as prophetically blind as the Pharisees and Sadducees.

Jesus also urged, "From the fig tree learn its lesson: as soon as its branch becomes tender and puts out its leaves, you know that summer is near. So also, when you see all these things, you know that he is near, at the very gates" (Matthew 24:32-33). Jesus indicates in this verse that God has revealed certain things so people who know the Bible can understand that a fulfillment of prophecy is taking place (or that the stage is being set for a prophecy to eventually be fulfilled). Jesus is thus instructing His followers to become accurate observers of the times so they will recognize the fulfillment of biblical prophecies (see also Luke 21:25-28).

A Qualification

I must be careful to emphasize that there are no signs that precede the rapture of the church. Scripture reveals that the rapture is an imminent event. The term *imminent* literally means "ready to take place" or "impending." Nothing must be prophetically fulfilled before the rapture occurs (see 1 Corinthians 1:7; 16:22; Philippians 3:20; 4:5; 1 Thessalonians 1:10; Titus 2:13; Hebrews 9:28; James 5:7-9; 1 Peter 1:13; Jude 21). The rapture is a signless event that can occur at any moment.

This is in contrast to the second coming of Christ, which is preceded by many events in the seven-year tribulation period (see Revelation 4–18).

> The signs we are seeing in the world today anticipate events that will occur after the Rapture in anticipation of Jesus' return. The Bible's end times prophecies refer to the seven-year Tribulation period and portend the second coming of Christ to rule and reign. But no sign presages the Rapture. Signs are for Christ's return, not the church's rapture. [4]

Does that mean that the signs of the times are irrelevant to us who live prior to the moment of the rapture? Not at all! We are currently witnessing many events in the world that are clearly setting the stage for the fulfillment of prophecies during the future tribulation period. Here then is my point. Any stage-setting which indicates that the tribulation period may be drawing near is an indication that the rapture is even nearer.

Dr. John F. Walvoord, one of my former mentors at Dallas Theological Seminary, gave an illustration that helps us to understand this. Walvoord compared the rapture to Thanksgiving and the second coming to Christmas. There are all kinds of signs that Christmas is drawing near—TV ads, radio ads, newspaper ads, manger scenes, Christmas lights and decorations...the signs are everywhere. But Thanksgiving can sneak up on us. We really don't see obvious signs that Thanksgiving is approaching. But one thing is for sure. If Thanksgiving has not yet taken place, and yet we're seeing clear signs that Christmas will arrive soon, we automatically know that Thanksgiving is all the nearer. By analogy, as we witness the stage being set today for events that will transpire during the tribulation period in anticipation of the second coming of Christ, we can know that the rapture is that much closer.

I believe that just as tremors (or foreshocks) often occur before major earthquakes, so preliminary manifestations of some of these signs are emerging, setting the stage for the tribulation period. Someone said that prophecies cast their shadows before them. I think this is true. Prophecies that relate specifically to the tribulation period are presently casting their shadows before them. The stage is now being set for their fulfillment.

Significant Current Events

Some Christians will continue to scoff at the signs of the times (particularly Christians in the preterist camp), but those of us who seek to follow Jesus's injunction to be accurate observers of the times have our eyes on some key events in the world. Here is a sampling of some of the more significant developments.

The Rebirth of Israel

The birth of the modern state of Israel in 1948 as a self-governing nation began an actual fulfillment of specific Bible prophecies about an international regathering of the Jews in unbelief before the judgment of the tribulation. This regathering was to take place after centuries of exile in various nations around the world.

In Ezekiel 36:10 God promised, "I will multiply people on you, the whole house of Israel, all of it. The cities shall be inhabited and the waste places rebuilt." God promised, "I will take you from the nations and gather you from all the countries and bring you into your own land" (verse 24). Israel would again be prosperous, for God promised, "I will make the fruit of the tree and the increase of the field abundant, that you may never again suffer the disgrace of famine among the nations" (verse 30).

In the vision of dry bones in Ezekiel 37, the Lord miraculously brings the bones back together into a skeleton, the skeleton is wrapped in muscles and tendons and flesh, and God then breathes life into the body. This chapter is undoubtedly speaking about Israel—"These bones are the whole house of Israel" (verse 11). So this chapter portrays Israel as becoming a living, breathing nation, brought back from the dead, as it were.

Therefore, 1948 is a year to remember. The backdrop is that in AD 70, Titus and his Roman warriors destroyed Jerusalem, definitively ending Israel's existence as a political entity (see Luke 21:20). Since then, the Jews have been dispersed worldwide for many centuries. In the year 1940, no one could have guessed that within a decade Israel would be a nation again. And yet it happened. Israel achieved statehood in 1948, and the Jews have been returning to their homeland ever since.

Israel currently remains in unbelief. But according to Joel 2:28-29, Israel will one day experience a spiritual awakening. Armageddon seems to be the historical context in which Israel finally becomes converted (Zechariah 12:2–13:1).

Meanwhile, even as I write in early 2014, Jewish people are continuing to stream back to the Holy Land. All eyes are on Israel!

The Escalation of Apostasy

The word *apostasy* comes from the Greek word *apostasia* and means "falling away." The word refers to a determined, willful defection from the faith, an abandonment of it.

Scripture clearly prophesies an escalation of apostasy in the end times. For example, 1 Timothy 4:1-2 warns, "The Spirit expressly says that in later times some will depart from the faith by devoting themselves to deceitful spirits and teachings of demons, through the insincerity of liars whose consciences are seared." Likewise, 2 Timothy 4:3-4 warns, "The time is coming when people will not endure sound teaching, but having itching ears they will accumulate for themselves teachers to suit their own passions, and will turn away from listening to the truth and wander off into myths." Who can doubt that these words have application to our own day?

Apostasy can include a denial of…

God (2 Timothy 3:4-5)	sound doctrine (2 Timothy 4:3-4)
Christ (1 John 2:18)	morals (2 Timothy 3:1-8)
Christ's return (2 Peter 3:3-4)	authority (2 Timothy 3:4)
the faith (1 Timothy 4:1-2)	

I have witnessed every one of these denials in the Christian church over the past decade. Sad to say, some famous Christian leaders and authors have actually communicated rank heresy in some of their teachings. These are days of deception.

The Craving for Peace in the Middle East

The entire Middle East has been an arena of conflict for more than 60 years. Consider this list of wars in the region.

> the War of Independence, or First Arab–Israeli War (1947–1948)
> the Suez War, Sinai Campaign, or Second Arab–Israeli War (1956)
> the Six-Day War (1967)
> the War of Attrition (1968–1970)
> the Yom Kippur War, or October War (1973)
> the Lebanese Civil War (1975–1976)
> the Iran–Iraq War, or First Persian Gulf War (1980–1988)
> the First Lebanon War (1982–1985)
> the Persian Gulf War (1991)
> the War with Iraq (1991–2003)
> the War on Terror (2001 to present)

Many wonder whether there will ever be peace in the Middle East.

People are crying out today for a leader who can take control of world crises and solve the Middle East problem. This yearning is setting the stage for what is to come. For Scripture prophesies that the antichrist—the leader of a revived Roman empire, a "United States of Europe"—will sign a covenant with Israel. To the amazement of everyone, he will appear to have solved the Middle East dilemma.

A Revived Roman Empire

The idea of a revived Roman Empire of the end times is based on Daniel 7, which makes reference to four beasts. These beasts represent kingdoms that play important roles in biblical prophecy.

The first, Daniel says, was "like a lion and had eagles' wings," but "its wings were plucked off" (verse 4). This imagery apparently represents the power and strength of Babylon.

Daniel then sees "another beast, a second one, like a bear" (verse 5), an animal of great strength. This kingdom is Medo-Persia, which was well known for its strength and fierceness in battle.

The third beast was "like a leopard, with four wings of a bird on its back. And the beast had four heads, and dominion was given to it" (verse 6). This imagery represents Greece under Alexander the Great, and the four heads are the four generals who divided the kingdom following Alexander's death.

The fourth beast was a mongrel beast composed of parts of a lion, bear, and leopard, and it was more terrifying and powerful than the three preceding beasts.

> There shall be a fourth kingdom on earth, which shall be different from all the kingdoms, and it shall devour the whole earth, and trample it down, and break it to pieces. As for the ten horns, out of this kingdom ten kings shall arise, and another shall arise after them; he shall be different from the former ones, and shall put down three kings. He shall speak words against the Most High (verses 23-25).

This wild imagery refers to the Roman Empire. Rome existed in ancient days but fell apart in the fifth century AD. It will be revived, however, in the end times, apparently comprised of ten nations ruled by ten kings. A smaller, eleventh horn (the antichrist) emerges from within this ten-nation confederacy. He apparently starts out in an insignificant way but grows powerful enough to uproot (or overtake) three of the existing horns (or rulers). He eventually comes into power and dominance over this revived empire.

Rome has never consisted of a ten-nation confederacy with ten co-rulers. This means this prophecy must deal with the future.

Related to this, in Daniel 2 we read of a prophetic dream that Nebuchadnezzar had. In this dream, this end-times Roman Empire was pictured as a mixture of iron and clay (verses 41-43). Daniel, the great dream-interpreter, saw this as meaning that this latter-day Roman Empire would be strong as iron. But just as iron and clay do not naturally mix with each other, so this latter-day Roman Empire would have some divisions. It would not be completely integrated.

Many modern biblical interpreters see the European Union as a primary prospect for the ultimate fulfillment of this prophecy. A common monetary currency is the first step in what will eventually be a common and unified political entity. Perhaps the stage is being set even now for the fulfillment of Daniel 2 and 7.

Globalism

In our day, we are witnessing major steps toward globalism. We see globalist policies emerging in economics, banking, commerce and trade, business, management, manufacturing, environmentalism, population control, education, religion, agriculture, information technologies, entertainment, publishing, science, medicine, and government. The book of Revelation tells us that the antichrist will ultimately lead an anti-God global union (see Revelation 13). It will be a political, economic, and religious union.

Considering the multiple cascading problems now facing humanity—including a declining oil supply, the Middle East conflict, terrorism, overpopulation, starvation, pollution, national and international crime, cyber warfare, and economic instability—more and more people are likely to believe that such problems can be solved only on a global level. They may think that the only hope for human survival is a strong and effective world government.

As danger continues to mount in the world, people worldwide are yearning for a leader who can take control and fix everything. The global economy is reeling, people are suffering, and there is a sense of urgency for a powerful leader who can finally chart a clear global course toward lasting stability. Such a leader is coming, and he may already be alive in the world. Scripture identifies him as the antichrist.

The technology that makes possible a world government— instant global media through television, radio, the Internet, and so on—is now in place. Technology has greased the skids for the emergence of globalism in our day.

Conclusion

We must ever seek to avoid two extremes when regarding the signs of the times—seeing signs everywhere and scoffing at the signs. Our best policy is to first become thoroughly acquainted with what Scripture teaches about the end times (including the signs of the times). Only then are we in a position to watch for legitimate correlations between current world events and biblical prophecy. When legitimate correlations become obvious, nothing is wrong with becoming enthused about God's "advance intel," but we must also seek to remain sober-minded and not sensationalistic.

6

Is America in Bible Prophecy?

The question of whether America is mentioned in biblical prophecy has been the subject of much debate through the years. Some say yes, and others say no. Many theories on the issue have been speculative and far-fetched. Others have taken a more reasoned approach. I will consider two major viewpoints in the debate: (1) America is only indirectly mentioned in Bible prophecy, and (2) America is not mentioned in Bible prophecy at all.

Only Indirectly Mentioned in Bible Prophecy

Some prophecy enthusiasts believe that Bible prophecy includes no direct references to the United States, but it may mention America indirectly. Here are some possible indirect references.

One of the Nations

Many suggest that a number of general prophetic references to "the nations" in the tribulation period are likely to include the United States.

- Events in Israel will become a cause of stumbling for the nations of the earth (Zechariah 12:2-3).
- God will "shake all nations" (Haggai 2:6-7).
- God will be glorified among the nations (Isaiah 66:18-20).

Of course, even though such passages may indeed include the United States, they do not tell us anything specific about the role of the United States in the end times.

Cooperation with Europe

Though the United States is not specifically mentioned in biblical prophecy, some suggest the possibility that a weakened United States—no longer a superpower—may become an ally with the United States of Europe (the revived Roman Empire) early in the tribulation period. After all, most citizens of the United States have roots in Europe and would likely be more open to allying with Europe than with any other geopolitical entity.

Eventually the antichrist, who begins as the ruler of the revived Roman Empire, will achieve global dominion. The United States will likely be subsumed in the globalism that will emerge and prevail during the tribulation. Even in our day, our present government administration seems to be moving us away from American national sovereignty and is open to handling more and more problems in a global way.

Related to this, when Armageddon breaks out at the end of the tribulation period, troops from around the world will stand against Israel, and troops from the United States may be included. After all, Zechariah 12:3 tells us, "On that day I will make Jerusalem a heavy stone for all the peoples. All who lift it will surely hurt themselves. And all the nations of the earth will gather against it." The phrase "all the nations of the earth" would seem to include the United States.

Zechariah 14:2 likewise states, "I will gather all the nations against Jerusalem to battle, and the city shall be taken and the houses plundered and the women raped. Half the city shall go out into exile, but the rest of the people shall not be cut off from the city." Again, "all the nations" would seem to include the United States.

Revelation 16:14 reveals that "the kings of the whole world" will be gathered together "for battle on the great day of God the Almighty." The "kings of the whole world" would apparently include the commander in chief of the US military.

You may be wondering how such a thing could ever happen. Keep in mind that following the rapture of the church, there will not be any Christians on the earth—including in the United States, where many Christians presently live. This means that many of the people in the United States who have long supported Israel will no longer be around to do so, but will be with the Lord in heaven. It is easy to see how a Christian-less United States could ally with the revived Roman Empire and then find itself in league with the antichrist during the tribulation period.

Babylon in Revelation 17–18

Some prophecy students have seen parallels between Babylon the great in the book of Revelation and the United States (or more narrowly, New York City). Both Babylon and the United States are dominant, both are militarily strong, both are immoral, both are excessively rich, and both think they are invulnerable. Therefore they must be one and the same.

This scenario is not very popular today. Most people recognize that such a view involves more eisegesis (reading a meaning into the text of Scripture) than exegesis (drawing the meaning out of the text of Scripture). Nevertheless, the theory continues to surface time and again.

The Land Divided by Rivers

Other prophecy students claim that the United States may be the fulfillment of Isaiah 18:1-7, which refers to a nation "whose land the rivers divide" (verse 2). This must be the United States, it is reasoned, since this country is divided by the Mississippi River. Verse 7 reveals that this nation is "a nation mighty and conquering," perhaps referring to the military might and expansionism of the United States.

This viewpoint has one major problem. Verse 1 clearly reveals that the nation under discussion is ancient Cush, which is modern Sudan.

The Land of Tarshish

Still other prophecy interpreters believe the United States may be included in the land of Tarshish referenced in Ezekiel 38:13. This passage informs us that when a great northern military coalition composed of Russia and a number of Muslim nations invades Israel, a small group of nations will offer a lame protest. "Sheba and Dedan and the merchants of Tarshish and all its leaders will say to you, 'Have you come to seize spoil? Have you assembled your hosts to carry off plunder, to carry away silver and gold, to take away livestock and goods, to seize great spoil?'"

Some believe ancient Tarshish is modern Spain. Others say it may be Great Britain. Still others say it may refer to the colonies of Western Europe and the nations that have subsequently arisen from them, including the United States, Canada, and Mexico. Still others say Tarshish might represent all the Western nations of the end times, which would include the United States.

This being so, Ezekiel 38:13 may indicate that the United States will be among the nations that lodge a protest against the massive Ezekiel invasion into Israel. But the protest is feeble and lacks military support.

My personal assessment is that this view is too speculative and has little scriptural support. Besides, no one is sure about the proper geographical identity of Tarshish.

Not Mentioned in Bible Prophecy at All

A second major viewpoint in this debate is that America is not mentioned in Bible prophecy at all. If this assessment is correct, the question is, *why* isn't America mentioned in Bible prophecy? Prophecy students have proposed a number of explanations.

Most Nations Are Not Mentioned in Bible Prophecy

Of course, most nations in the world are not mentioned in Bible prophecy. Therefore it may be insignificant that the United States is not mentioned.

Still, some people reason that the United States is the world's single remaining superpower and Israel's principal ally. One therefore might naturally expect at least a passing reference to the United States in Bible prophecy.

No Significant Role

A second possibility is that America is not mentioned in Bible prophecy simply because America plays no significant role in the unfolding of God's end-time plans. Again, however, one might naturally expect at least some reference given America's relationship with Israel and place in the world. So again, why is there no reference?

Possible Moral Implosion

Some suggest that America is not mentioned in Bible prophecy because it may eventually implode due to ever-escalating moral and spiritual degeneration.[1] This is a real possibility. Alarming statistics reveal the moral and spiritual trouble in this country.

- Four out of five adults—some 83 percent—say they are concerned about the moral condition of the United States.

- Most Americans believe that gambling (61 percent), cohabitation (60 percent), and sexual fantasies (59 percent) are morally acceptable.

- Nearly half of Americans believe that having an abortion (45 percent) and having a sexual relationship with someone of the opposite sex other than their spouse (42 percent) are morally acceptable.

- About one-third of Americans give the stamp of approval to pornography (38 percent), profanity (36 percent), drunkenness (35 percent) and homosexual sex (30 percent).

If the moral fiber of this country continues to erode, the demise of this country may be only a matter of time.

Nuclear Attack

Another possibility is that the United States is not mentioned in Bible prophecy because it will be destroyed or greatly weakened by a nuclear attack and will play no significant role in the end times. This scenario may be hard to swallow for some Americans. However, there is certainly a good chance that the United States will be attacked with nuclear weapons at some point in the future. Government advisors are presently saying that a nuclear attack on US soil within the next ten years is more likely than not.

I personally think it's a stretch to say the entire United States could be destroyed. However, if a major city—New York City, Los Angeles, or Chicago for example—were destroyed, this would have a devastating and long-lasting effect on the US economy.

Nuclear terrorism is not merely the talk of sensationalists or alarmists. Some of the greatest thinkers in our land are sounding warning bells. National security experts say the risk of attack by weapons of mass destruction within the next decade may be as high as 70 percent. Some US senators are saying the United States faces an existential threat from terrorists who may get their hands on weapons of mass destruction. In the next decade, they say, we face the very real possibility of nuclear jihad.

The United States faces the problem of having many easy entrances. A terrorist could easily smuggle a nuclear bomb across US borders or into its ports. Only 5 percent of the 50,000 cargo containers shipped into the United States each day get screened. That leaves 95 percent that remain unscreened. A bomb could easily make its way into the country in one of the unscreened containers.

A terrorist group could also launch a nuclear weapon from a commercial ship off the coast of the United States. About 75 percent of the US population lives within 200 miles of the coast. With more than 130,000 registered merchant ships sailing off US coastal waters, the nuclear danger is obvious.

EMP Attack

Yet another possibility is that the United States is not mentioned in Bible prophecy because the country may become incapacitated due to an electromagnetic pulse (EMP) attack. This realistic possibility is documented in a report issued in 2004 by a blue-ribbon commission created by Congress. In the report, titled "Commission to Assess the

Threat to the United States from Electromagnetic Pulse Attack," some government officials lamented that the technology is now here to bring the American way of life to an end.

According to the report, a single nuclear weapon delivered by a missile to an altitude of a few hundred miles and detonated over the United States would yield catastrophic damage to the nation. Such a missile could easily be launched from a freighter off the coast of the United States. The commission explained that the higher the altitude of the weapon's detonation, the larger the affected geographic area would be. At a height of 300 miles, the entire continental United States would be exposed along with parts of Canada and Mexico.

The electromagnetic pulse produced by such a weapon would be likely to severely damage or knock out electrical power systems, electronics, and information systems—which Americans daily depend on. At high risk would be electronic control, the infrastructures for handling electric power, sensors and protective systems of all kinds, computers, cell phones, telecommunications, cars, boats, airplanes, trains, fuel and energy, banking and finance, emergency services, and even food and water. Anything controlled or delivered electronically is at risk.

American society would be catastrophically affected because the infrastructure of our society—civilian and military—virtually runs on electricity and electronic components. The commission estimated that it could take "months to years" to fully recover from such an attack.

Starvation and disease could even follow in some parts of the United States following an EMP attack. Expert testimony presented before the US Congress indicated that an EMP attack could reduce the United States to a pre–Industrial Age capacity in terms of transportation options and the ability to provide food and water to the general population. Instead of cars, buses, and trains, people would be reduced to using bikes, horses, and buggies.

The Muslim Threat: Jihad

Perhaps America is not mentioned in Bible prophecy because it will be victimized by Islamic jihad. Some Muslim leaders today teach that

jihad is a foreign policy option that can help expand Islamic authority all over the world. Many Shiite Muslims believe that at the apocalyptic end of days, a great, armed jihad will result in the subjugation of
the entire world to Islam.[2]

Many such Shiite Muslims have long believed in the eventual
return of the Twelfth Imam, believed to be a direct (bloodline) descen-
dant of Muhammad's son-in-law, Ali (whose family, it is believed, constitutes the only legitimate successors to Muhammad). The Twelfth
Imam—who disappeared as a child in AD 941—will allegedly return
in the future as the Mahdi ("the rightly guided One"). He will reportedly create a messianic era of global order and justice for Shiites in
which Islam will be triumphant.

The appearance of the Twelfth Imam can supposedly be hastened
through apocalyptic chaos and violence—that is, by unleashing an
apocalyptic holy war against Christians and Jews. So some Muslim
extremists believe they could influence the divine timetable and bring
about the end of days.

The radical Muslim goal is to attain a world without America and
Zionism, and once this goal is reached, the Twelfth Imam can be
expected to return. Some of these radical Muslims claim that humanity
will soon know what it is like to live in a Jew-free and USA-free world.

A Muslim who loses his or her life in service to Allah is guaranteed
entrance into paradise (Hadith 9:459). This provides a religious motivation for Muslims to participate in jihad. According to Muslim tradition, Muhammad said, "The person who participates in (holy battles)
in Allah's cause and nothing compels him to do so except belief in Allah
and His Apostles, will be recompensed by Allah either with a reward, or
booty (if he survives) or will be admitted to Paradise (if he is killed in
the battle as a martyr)" (Hadith 1:35). This is highly significant to Muslims, for it is the only way a Muslim can be assured of going to paradise.

Other radical Muslims are pushing not for the destruction of the
United States but rather its complete conversion to Islam. The establishment of a global Islamic state is a common goal of radical Muslims.
This would certainly include the United States. Citing Quran 3:85,
many Muslims stress that Allah will never accept any religion other

than Islam. Some Muslim leaders teach that the whole world must be under the rule of Islam, without exception.

One Muslim leader has warned people alive today that before Allah closes our eyes for the last time, we will witness Islam grow from the second-largest religion in America (which it presently is) to the largest. Toward this end, some rich Muslims—some Saudis, for example—are contributing countless millions of dollars to American universities to endow academic departments of Middle Eastern studies. These could significantly contribute to the expansion of Islam. Muslims also finance the building of Islamic centers, mosques, and schools for educating Muslim children in America.

Weakened by the Rapture

Still other Christians suggest that the United States is not mentioned in Bible prophecy because the United States will be decimated by the rapture. It seems fair to say that because of the large population of Christians in the United States, the negative effect of the rapture will be greater in America than in most other nations.

Following the moment of the rapture, many employees will no longer show up for work, many bills and mortgages will go unpaid, many college tuition bills and loans will go unpaid, many business leaders will no longer show up to lead their companies, many law enforcement personnel will no longer be here to keep the peace, and the stock market will likely crash because of the ensuing panic. This and much more will result following the rapture.

A Combination Scenario

Several of these scenarios could take place concurrently, and their combined effect could greatly weaken the United States.[3] For example, America could morally implode, a nuclear weapon could detonate in an American city, and the rapture could happen. The combined effect would cause the United States to plummet.

Of course, as an American patriot, I want only the best for this country. However, the scenarios I have described above are entirely possible. They are consistent with what we know of Bible prophecy.

A Historical Note: Great Civilizations Can Fall

Many great nations have risen and fallen throughout human history. In each case, the nation probably had no expectation of its impending demise. Most of the citizens of these nations were not likely to expect their nation to fall. The harsh reality of documented history, however, is that great nations do fall.

- The Babylonians never thought Babylon would fall, but its demise came in less than a century.
- The Persians never thought the Persian Empire would fall, but it finally capitulated after about two centuries.
- The Greeks never thought Greece would fall, but it waned in less than three centuries.
- No one thought the mighty Roman Empire would decline, but it waned after holding out for nine centuries.

Is the United States invincible? We tend to think we are special—that we will succeed where others have failed. But such a mentality may be as arrogant as it is unwise. Research demonstrates that many of the fallen civilizations in history also thought they were superior to their neighbors and forebears. Few of their citizens could imagine their society would one day collapse.

God Controls Nations

God is absolutely sovereign over human affairs. God rules the universe, controls all things, and is Lord over all (see Ephesians 1). Nothing can happen in this universe that is beyond the reach of His control. All forms of existence are within the scope of His absolute dominion. God asserts, "My counsel shall stand, and I accomplish all my purpose" (Isaiah 46:10). God assures us, "As I have planned, so shall it be, and as I have purposed, so it shall stand" (Isaiah 14:24).

God is certainly sovereign over the affairs of individual nations in the world. Scripture reveals that God "makes nations great, and he destroys them; he enlarges nations, and leads them away" (Job 12:23).

We are told that "he made from one man every nation of mankind to live on all the face of the earth, having determined allotted periods and the boundaries of their dwelling place" (Acts 17:26).

What does this mean for the United States? God is absolutely sovereign over the nations, and He is a holy God of judgment. Therefore, is it possible that God may sovereignly judge America in the end times for turning away from Him?

Those who doubt this possibility should consult what the apostle Paul says in Romans 1:18-28. If this passage tells us anything, it warns that when a nation willfully rejects God and His Word, God eventually reveals His wrath against that nation. One way God reveals His wrath is by allowing the people of that nation to experience the full brunt of the ravaging consequences of their sin.

Consider America's high prevalence of pornography, premarital sex, extramarital sex, homosexuality, same-sex marriages, abortions, alcohol and drug abuse, divorce, and much more. America is presently in a dangerous place!

God's judgment on America for its moral and spiritual degeneracy in the end times could be just one more reason why global power will shift away from the United States of America to the United States of Europe in the end times. Rome will rise again with the antichrist as her ruler.

Conclusion

My personal assessment is that America is not mentioned in Bible prophecy. I also believe America is likely to weaken in the end times. More specifically, I believe that America will continue to plummet morally, that weapons of mass destruction may well be detonated on American soil, and that when the rapture occurs, America will suffer more than most other countries.

7

Can We Know When the Ezekiel Invasion Will Occur?

S ome 2600 years ago, the prophet Ezekiel announced that the Jews would be regathered from many nations to the land of Israel in the end times (Ezekiel 36–37). He then prophesied that sometime later, a massive northern assault force would conduct an all-out invasion of Israel. Russia will lead this coalition of Muslim nations, which will include modern Iran, Sudan, Turkey, and Libya. Their goal will be to utterly obliterate the Jews.

The question is, when does this invasion take place? Multiple options have been suggested. Some say it takes place before the tribulation and before the rapture. Others say it takes place after the rapture but before the tribulation. Others say it happens in the first half of the tribulation period. Others say it takes place at the end of the tribulation. Still others say it takes place after the tribulation but before the millennial kingdom. Finally, some people place it at the beginning or the end of the millennial kingdom. The debate is a complicated one, and many interpretive variables are involved.

I will briefly consider each view. First, however, I want to summarize some general considerations as to the timing of the invasion. These general considerations will help us to properly assess the various views Christians have offered.

General Considerations

Scripture points to five general considerations that can help guide our thinking on the timing of the Ezekiel invasion.

The Last Days

Foundationally, the invasion will take place in the "latter years," or "latter days," which can only be taken to mean the end times. The Old Testament use of the term *last days* (and similar terms) refers to the time leading up to the coming of the Messiah to set up His millennial kingdom on earth.[1] More specifically, such terms are generally used to depict a time when Israel is in her time of tribulation.[2] Dallas Theological Seminary professor J. Dwight Pentecost, after a broad examination of Scripture, affirms that the term *last days*, used with respect to Old Testament Jews, "has specific reference to the latter years and days of God's dealing with the nation Israel, which, since it is before the millennial age (Ezek. 40), must place it during God's dealing with Israel in the seventieth week of Daniel's prophecy."[3]

Harold Hoehner, who earned his PhD at Cambridge University and has done postdoctoral studies at Tubingen University, likewise affirms that "the familiar expressions 'after many days,' 'in the latter days' (38:8), and 'in the last days' (38:16) refer to the time of the tribulation (Deut. 4:27-30; Dan. 2:28; 8:19, 23; 10:14) and/or the millennial restoration (Isa. 2:2-4; Mic. 4:1-7). The context must determine the setting. Here in Ezekiel 38–39 it must refer to the time of great tribulation for Israel."[4]

Yet to Come

No invasion on the magnitude of Ezekiel 38–39 has ever taken place in Israel's history. To be sure, Israel has encountered innumerable battles and invasions. But there has never been an invasion in which...

- a massive alliance composed of nations in the territories of modern Russia, Iran, Turkey, Sudan, and Libya attacked Israel;
- the alliance was utterly and horrifically destroyed by God with a massive earthquake, with fire and brimstone from heaven, with infighting among the troops, and with disease; and

- the number of casualties was so great that it required seven months to bury all the dead bodies in a big valley (Ezekiel 39:11-12).

The invasion clearly hasn't happened yet, so it will happen in the future (the "last days").

Israel Restored to Its Land

Before the invasion occurs, Israel must first be restored to the land. Of course, if Israel is not in the land, the nation cannot be invaded. Ezekiel 38:8 refers to the Holy Land, "whose people were gathered from many peoples upon the mountains of Israel." In 1948, for the first time in 19 centuries, Israel became a nation again. With Israel back in the land after a long and worldwide dispersion of Jews in many nations, a key piece of the puzzle is now in place, setting the stage for the future invasion of Israel by the northern military coalition.

Security and Rest

Scripture affirms that Israel will be living in security and at rest at the time of the Ezekiel invasion (see Ezekiel 38:8,11). Some interpreters view Israel as being in a state of security at the present because of Israel's well-equipped army, first-rate air force, effective missile defense system, strong economy, and strong relationship with the United States.

Other Christians believe that since Israel became a nation in 1948, she has remained on high alert because of her tense relations with her Arab neighbors. In view of this, many believe Israel will experience true security only when the leader of a revived Roman Empire—a European superstate—signs a peace pact or covenant with Israel, an event that will officially begin the tribulation period (Daniel 9:27). Some interpreters suggest that the Ezekiel invasion will take place sometime after this covenant is signed.

National Alliances

National alliances—formal or informal—must be in place among the invading nations. We can expect alliances to develop between certain Muslim nations (such as Iran, Turkey, Sudan, and Libya) as well as between these Muslim nations and Russia. These alliances have already developed in our day.

Now let's shift our attention to contending views in the debate over when this invasion will transpire.

Viewpoint 1: Before the Tribulation and Before the Rapture

A popular view in recent days is that the Ezekiel invasion into Israel will take place before the tribulation and even before the rapture. This scenario was portrayed in the popular Left Behind series by Tim LaHaye and Jerry Jenkins as well as in some of Joel Rosenberg's books. Here is the reasoning.

1. This view incorporates the seven-year tribulation period. The seven years to burn the weapons following this invasion (Ezekiel 39:9) are the seven years of the tribulation period.

2. This view may best explain why Israel is able to rebuild its temple. If all the invading Muslim armies are destroyed by God prior to the beginning of the tribulation period, Israel could more easily rebuild its temple on the temple mount in Jerusalem. There would be much less resistance.

3. This is the most feasible scenario. For example, it seems highly unlikely that the invasion could be placed during Christ's millennial kingdom or even at the end of the trib- ulation period.

Those who hold to other views find some problems with this viewpoint.

1. The idea that the invasion takes place before the rapture seems to contradict Ezekiel's indication that the invasion takes place in the "last days" or "latter years" (Ezekiel 38:8,16). When these phrases are used of Israel, they seem to point to the tribulation period.

2. The idea that the invasion takes place before the rapture

contradicts Ezekiel's prophecy that the invasion will take place when Israel is living in security and at rest (Ezekiel 38:11), something that will be brought about when the antichrist signs a covenant with Israel (which begins the tribulation period).

3. The New Testament consistently teaches that the rapture is imminent—that is, nothing must be prophetically fulfilled before the rapture occurs. So one cannot say this invasion must occur before the rapture.

4. Second Thessalonians 2:6-8 indicates that the antichrist (the "lawless one") cannot emerge until He who restrains is taken out of the way.

In view of this fourth point, the following argument might be plausible.

- Israel will not have security until the antichrist signs a peace pact with Israel—an event which begins the tribulation.

- However, the antichrist cannot emerge until after the rapture because that is when the Restrainer—the Holy Spirit—will be removed.

- Therefore Israel will not be in security until after the rapture.

- Consequently the Ezekiel invasion cannot occur until after this time.

Viewpoint 2: After the Rapture but Before the Tribulation

Prophecy expert Thomas Ice offers a different view, holding that the Ezekiel invasion "will be during the interval of days, weeks, months, or years between the rapture and the start of the seven-year tribulation."[5] He offers this evidence in support of his view.

1. The world will be in a state of absolute chaos following the rapture. The United States has a heavy population of Christians, so the rapture will have a devastating effect on the

United States. Russia and her Muslim allies may therefore seize the moment and consider this the ideal time to invade Israel.

2. Once God destroys Russia and the Muslim invaders prior to the tribulation, the door may be open for the rapid rise of the antichrist as the leader of the revived Roman Empire— a European superstate.

3. With the Muslim invaders destroyed before the tribulation, the antichrist could more easily sign a peace pact with Israel (Daniel 9:27), guaranteeing that Israel will be protected.

4. This scenario may account for Israel's ability to construct the Jewish temple on the temple mount in Jerusalem. With Muslim forces destroyed, Muslim resistance will be greatly minimized.

5. If the invasion takes place after the rapture and the rapture takes place at least three and a half years before the tribulation, this scenario would allow for the invaders' weapons to be completely burned for seven years prior to the midpoint of the tribulation, when the antichrist sets up his headquarters in Jerusalem and Israel must take flight.

Those who hold to other views find some problems with this viewpoint.

1. Some believe the idea that the Ezekiel invasion precedes the tribulation contradicts the fact that the invasion takes place in the "last days" or "latter years" (Ezekiel 38:8,16). As noted previously, some believe these phrases—when used of Israel—point to the tribulation period.

2. The idea that the invasion takes place before the tribulation contradicts Ezekiel's prophecy that the invasion will take place when Israel is living in security and at rest (Ezekiel 38:11), something that will be brought about when the antichrist signs a covenant with Israel.

Viewpoint 3: In the First Half of the Tribulation

Other prophecy experts—including John F. Walvoord, J. Dwight Pentecost, Charles C. Ryrie, Herman Hoyt, and Mark Hitchcock—place the Ezekiel invasion in the early part of the tribulation. They offer these supportive considerations.

1. This position easily satisfies the precondition of Israel being secure and at rest prior to the invasion. This state of security and rest will be based on Israel signing a covenant with the leader of the revived Roman Empire (the antichrist).

2. God's destruction of the Russian and Muslim invading force during the first half of the tribulation will create a power vacuum and allow for the quick ascendancy of the antichrist.[6]

3. The destruction of Muslim forces in the first half of the tribulation will also allow for the easy emergence of a one-world religion. Christians will have already been raptured, and now the Muslim forces will have been destroyed.

Those who hold to other views find some problems with this viewpoint.

1. Any view which has this invasion taking place in the first half of the tribulation has a hard time being reconciled with the burning of weapons for seven years. For example, if the invasion takes place in year two of the tribulation period, this means the seven-year burning of weapons would continue beyond the tribulation and into the millennial kingdom.

2. Those who hold to this view may not properly appreciate the level of persecution of the Jews in the second half of the tribulation. Burning weapons for seven years under this heavy persecution would difficult.

3. It is hard to see why God would intervene on Israel's behalf by destroying the northern intruder during the first half of the tribulation, only to then allow events in the second

half of the tribulation that do great damage to Israel.[7] It seems better to place the invasion some years prior to the tribulation.

Viewpoint 4: At the End of the Tribulation

Other Bible expositors suggest that the Ezekiel invasion into Israel will take place at the end of the tribulation. They equate this invasion with Armageddon. Several arguments are offered in support of this view.

1. Armageddon takes place during the tribulation, and Ezekiel's invasion is in the "last days" and "latter years" (terms which some believe indicate the tribulation), so these events must be equated.

2. Birds and predatory animals will feast on the dead bodies following God's destruction of the Ezekiel invaders (Ezekiel 39:4,17-20). The same thing will happen after Armageddon (Revelation 19:17-18). Therefore the northern invasion and Armageddon must be one and the same.

3. Zechariah 12:10 tells us that large numbers of Jews will turn to the Lord at the end of the tribulation (following Armageddon). In like manner, Ezekiel 39:22,29 seems to indicate Jewish conversions after the Ezekiel invasion. They must therefore be the same.

Those who hold to other views find some problems with this viewpoint.

1. Armageddon involves all the nations of the earth (Joel 3:2; Zephaniah 3:8; Zechariah 12:3; 14:2), whereas the Ezekiel invaders includes only specific nations—Russia, Iran, Sudan, Turkey, Libya, and some other Muslim nations (see Ezekiel 38:1-6).

2. The locations are different. At Armageddon the destruction takes place at the Mount of Megiddo, about 60 miles north

of Jerusalem. The destruction depicted by Ezekiel takes place on the mountains of Israel.

3. The casualties of Armageddon take place as a result of the personal appearance of Jesus Christ at His second coming (Revelation 19:15). The casualties of the Ezekiel invasion result from a great earthquake, infighting among the troops, the outbreak of disease, torrential rain, and fire and brimstone falling on the troops (Ezekiel 38:20-22).

4. The Jews at the end of the tribulation (when Armageddon will occur) will not be living in security and at rest, for they will be enduring great persecution at the hands of the antichrist. By contrast, the Jews during the first half of the tribulation will be living in relative security and rest, which is when many believe Ezekiel's invasion takes place.[8]

5. If Ezekiel's invasion is equated with Armageddon, the seven-year burning of weapons will extend well into the millennial kingdom.

6. At Armageddon the beast (or antichrist) is the head of the invasion campaign (Revelation 19:19). Gog is the head of the invading force in Ezekiel's prophecy (Ezekiel 38:2).

7. The armies gathered at Armageddon array themselves against Jesus Christ at the second coming (Revelation 19:19). This is not true of Ezekiel's northern military coalition.

Viewpoint 5: After the Tribulation and Before the Millennium

Other Christians see an interlude between the tribulation and the millennial kingdom during which the Ezekiel invasion takes place. They support this position with these considerations.

1. If there could be an interlude between the rapture and the tribulation, then to be consistent, there may be an interlude between the tribulation and the millennium.

2. Israel will truly be living in security and rest following the second coming, so the invasion must take place at this point.

Those who hold to other views find some problems with this viewpoint.

1. The big problem with this view is that the interlude between the tribulation and the millennial kingdom wouldn't be long enough to accommodate all the details of Ezekiel 38–39 (including burning weapons for seven years). Scripture provides no evidence for such a lengthy interlude.

2. It seems impossible to fathom that a military force would attempt to attack Israel following Christ's glorious second coming. Besides, when the King of kings and Lord of lords comes, "From his mouth comes a sharp sword with which to strike down the nations" (Revelation 19:15). The enemies of Christ are not likely to last long enough to launch an invasion against Israel.

Viewpoint 6: At the Beginning of the Millennium

Yet other Bible expositors—Arno Gaebelein being one of the more popular—suggest that the Ezekiel invasion takes place at the beginning of the millennial kingdom. The primary argument cited in favor of this viewpoint is that Israel will certainly be at peace and at rest in Christ's millennial kingdom.

Those who hold to other views find some problems with this viewpoint.

1. Isaiah 2:4 explicitly tells us that there will be no war in Christ's millennial kingdom. This would seem to preclude any possibility of an invasion into Israel by the Ezekiel invaders.

2. An invasion into Israel early in the millennium would be virtually impossible because after the second coming of Christ, all unbelievers will be executed at the judgment of

the nations (Matthew 25:31-46). Jeremiah 25:32-33 affirms that the Lord will destroy all the wicked of the earth at His return (see also Revelation 19:15-18). Only believers enter into Christ's millennial kingdom. [9]

3. Ezekiel 39:12 tells us that following the Ezekiel invasion, the land will be defiled for seven months until all the dead bodies are buried. It is difficult to believe that the land will be defiled for seven months during the inaugural period of Christ's millennial kingdom.

4. Isaiah 9:4-5 tells us that all weapons of war will be destroyed following the beginning of Christ's millennial kingdom. Where would the Ezekiel invaders obtain weapons? [10]

5. Many today view the Muslim hatred of the Jewish people to be satanically inspired. At the beginning of the millennium, however, Satan will be bound up until the end of the millennium (Revelation 20:1-3).

6. No nation would try to attack Israel when Christ Himself—the King of kings and Lord of lords—is ruling. Such would be the height of madness.

Viewpoint 7: At the End of the Millennium

A final view is that the Ezekiel invasion will take place at the end of the millennial kingdom. This view has been predominant among non-evangelicals. [11]

1. "When the thousand years [the millennial kingdom] are ended, Satan will be released from his prison and will come out to deceive the nations that are at the four corners of the earth, Gog and Magog, to gather them for battle; their number is like the sand of the sea. And they marched up over the broad plain of the earth and surrounded the camp of the saints and the beloved city, but fire came down from heaven and consumed them, and the devil who had deceived them

was thrown into the lake of fire and sulfur where the beast and the false prophet were, and they will be tormented day and night forever and ever" (Revelation 20:7-10). This passage refers to Gog and Magog, so this must be the same invasion as described in Ezekiel 38–39.

2. The Ezekiel invasion is by "a great host" (Ezekiel 38:4) and "a mighty army" (verse 15), and God tells the leader, "many peoples are with you" (verse 6). The invasion force mentioned in Revelation is also described as being massive—"Their number is like the sand of the sea" (Revelation 20:8). Therefore these must be the same invasion.[12]

3. This view best explains the tremendous prosperity of Israel at the time this invasion begins (Ezekiel 38:12).

4. In both cases, God Himself defeats the invaders (Ezekiel 39:3-6; Revelation 20:9).

Those who hold to other views find some problems with this viewpoint.

1. The chronology does not fit. The invasion described by Ezekiel in Ezekiel 38–39 is sometime after the restoration of Israel (Ezekiel 36–37), when Jews stream back to the Holy Land from many nations around the world. Such will not be the case at the end of the millennium.

2. The invasion prophesied by Ezekiel is eventually followed by the establishment of the millennial kingdom (Ezekiel 40–48). The invasion prophesied in Revelation 20:7-10 is immediately followed by the establishment of the eternal state (Revelation 21).

3. Ezekiel 39:12 says it will take the Jews seven months to bury all the dead bodies. This burial would not be likely to happen at the end of the millennial kingdom. In this scenario, the Israelites spend seven hard months burying the wicked dead who invaded them. Immediately following this, according

to the book of Revelation, these same wicked dead are resurrected in order to take part in the great white throne judgment and be thrown into the lake of fire. Such a scenario is infeasible. Besides, Revelation 20:9 tells us that "fire came down from God out of heaven and consumed them." There won't be any bodies left to bury. They'll all be incinerated.

4. The next event in the book of Revelation after the great white throne judgment is the beginning of the eternal state (Revelation 21). This naturally brings up the problem of the burning of weapons for seven years. If this invasion takes place at the end of the millennial kingdom, then the burning of weapons would have to go beyond the millennial kingdom and into the eternal state, which doesn't make any sense at all.

5. The Ezekiel invading force involves a coalition of localized nations (Russia and a number of Muslim nations) who invade from the north. The millennial invaders will be an international army—"the nations that are at the four corners of the earth" (Revelation 20:8).

6. The apostle John may have been using the terms Gog and Magog as a shorthand metaphor, just as we do today. For example, the name Wall Street is now a metaphor for the stock market. Likewise, in New Testament times, terms like Corinthian and Nazarene became metaphors for people with less-than-desirable qualities. When John used the terms Gog and Magog in Revelation 20:7-10, his readers no doubt immediately drew the right connection and understood that this invasion at the end of the millennium would be similar to what Ezekiel described—a confederation of nations will attack Israel but will not succeed.[13]

Conclusion

In view of the wide diversity of opinions on this issue, it is probably wise not to be dogmatic on it. As one scholar put it, "The plethora of interpretations for this passage cautions the student concerning dogmatism in his conclusions."[14] Many fine scholars have debated this issue back and forth through the centuries, and that fact alone calls for humility in the face of this interpretive difficulty. My personal opinion is that the invasion will likely take place either after the rapture but about three and a half years before the tribulation period, or perhaps at the very beginning of the tribulation period.

DEBATE 4

Which View of the Rapture Is Correct?

8

The Case for Pretribulationism

The rapture is that glorious event in which the dead in Christ will be resurrected, living Christians will be instantly translated into their resurrection bodies, and both groups will be caught up to meet Christ in the air and taken back to heaven (John 14:1-3; 1 Corinthians 15:51-54; 1 Thessalonians 4:13-17). This means that one generation of Christians will never pass through death's door. They will be alive on earth one moment, and the next moment they will be translated into their resurrection bodies and caught up to meet Christ in the air. What an awesome moment that will be!

Christians often debate the timing of the rapture. Five different views have emerged in the debate:

> pretribulationism,
> midtribulationism,
> posttribulationism,
> the pre-wrath view, and
> the partial rapture view.

I will address each of these, beginning in this chapter with pretribulationism. This view—espoused by such scholars as John F. Walvoord, Charles C. Ryrie, and J. Dwight Pentecost—is the one I personally subscribe to.[1]

Pretribs point to prophetic chronological clues that they believe indicate that the rapture will take place prior to the tribulation period. If this view is correct, as I believe it is, this means the church will not go through the judgments prophesied in the book of Revelation (chapters 4–18). This view is most consistent with a literal interpretation of biblical prophecy.

Kept from the Hour of Trial

In Revelation 3:10 God promises the church in Philadelphia, "I will keep you from the hour of trial that is coming on the whole world, to try those who dwell on the earth." The seven churches in Revelation 2–3 were historical churches in Asia Minor, but many scholars believe these churches may also point in a secondary way to churches in the succeeding centuries of church history. If this is correct, then Jesus may have been referring to the future rapture in Revelation 3:10.

Many scholars note that there is a definite article (*the*) before the word *hour* in Revelation 3:10. Definite articles in the English language do not hold too much significance. But in the Greek language they are very important. Among other things, definite articles can indicate specificity. The definite article in Revelation 3:10 may point to a specific and distinctive time period, not just any hour of trial. The reference may therefore be to the future tribulation period, the seven-year hour of trial described in detail in Revelation 4–18. The church is to be kept from this period of trial.

This verse reveals that the church saints will be kept from the actual hour of testing, not just the testing itself. If the Lord meant to communicate that He would preserve them in the midst of the testing itself, He would have omitted the words *hour of* and simply said, "I will keep you from the trial that is coming…"

The Greek preposition *ek*, translated "from" in this verse, carries the idea of separation from something. This means that believers will be completely separated from the hour of trial by being raptured before the period even begins.

Renald Showers makes this observation in his book *Maranatha: Our Lord Come!*

The language in Jesus' reference to this future period of worldwide testing implied that it was well-known to the church saints. It was well-known because both Old and New Testament Scriptures, written years before Revelation, foretold this unique, future period of testing or Tribulation, which would take place prior to the coming of the Messiah to rule the world in the Messianic Age or Millennium (Isa. 2:10-21; Dan. 12:1; Zeph. 1:14-18; Mt. 24:4-31).[2]

This verse promises that only church saints will be kept out of this hour of trial coming on the whole world. Those who become believers during the hour of trial itself, whom we might call tribulation saints, will go through the remainder of the tribulation. This is an important observation, as noted by prophecy expert Arnold Fruchtenbaum in his book *The Footsteps of the Messiah*.

> Throughout the Tribulation, saints are being killed on a massive scale (Rev. 6:9-11; 11:7; 12:11; 13:7,15; 14:13; 17:6; 18:24). If these saints are Church saints, they are not being kept safe and Revelation 3:10 is meaningless. Only if Church saints and Tribulation saints are kept distinct does the promise of Revelation 3:10 make any sense.[3]

Absent from Tribulation Passages

No Old Testament passage on the tribulation mentions the church (for example, see Deuteronomy 4:29-30; Jeremiah 30:4-11; Daniel 8:24-27; 12:1-2). Likewise, no New Testament passage on the tribulation mentions the church (for example, Matthew 13:30,39-42,48-50; 24:15-31; 1 Thessalonians 1:9-10; 5:4-9; 2 Thessalonians 2:1-11).

In the book of Revelation, the word *church(es)* is used 19 times in the first three chapters. However, the section dealing with the tribulation (chapters 4–18) never mentions the church. The church is then mentioned again in the context of the second coming of Christ in chapter 19. The church's complete absence would seem to indicate that it is not on earth during the tribulation.

Further, a pretribulational rapture best explains the massive apostasy that engulfs the world following the removal of the restrainer—apparently the Holy Spirit (2 Thessalonians 2:3-7). The Holy Spirit indwells all believers (John 14:16; 1 Corinthians 3:17), so He will essentially be removed when the church is raptured, thus making possible the fast eruption of apostasy throughout the world.

Delivered from the Wrath to Come

Scripture assures us that the church is not destined for wrath (1 Thessalonians 5:9; see also Romans 5:9). This means the church cannot go through the "great day of [God's] wrath" in the tribulation period (Revelation 6:17; see also 14:10,19; 15:1,7; 16:1).

First Thessalonians 1:10 explicitly states that Jesus "delivers us from the wrath to come." The Greek word translated *delivers* means "to draw or snatch out to oneself, to rescue, to save, to preserve." Greek scholar Marvin Vincent, author of *Word Studies in the New Testament*, says the verb literally means "to draw to one's self" and "almost invariably" refers to deliverance from "some evil or danger or enemy."[4] This clearly seems to be referring to the rapture of the church before the tribulation period. In fact, the deliverance from wrath in 1 Thessalonians 1:10 sounds similar to the description of the rapture in 1 Thessalonians 4:16-17:

> For the Lord himself will descend from heaven with a cry of command, with the voice of an archangel, and with the sound of the trumpet of God. And the dead in Christ will rise first. Then we who are alive, who are left, will be caught up together with them in the clouds to meet the Lord in the air, and so we will always be with the Lord.

The phrase *caught up* here literally means "snatch up or take away."

Moreover, the Greek preposition *ek* ("from") is used in this verse, just as it is used in Revelation 3:10. The term carries the idea of "separation from." Believers will be delivered from this wrath by being completely separated from it, which requires the rapture.

Rescue Before Judgment

Throughout Scripture, God is seen protecting His people before judgment falls (see 2 Peter 2:5-9).

- Enoch was transferred to heaven before the judgment of the flood.

- Noah and his family were in the ark before the judgment of the flood.

- Lot was taken out of Sodom before judgment was poured out on Sodom and Gomorrah.

- The firstborn among the Hebrews in Egypt were sheltered by the blood of the Paschal Lamb before judgment fell.

- The spies were safely out of Jericho and Rahab was secured before judgment fell on Jericho.

So, too, will the church be secured safely—by means of the rapture—before judgment falls in the tribulation period. God's modus operandi seems to be to rescue His people before His judgment falls on unbelievers.

Noteworthy Parallels

The description of the rapture in 1 Thessalonians 4:16-18 shares some interesting parallels with 1 Thessalonians 5:10-11. The latter passage says, "[Christ] died for us so that whether we are awake or asleep we might live with him. Therefore encourage one another and build one another up, just as you are doing." Note these similarities:

1 Thessalonians 4:16-18	1 Thessalonians 5:10-11
"the dead in Christ"	"asleep"
"we who are alive"	"awake"
"encourage one another with these words"	"encourage one another and build one another up"

In view of this, a number of scholars believe 1 Thessalonians 5:10-11 refers to the rapture just as 1 Thessalonians 4:13-17 does. First Thessalonians 4:13-18 also seems to share some parallels with Jesus's description of the rapture in John 14:1-3.

John 14:1-3	1 Thessalonians 4:13-18
"I will come again."	"The Lord himself will descend from heaven."
"I will…take you to myself."	Believers will be "caught up together."
"…that where I am you may be also."	"We will always be with the Lord."
"Let not your hearts be troubled."	"That you may not grieve… encourage one another with these words."

These similarities clearly indicate that both passages are referring to the same event—the rapture of the church. And the scriptural evidence reveals that it takes place prior to the beginning of the tribulation.

The Rapture and the Second Coming

At the rapture, Christ will come *for* His saints in the air prior to the tribulation, whereas at the second coming, He will come *with* His saints to the earth to reign for 1000 years (Revelation 19; 20:1-6). The fact that Christ comes with His holy ones (redeemed believers) at the second coming presumes they have been previously raptured. In other words, Christ cannot come *with* them until He has first come *for* them.

Every eye will see Jesus at the second coming (Revelation 1:7), but the rapture is never described as being visible to the whole world. At the rapture, Christians meet Jesus in the air (1 Thessalonians 4:13-17), whereas at the second coming, Jesus's feet touch the Mount of Olives (Zechariah 14:4). At the rapture, Christians are taken and unbelievers are left behind (1 Thessalonians 4:13-17), whereas at the second coming unbelievers are taken away in judgment (Luke 17:34-36) and mortal believers remain to enter into Christ's millennial kingdom (Matthew 25:31-46).

At the rapture, Jesus will receive His bride, whereas at the second coming He will execute judgment (Matthew 25:31-46). The rapture will take place in the blink of an eye (1 Corinthians 15:52), whereas the second coming will be more drawn out, and every eye will see Him (Matthew 24:30; Revelation 1:7).

The Bride and the Bridegroom

Scripture portrays Christ as the Bridegroom (John 3:29) and the church as the bride of Christ (Revelation 19:7). The backdrop to this imagery is rooted in Hebrew weddings, which included three phases.

1. The marriage was legally established by the parents of the bride and groom, after which the groom went to prepare a place to live in his father's house.

2. The bridegroom returned to claim his bride.

3. The marriage was celebrated with a feast that lasted several days.

All three of these phases are seen in Christ's relationship to the church, or bride of Christ.

1. As individuals living during the church age come to salvation, under the Father's loving and sovereign hand, they become a part of the bride of Christ (the church). Meanwhile, Christ, the Bridegroom, is in heaven, preparing a place for the bride of Christ to live in His Father's house.

2. The Bridegroom returns to claim His bride at the rapture, at which time He takes His bride to heaven, where He has prepared a place for her (John 14:1-3). The actual marriage takes place in heaven (Revelation 19:7-9) prior to the second coming (verses 11-16).

3. Many believe the marriage supper of the Lamb follows the second coming, prior to Christ's institution of the millennial kingdom (during the gap mentioned in Daniel 12:11-12; compare with Matthew 22:1-14; 25:1-13).

There are other parallels as well. Jewish grooms paid a purchase price to establish the marriage covenant, and Jesus paid a purchase price for the church (1 Corinthians 6:19-20). A Jewish bride was declared sanctified or set apart in waiting for her groom, and the church is declared sanctified and set apart for Christ the Bridegroom (1 Corinthians 6:11; Ephesians 5:25-27). A Jewish bride was unaware of the exact time her groom would come for her, and the church is unaware of the exact time that Jesus the Bridegroom will come at the rapture, though His coming is imminent.

The Blessed Hope

The term "blessed hope" in Titus 2:13 is a reference to the rapture of the church. This event is blessed in the sense that it brings blessedness to believers. The term carries the idea of joyous anticipation. Believers can hardly wait for it to happen!

In this passage, the apostle Paul says Christians are "looking for the blessed hope and the appearing of the glory of our great God and Savior, Christ Jesus" (NASB). At this momentous event, the dead in Christ will be resurrected, and believers still alive on earth will be instantly translated into their resurrection bodies (see Romans 8:22-23; 1 Corinthians 15:51-58; Philippians 3:20-21; 1 Thessalonians 4:13-18; 1 John 3:2-3). These bodies will never again be subject to sickness, pain, and death. As we continue to pass through this fallen world as pilgrims, we are empowered by this magnificent hope.

The Imminence of the Rapture

The term *imminent* means "ready to take place" or "impending." The New Testament teaches that the rapture is imminent (see 1 Corinthians 1:7; 16:22; Philippians 3:20; 4:5; 1 Thessalonians 1:10; Titus

2:13; Hebrews 9:28; James 5:7-9; 1 Peter 1:13; Jude 21). The rapture is a signless event that can occur at any moment—nothing must be prophetically fulfilled before the rapture occurs. This is in contrast to the second coming of Christ, which is preceded by many events that transpire during the seven-year tribulation period (see Revelation 4–18).

The imminence of the rapture is certainly implied in the apostle Paul's words in Romans 13:11-12.

> You know the time, that the hour has come for you to wake from sleep. For salvation is nearer to us now than when we first believed. The night is far gone; the day is at hand. So then let us cast off the works of darkness and put on the armor of light.

The word *salvation* in this context must be eschatological, referring to the rapture, for Paul refers to it as a specific future event. At the end of each day, the Christian is that much closer to the rapture.

The imminence of the rapture is also implied in James 5:7-9.

> Be patient, therefore, brothers, until the coming of the Lord. See how the farmer waits for the precious fruit of the earth, being patient about it, until it receives the early and the late rains. You also, be patient. Establish your hearts, for the coming of the Lord is at hand. Do not grumble against one another, brothers, so that you may not be judged; behold, the Judge is standing at the door.

Imminence makes sense only in pretribulationism. In midtribulationism, the rapture takes place three and a half years after the tribulation begins. In posttribulationism, the rapture follows the tribulation. Imminence is impossible in these systems.

The fact that the rapture is a signless event and could occur at any moment ought to spur the Christian to live in purity and righteousness (see Titus 2:13-14).

> The fact that the glorified, holy Son of God could step through the door of heaven at any moment is intended by

God to be the most pressing, incessant motivation for holy living and aggressive ministry (including missions, evangelism, and Bible teaching) and the greatest cure for lethargy and apathy. It should make a difference in every Christian's values, actions, priorities, and goals.[5]

9

The Case for Midtribulationism

Midtribulationism is the view that Christ will rapture the church in the middle of the tribulation period. Well-known proponents of this position include Gleason Archer (1916–2004), J. Oliver Buswell (1895–1977), and Merrill Tenney (1904–1985).[1]

Midtribulationists typically argue that a number of prophetic passages place emphasis on the midpoint of the tribulation period and on the severe tribulations of its final three and a half years. For example, Daniel 9:27 says the antichrist "shall make a strong covenant with many for one week, and for half of the week he shall put an end to sacrifice and offering." In other words, the antichrist will put a stop to Jewish sacrifices in the temple at the midpoint of the tribulation.

Revelation 13:5 also speaks of the antichrist, affirming that "the beast was given a mouth uttering haughty and blasphemous words, and it was allowed to exercise authority for forty-two months." Forty-two months is equivalent to three and a half years. This means that the antichrist will come into great power in the last three and a half years of Daniel's seventieth week.

Scripture reveals that things become especially bad during the second half of the tribulation. Revelation 11:2 says the holy city (Jerusalem) will be trampled for 42 months. Revelation 12:6 indicates that the Jewish remnant will flee into the wilderness, where it will be sustained for 1260 days (also three and a half years). Verse 14 continues speaking of the Jewish remnant: "The woman was given the two wings of the great eagle so that she might fly from the serpent into the wilderness, to the place where she is to be nourished for a time, and times, and half a time" (again, three and a half years).

Because prophetic Scripture speaks often of the midpoint of the tribulation period, pointing to the great severity of the last three and a half years, a midtribulational rapture makes great sense to many people. In this scenario, the rapture will occur after the "beginning of sorrows" (Matthew 24:8 NKJV), which refers to all seven seal judgments and the first six trumpet judgments of Revelation 6–9, but before the "great tribulation" (verse 21 NKJV). "The beginning of sorrows" is the first half of the tribulation, and "the great tribulation" is the second half. The church will go through the first half but be spared from the second half.

Midtribulationists believe that what Christians will experience during the first three and a half years of the tribulation period will be difficult, just as Christians of all ages have had to suffer tribulations (see Acts 14:22; Romans 8:18; 2 Corinthians 4:17; 1 Peter 1:6). But the tribulations of this first half of Daniel's seventieth week will involve man's wrath against man, not God's wrath against man. God's wrath allegedly does not fall until the last three and a half years of the tribulation period. The church will be raptured before this time.

Midtribulationists point to 1 Thessalonians 5:9, where the apostle Paul writes that God "has not destined us [believers] for wrath, but to obtain salvation." The wrath in this verse is interpreted to be God's wrath that falls in the second half of the tribulation. In this view, then, the last half of the seventieth week of Daniel (Daniel 9:24-27) is much more severe than the first half. Midtribulationism is sometimes referred to as a form of pretribulationism because it teaches that the rapture precedes the tribulations (or wrath) of the second half of the seven-year period.[2]

This view is supported by the suggestion that the two prophetic witnesses of Revelation 11, who are caught up to heaven after they are resurrected, represent the church. These two are resurrected and raptured to heaven at the midpoint of the tribulation, so this must mean the church is raptured at this time.

The rapture will occur "with the sound of the trumpet of God" (1 Thessalonians 4:16). Midtribs equate this with "the last trumpet" (1 Corinthians 15:52) and the seventh trumpet judgment (Revelation 11:15-19), which comes at the midpoint of the tribulation.

Midtribulationists also appeal to 2 Thessalonians 2:1-4 in support of their view.

> Now concerning the coming of our Lord Jesus Christ and our being gathered together to him, we ask you, brothers, not to be quickly shaken in mind or alarmed, either by a spirit or a spoken word, or a letter seeming to be from us, to the effect that the day of the Lord has come. Let no one deceive you in any way. For that day will not come, unless the rebellion comes first, and the man of lawlessness is revealed, the son of destruction, who opposes and exalts himself against every so-called god or object of worship, so that he takes his seat in the temple of God, proclaiming himself to be God.

Midtribs suggest that specific signs—the rebellion and the revealing of the man of lawlessness—must precede the rapture of the church. They say this disproves the pretribulational rapture and lends credence to a midtribulational rapture.

Yet another argument offered in support of midtribulationism (and against posttribulationism) is that this view allows for the emergence of a group of people who become Christians in the second half of the tribulation. This is necessary because Scripture reveals that following the second coming, Christ will invite unresurrected believers who survive the tribulation into the millennial kingdom (Matthew 25:31-46; see also Revelation 20:7-8).

In a posttribulational scenario, no Christians would be available to enter the millennial kingdom in their mortal bodies. After all, every believer will receive a glorified resurrection body at the rapture. No mortal (unresurrected) Christians would be left in such a scenario. Midtribulationism solves this problem.

Midtribs suggest that Revelation 3:10 predicts a midtribulational rapture: "Because you have kept my word about patient endurance, I will keep you from the hour of trial that is coming on the whole world, to try those who dwell on the earth." The "hour of trial" allegedly refers specifically to the last three and a half years of Daniel's seventieth week.

My Assessment

I believe the pretribulational view of the rapture holds the most biblical support. However, I do not lightly dismiss the midtribulational viewpoint. Here are the reasons why I respectfully reject arguments supporting it.

Two Periods of the Tribulation

The tribulation period is in fact divided into two periods of three and a half years each, and specific events occur at the midpoint of the tribulation period. For example, we know that the antichrist will prohibit sacrifices in the Jewish temple (Daniel 9:27) and Jews will flee out of Jerusalem into the wilderness (Revelation 12:6,14) at that time. And the second half of the tribulation period is indeed worse than the first half. The judgments get progressively worse.

But midtribulationists read far too much into this. The rapture is nowhere mentioned or even alluded to at the midpoint of the tribulation period. It is simply not there. In fact, it is fair to say that while the Bible specifies that certain events will transpire at the midpoint of the tribulation, it is deafeningly silent on any rapture taking place at that point.

God's Wrath

Pretribulationists cannot go along with the idea that the wrath of God is evident only in the second half of the tribulation period. Rather, the entire seven-year period is characterized by the wrath of God. Consider Zephaniah 1:15,18, which describes the entire tribulation period as "a day of wrath" and "the day of the wrath of the LORD."

Midtribulationists say Revelation 6–9 refers only to the beginning of sorrows. But Revelation 6:17 says "the great day of their wrath has come, and who can stand?" "Their wrath" specifically refers to the wrath of the Father and the Lamb, Jesus Christ. Christ Himself is the one who opens each of the seven seals, so He initiates each of these judgments. Clearly then, the wrath of God begins falling on humankind in the first half of the tribulation.

Granted, we witness examples of what might be called the wrath of man in the first half of the tribulation period. However, divine wrath can be expressed through human agency. Is this not what we witness throughout biblical history? For example, God showed His displeasure against Israel in Old Testament times by allowing the Assyrians or Babylonians to take them into captivity. God used human beings as His whipping rods against Israel. We may witness examples of man's wrath in the first half of the tribulation period, but that does not mean God's wrath is not being expressed.

Different Trumpets

Midtribs make the case that the rapture occurs at the last trumpet (1 Thessalonians 4:16-17). They equate this with the seventh trumpet, which sounds in the middle of the tribulation (Revelation 11:15-19). This must mean, they reason, that the rapture occurs at the midpoint of the tribulation. But theologian Charles C. Ryrie notes that this logic is flawed.

> This is a somewhat simplistic argument that assumes that all blowing of trumpets must indicate the same kind of event. This is not true. In Jewish apocalyptic literature, trumpets signaled a variety of great eschatological events, including judgments, the gathering of the elect, and resurrection.[3]

The various eschatological trumpets are sounded in different contexts. For example, the trumpet in 1 Corinthians 15 relates specifically to the rapture and glorification. The same is true of the trumpet mentioned in 1 Thessalonians 4:13-17. However, the trumpet of Revelation 11 is not related to the rapture. Rather, it deals specifically with the

unleashing of judgment. The trumpet argument for midtribulationism is unsound.

The Two Prophetic Witnesses

Midtribulationists assert that the resurrection and ascension of the
two prophetic witnesses of Revelation 11 represent the rapture of the
church. Such an idea, however, appears to be more eisegesis (reading
a meaning into the text) than exegesis (deriving the meaning from the
text itself). The text of Revelation offers virtually no indication that the
two witnesses represent the church.

Scripture simply indicates that during the tribulation period, God
will raise up two mighty witnesses who will testify to the true God
with astounding power. In fact, the power of these witnesses brings to
mind Elijah (1 Kings 17; Malachi 4:5) and Moses (Exodus 7–11). In
the Old Testament, two witnesses were required to confirm testimony
(see Deuteronomy 19:15; see also Matthew 18:16; John 8:17). So these
two witnesses will supernaturally confirm God's truth during the tribulation period.

Some believe it seems more natural to relate the two witnesses to
Israel. In support of this, many expositors believe the two witnesses will
actually be Moses and Elijah. After all, God deals with the Jews during
the tribulation, just as He did in the first 69 weeks of Daniel (see Daniel
9:26-27). Moses and Elijah are unquestionably two of the most influential figures in Jewish history, so their presence during the tribulation
period makes sense. Even if the two witnesses are not Moses and Elijah, however, there is still no indication that they represent the church.

All things considered, the account of the two witnesses offers no real
support to midtribulationism.

A Denial of Imminence

If the midtribulationist scenario is correct, the doctrine of the
imminence of the rapture must be dismissed. A midtribulational rapture must necessarily be preceded by three and a half years of signs.
The tribulation begins when the antichrist signs a covenant with Israel
(Daniel 9:27), and this would essentially begin a three-and-a-half-year

countdown to the day of the rapture. Any idea of the rapture occurring any moment is out the back door in this scenario.

> When these theologians locate the rapture of the church in the middle of the seventieth week of Daniel, which is measured by years, months, and days, it is no longer true that believers may expect the coming of Christ for the church at any time. A certain period of time must pass and certain prophesied events must take place before Christ can come for the church.[4]

The New Testament, however, clearly teaches an imminent rapture (see Romans 13:11-12; 1 Corinthians 1:7; 16:22; Philippians 3:20; 4:5; 1 Thessalonians 1:10; Titus 2:13; Hebrews 9:28; James 5:7-9; 1 Peter 1:13; Jude 21). The rapture is portrayed as a signless event that can occur at any moment.

Obviously, imminence makes sense only in pretribulationism. In midtribulationism, the rapture is at least three and a half years into the tribulation. In posttribulationism, the rapture follows the tribulation. Imminence is impossible in these two systems.

2 Thessalonians 2

Midtribulationists argue that specific signs—the rebellion and the rise of the antichrist—must precede the rapture of the church. However, this is an incorrect understanding of 2 Thessalonians 2. The text reveals that the signs specified take place during the tribulation period ("the day of the Lord"), not prior to the rapture.

The apostle Paul had earlier taught the Thessalonian Christians that they would be raptured prior to the tribulation period. But some false teachers had come to Thessalonica and told the believers there that they were already experiencing the day of the Lord. This understandably unsettled the Thessalonians. So in 2 Thessalonians the apostle Paul clarifies the matter for them. He points out that the major events of the tribulation period (such as the rise of the antichrist) had not yet occurred, so they were obviously not yet in the tribulation period.

Paul then told them that the antichrist cannot rise until the restrainer is removed (2 Thessalonians 2:7). Who is the restrainer? It is apparently the Holy Spirit, who will be removed when the church is raptured from the earth (because the church is the temple of the Holy Spirit—see 1 Corinthians 3:16; 6:19).

Thus 2 Thessalonians 2 offers no real support to the midtribulational view of the rapture but rather supports the pretribulational view.

Populating the Millennium

Scripture reveals that mortal Christians (who have not received their resurrection bodies) will enter into Christ's millennial kingdom (see Matthew 25:31-46). Midtribulationists claim that these people become Christians in the second half of the tribulation period, after a midtribulational rapture. However, pretribulationism also recognizes that tribulation converts will enter into Christ's millennial kingdom in their mortal bodies. The case for the timing of the rapture must rest on the other evidence cited above.

Conclusion

I respect those who hold to midtribulationism, but I believe that pretribulationism is the correct biblical view. In my thinking, midtribulationism simply does not sync with all the biblical data on the rapture.

10

The Case for Posttribulationism

The posttribulational view—espoused by such scholars as George Eldon Ladd, Alexander Reese, and Robert Gundry—is the view that Christ will rapture the church after the tribulation period at the second coming of Christ.[1] They offer a number of arguments in support of this view.

For example, Scripture confirms that Christians will experience tribulation. In John 16:1-2, Jesus tells His disciples, "I have said all these things to you to keep you from falling away. They will put you out of the synagogues. Indeed, the hour is coming when whoever kills you will think he is offering service to God." In Acts 14:22 we are told, "Through many tribulations we must enter the kingdom of God." Romans 12:12 exhorts believers, "Be patient in tribulation." Therefore, the idea that Christians will go through tribulation is intrinsic to Scripture.

Posttribulationists are careful to emphasize that even though the church will go through the time of judgment prophesied in the book of Revelation, it will be "kept through" the trials—especially those relating to Satan's wrath. They believe Revelation 3:10 supports this idea: "Because you have kept my word about patient endurance, I will keep you from the hour of trial that is coming on the whole world, to try those who dwell on the earth." The phrase "keep you from," allegedly means "keep you through."

Posttribulationists also cite Revelation 20:4-6 in support of their view.

> Then I saw thrones, and seated on them were those to whom the authority to judge was committed. Also I saw the souls of those who had been beheaded for the testimony of Jesus and for the word of God, and those who had not worshiped the beast or its image and had not received its mark on their foreheads or their hands. They came to life and reigned with Christ for a thousand years. The rest of the dead did not come to life until the thousand years were ended. This is the first resurrection. Blessed and holy is the one who shares in the first resurrection! Over such the second death has no power, but they will be priests of God and of Christ, and they will reign with him for a thousand years.

In the posttrib scenario, believers who die during the tribulation period come to life just before the millennium and reign with Christ. This "first resurrection" is equated with the rapture.

Posttribs also note that saints are on earth during the tribulation period (see Revelation 13:7; 14:12; 17:6). This must mean the rapture has not yet occurred.

The vocabulary of the New Testament is also cited as a support for posttribulationism. The same Greek word (*parousia*) is used to describe the rapture and the second coming, so the two events must occur at the same time. The word *parousia* literally means "coming," "arrival," or "presence." The word is used of the rapture in 1 Thessalonians 4:15 and of the second coming in Matthew 24:27. The events belong together.

Matthew 24:37-42 provides more support.

> For as were the days of Noah, so will be the coming of the Son of Man. For as in those days before the flood they were eating and drinking, marrying and giving in marriage, until the day when Noah entered the ark, and they were unaware until the flood came and swept them all away, so

will be the coming of the Son of Man. Then two men will
be in the field; one will be taken and one left. Two women
will be grinding at the mill; one will be taken and one left.
Therefore, stay awake, for you do not know on what day
your Lord is coming.

Posttribs believe this passage refers to the rapture, for "two men will
be in the field; one will be taken and one left," and "two women will
be grinding at the mill; one will be taken and one left." These are in the
context of the second coming, so the rapture must happen at the second coming and not prior to the tribulation period.

Besides, posttribs say, pretribulationism is a novel view that emerged
late in church history. It finds its origin in John Nelson Darby (1800–
1882), who allegedly got it from Edward Irving (1792–1834). This
means that the majority of church history knew nothing of this view.
Because it is a recent view, it must not be correct.

My Assessment

Posttribulationism is certainly held by many Christians I respect. I
do not personally accept the view, but I nevertheless acknowledge that
proponents of the view have sought to be biblical in their approach.
Here are some of the reasons I opt for pretribulationism rather than
posttribulationism.

Christians and Tribulation

No pretrib denies that Christians will experience tribulation in the
world (Acts 14:22). However, Scripture uses the word *tribulation* in at
least two senses—a general sense and a specific sense. Sometimes the
word is used generally to refer to the trials and tribulations that we all
face in living on the earth. For example, Jesus said, "In the world you
will have tribulation. But take heart; I have overcome the world" (John
16:33). Other times, however, the word refers to a specific seven-year
period just preceding the second coming of Christ (Matthew 24:29).
Christians will be delivered only from this period of tribulation.

Kept Through the Tribulation

It seems unreasonable to say that Christians will be kept through (or kept safe from) the many tribulations—especially those relating to Satan's wrath—that are unleashed during the tribulation period. Many of the calamities that fall during the tribulation are indiscriminate. For example, devastating earthquakes do not somehow steer clear of Christians and afflict only unbelievers. Wormwood—apparently a large asteroid that will make deep impact on earth—will likewise afflict everyone, both believers and unbelievers. Believers could hardly be "kept through" such horrific events.

Scripture reveals that the entire tribulation period is characterized by wrath (Zephaniah 1:15,18), judgment (Revelation 14:7), fury (Isaiah 26:20-21), trial (Revelation 3:10), distress (Jeremiah 30:7), destruction (Joel 1:15), darkness (Amos 5:18), desolation (Daniel 9:27), and punishment (Isaiah 24:20-21). Simply put, no passage can be found to alleviate to any degree whatsoever the severity of this time.

Believers who live during the tribulation period will be persecuted by the devil. Revelation 2:10 urges believers, "Do not fear what you are about to suffer. Behold, the devil is about to throw some of you into prison, that you may be tested, and for ten days you will have tribulation. Be faithful unto death, and I will give you the crown of life." We are also told that the antichrist (the beast) persecutes Christians: "It was allowed to make war on the saints and to conquer them" (Revelation 13:7). Notice that the saints are not "kept through" this war, but are conquered.

Moreover, Revelation 3:10 does not actually support posttribulationism. It indicates that believers will be saved "out of" or "separated from" (Greek: *ek*) the actual time period ("hour of trial") of the tribulation.

One must not miss the clear statement in Revelation 3:10 that the tribulation period is "the hour of trial that is coming on the whole world." No one seems to be exempt. No one seems to be "kept through" the tribulation. Isaiah likewise speaks of the tribulation as being global: "Behold, the LORD will empty the earth and make it desolate, and he will twist its surface and scatter its inhabitants" (Isaiah 24:1). "Terror and the pit and the snare are upon you, O inhabitant of the earth" (verse 17). It seems fair to say that anyone who lives on the earth during the tribulation period will experience significant suffering.

Tribulation Saints

Saints will be on the earth during the tribulation period (for example, Revelation 6:9-11). However, pretribs believe these are people who were left behind at the rapture and then become believers during the tribulation period. Perhaps these people become convinced of the truth of Christianity after they see millions of Christians supernaturally vanish off the planet at the rapture. (Many Bibles and Christian books will be left behind to explain the event.) Perhaps they become believers as a result of the ministry of the 144,000 Jewish evangelists introduced in Revelation 7—who themselves apparently come to faith in Christ after the rapture. And many could become believers as a result of the miraculous ministry of the two witnesses of Revelation 11, prophets whose powers are similar to Moses's and Elijah's. The book of Revelation indicates that many people will respond to the gospel of the kingdom during the tribulation (Revelation 7:9-14).

A Resurrection After the Tribulation

Pretribulationists and posttribulationists agree that a resurrection will occur between the tribulation period and the millennial kingdom (Revelation 20:4-6). They also agree that this event will be part of the "first resurrection." Pretribs note, however, that not all resurrections happen at the same time. One resurrection of believers happens in conjunction with the rapture before the tribulation period (1 Thessalonians 4:13-17). Another resurrection of believers takes place after the tribulation period (Revelation 20:4-6). And both are part of the first resurrection.

To clarify, the Scriptures indicate that there are two types of resurrection. The first is appropriately called the "first resurrection" (Revelation 20:5), the "resurrection of life" (John 5:29), the "resurrection of the just" (Luke 14:14), and the "better resurrection" (Hebrews 11:35 NASB). The second resurrection is called the resurrection of judgment

(John 5:29; see also Daniel 12:2; Acts 24:15). The first resurrection is the resurrection of Christians, and the second resurrection is the resurrection of the wicked.

The first resurrection therefore includes all the resurrections of the righteous even though they are widely separated in time. There is one resurrection of the righteous at the rapture (before the tribulation—1 Thessalonians 4:13-17), another during the tribulation (the two witnesses—Revelation 11:3,11), another at the end of the tribulation (the martyred dead—Revelation 20:4-5), and still another at the end of the 1000-year millennial kingdom. They all are "first" in the sense of being before the second (final) resurrection of the wicked dead. Accordingly, the term *first resurrection* applies to all the resurrections of the saints regardless of when they occur, including the resurrection of Christ the firstfruits (1 Corinthians 15:23).

The second resurrection, or last resurrection, is an awful spectacle. All the unsaved of all time will be resurrected at the end of Christ's millennial kingdom, judged at the great white throne judgment, and cast alive into the lake of fire (Revelation 20:11-15).

The Vocabulary of the New Testament

Pretribulationists grant that the Greek word *parousia* means "coming," "arrival," or "presence." However, this simply means that both the rapture and the second coming—one before the tribulation and the other after it—are characterized by the coming, arrival, and presence of Jesus Christ. Theologian Charles C. Ryrie offers this illustration of how the same word can refer to two different events.

> Suppose proud grandparents should say to their friends, "We are looking forward to enjoying the presence (*parousia*) of our grandchildren next week"; then later in the conversation add, "Yes, we expect our grandchildren to be present at our golden wedding celebration." If you heard those statements you could draw one of two conclusions. (1) The grandchildren are coming next week for the golden wedding anniversary. In other words, the grandparents were speaking of the coming and the anniversary

as a single event, occurring at the same time. Or (2) the grandchildren will be making two trips to see their grandparents—one next week (perhaps as part of their vacation) and another later to help celebrate the golden wedding anniversary.[2]

Ryrie's point, of course, is that *parousia* can refer to two separate events—the rapture and the second coming. The truth of the matter is that the use of the term *parousia* does not prove either posttribulationism or pretribulationism. The timing of the rapture depends on other factors, such as those discussed above.

One Will Be Taken

Pretribulationists grant the importance of Matthew 24:37-41, which affirms that after the tribulation period, "two men will be in the field; one will be taken and one left. Two women will be grinding at the mill; one will be taken and one left." Pretribs deny, however, that this passage refers to the rapture. The parallel passage in Luke 17:34-37 indicates that those who are taken are taken not in the rapture but rather are taken in judgment.

> "I tell you, in that night there will be two in one bed. One will be taken and the other left. There will be two women grinding together. One will be taken and the other left." And they said to him, "Where, Lord?" He said to them, "Where the corpse is, there the vultures will gather."

So, where will they be taken? They will be taken to a place where vultures feed on dead corpses. In other words, these people are taken away in judgment. They are not taken to heaven, so this passage and the parallel in Matthew 24 provide no support for posttribulationism.

Pretribulationism—a Recent View?

Posttribulationists assert that pretribulationism is a relatively recent view that emerged in the 1800s. Most of church history is said to have known nothing about this view.

Pretribs respond in several ways to this line of argumentation. First, to pretribs, the key issue is to determine what the Bible actually teaches and not when a belief first emerged in church history. If the Bible clearly teaches a doctrine, people should be very cautious in so easily dismissing it.

Further, pretribs note that some in the early church held to false doctrines, such as baptismal regeneration. A doctrine may have been held early in church history, but that does not necessarily mean it is correct. Conversely, a doctrine may have developed late in church history, but that does not necessarily mean it is incorrect.

Many believe that as doctrine developed through the centuries, eschatology naturally became a focus later in church history. Besides, many throughout church history—as early as the first century—have held to the doctrine of the imminent return of Christ, which is a key feature of pretribulationism.

Populating the Millennial Kingdom

The judgment of the nations, discussed in Matthew 25:31-46, reveals that Christ will separate the sheep from the goats according to how they treated Christ's brothers. The sheep are invited directly into Christ's millennial kingdom in their mortal (unresurrected) bodies. These mortal believers will marry, bear children, grow old, and die during the millennial kingdom (Isaiah 65:17-25). Such things could not happen if they were already resurrected.

This is a problem for posttribulationism. If the rapture happens after the tribulation period, at which point virtually all believers are resurrected, then what mortal (unresurrected) believers are left to enter into Christ's millennial kingdom? None! If all believers are raptured at the second coming, none are left to enter the millennium in their mortal bodies. This is no problem for pretribulationism, which teaches that after the rapture, many will become believers during the tribulation (see Revelation 7:9-17). These post-rapture believers will enter into the millennial kingdom in their mortal bodies.

Conclusion

I am personally acquainted with some quality Christians who hold to the posttribulational view. Posttribulationism is certainly a viable theological perspective. However, I am convinced it falls short of adequately dealing with all of the biblical data, some of which is cited above. I remain thoroughly convinced of pretribulationism.[3]

11

The Case for the Pre-wrath View

The pre-wrath view—espoused by Robert Van Kampen and Marvin Rosenthal—holds that the rapture occurs toward the end of the tribulation before the great wrath of God falls (2 Thessalonians 1:5-10).[1] Marvin Rosenthal preached the pretribulationist view for some 35 years before he abandoned it in favor of the pre-wrath view.

Rosenthal believes that since the word *wrath* does not appear in the book of Revelation until after the sixth seal, God's wrath will not be poured out until the seventh seal (see Revelation 6:12–8:1). This subsequently means that the rapture must take place between the sixth and seventh seals, near the end of the tribulation period.

Rosenthal declares that the term *tribulation period* should be omitted from discussions about the rapture. It should not be used as a synonym for the entire seventieth week of Daniel, for such a term allegedly predisposes one toward pretribulationism. He claims that pretribulationists have coined a technical phrase and superimposed it onto the Scriptures.

Rosenthal divides the seventieth week of Daniel into three clearly recognizable periods—the beginning of sorrows, the great tribulation, and the frequently predicted day of the Lord. More specifically, the first three and a half years are the beginning of sorrows. The midpoint of the seventieth week of Daniel begins the great tribulation, which lasts just one and three-fourths years (21 months). The final 21 months—the fourth quarter of the seven-year period—is the day of the Lord, in which alone falls the wrath of God.

In this line of thought, the rapture occurs just prior to the day of the Lord at the sounding of the seventh trumpet. Put another way, the rapture occurs between the end of the third quarter and the beginning of the fourth quarter of Daniel's seventieth week. This allows the church to escape the unleashing of God's wrath.

Not surprisingly, since the rapture is placed rather precisely after three-quarters of the seventieth week of Daniel, Rosenthal considers the doctrine of imminence untenable. No longer can Christians look forward to the possibility of the rapture occurring at any moment.

Rosenthal acknowledges that pretribulationists—such as John F. Walvoord, Charles C. Ryrie, and J. Dwight Pentecost—were formerly his heroes when it came to prophecy. Now he laments that their interpretation of Scripture is untrustworthy.[2] By contrast, he dogmatically asserts that his own interpretations are indisputable and beyond refutation.

My Assessment

Robert Van Kampen and Marvin Rosenthal have come up with an interesting and novel theory, but I believe it is flawed at its very foundation. That foundation has to do with precisely when the wrath of God is unleashed during the tribulation period.

The Word *Tribulation*

As noted above, Rosenthal rejects the use of the term *tribulation period*, which he says pretribulationists have turned into a technical term. The truth is that pretribulationists don't use this phrase as a technical term at all. Rather, they use it as a descriptive term. We have seen that Scripture describes the seventieth week of Daniel as a seven-year period characterized by wrath, judgment, fury, and much more. The term *tribulation period* is therefore an accurate designation of it.

The Tribulation and God's Wrath

Pretribulationists believe that God's wrath is poured out on the earth far prior to the seventh seal. Zephaniah 1:15 describes the entire future tribulation period this way: "A day of wrath is that day, a day of distress and anguish, a day of ruin and devastation, a day of darkness and gloom, a day of clouds and thick darkness." The entire tribulation period is characterized by God's wrath.

The apostle Paul tells us in 1 Thessalonians 1:10 that Jesus "delivers us from the wrath to come." Notice the definite article, *the*. In English, definite articles are not that significant. But in the Greek language they are extremely significant. Many believe "*the* wrath" points to a definite and specific future period of wrath. This period of wrath is most naturally interpreted as being the entire seven-year tribulation (Daniel 9:27), which is elsewhere called "the time of Jacob's trouble" (Jeremiah 30:7; see also Revelation 6:17; 14:7,10; 19:2).

The Seven Seals and God's Wrath

Scripture pictures the seven seals all coming as a sequence from the same ultimate source—God (Revelation 6; 8:1-5). This sequence features divine judgments that increase in intensity with each new seal. Human beings and warfare are instruments of God's wrath during the first six seals. Even the unsaved who experience this wrath recognize it as the "wrath of the Lamb" (Revelation 6:15-16). This recognition is appropriate, for Christ Himself—the Lamb of God—opens each seal, releasing each judgment (see Revelation 6:1,3,5,7,9,12; 8:1). Therefore, to argue that the wrath of God does not begin until the seventh seal hardly seems feasible.

The word *wrath* is not used until the seventh seal, but that does not mean that God's wrath has not fallen prior to that time. Theologian Norman Geisler explains, "The word *wrath* does not appear in Genesis, yet God's wrath was poured out during the Flood (6–8) and on Sodom and Gomorrah (19)."[3] In Bible times, people often experienced God's wrath even when the word *wrath* is not used in the biblical text.

Pre-wrath proponents rebut that during the first six seal judgments, people suffer the wrath of man, not the wrath of God. However, again, notice that Christ is the one who unrolls each seal, thereby initiating

115

each judgment on earth. This is a clear instance of God (Christ) using human agency as a means of expressing His wrath. God has often done this in the past. When God needed to chasten the Israelites in Old Testament times, He sent them into captivity under the Assyrians and Babylonians. God's wrath was expressed through human agency. Thus those on earth who experience the sixth seal judgment recognize it directly as the "wrath of the Lamb."

Notice also that each of the four horsemen of the Apocalypse is released when the Lamb opens a seal and one of the four "living creatures," who descend from the very presence of God (Revelation 4:6-8), says, "Come!" This, too, indicates that the seal judgments are expressions of the wrath of God.

Further, the first four seal judgments are typical of the expressions of divine wrath in Bible days—the sword, famine, pestilence, and wild beasts (Leviticus 26:22,25; Deuteronomy 28:21-25; Jeremiah 15:2-3; 16:4; Ezekiel 5:12,17; 14:21). The argument that the seal judgments represent only the wrath of man is untenable.

The Day of the Lord

The expression *the day of the Lord* denotes a time in which God actively controls and dominates history in a direct way instead of working through secondary causes. The day of the Lord is characterized by God actively intervening supernaturally in order to bring judgment against sin in the world. The New Testament writers used the term to describe the judgments that will be unleashed in the future seven-year tribulation period (1 Corinthians 5:5; 1 Thessalonians 5:2; 2 Thessalonians 2:2; 2 Peter 3:10). Most prophecy experts believe the day of the Lord is properly placed after the rapture in conjunction with the beginning of the tribulation period.

Rosenthal rejects this idea and calls it the single greatest error people make in terms of the proper timing of the rapture. As we have seen, Rosenthal holds to three periods within the seventieth week of Daniel: the beginning of sorrows (lasting three and a half years), the great tribulation (lasting 21 months, the third quarter of Daniel's seventieth week), and the day of the Lord (also lasting 21 months, the last quarter of Daniel's seventieth week). The day of the Lord allegedly begins with the opening of the seventh seal (Revelation 8).

Contrary to this view, Scripture typically points to the entire tribulation period as constituting the day of the Lord (see Joel 2:1-2). The day of the Lord includes the first six seal judgments. Rosenthal claims that the first six seal judgments represent the wrath of man, but some of the judgments are clearly beyond man's capabilities.

> When he opened the sixth seal, I looked, and behold, there was a great earthquake, and the sun became black as sackcloth, the full moon became like blood, and the stars of the sky fell to the earth as the fig tree sheds its winter fruit when shaken by a gale. The sky vanished like a scroll that is being rolled up, and every mountain and island was removed from its place (Revelation 6:12-14).

How can this possibly be categorized as the wrath of man? This is clearly the wrath of God, which occurs before Rosenthal's fourth quarter of Daniel's seventieth week.

When one combines this with what I noted previously—that each of the seven seals is opened by Jesus Christ and represents the wrath of the Lamb—to say that the wrath of God does not fall until the seventh seal makes no sense.

Conclusion

Rosenthal presents an inadequate theological system. Sadly, he also speaks ungraciously of such men as John F. Walvoord, Charles C. Ryrie, and J. Dwight Pentecost (all with whom I have personally interacted with in the past) and sets up his own view as indisputable and beyond refutation. Such dogmatism always raises a red flag in my mind.

12

The Case for the Partial Rapture View

The partial rapture theory is expressed in the writings of Robert Govett, J.A. Seiss, G.H. Pember, G.H. Lang, and Witness Lee.[1] This view teaches that only those believers who are watching and waiting for the Lord's return will be found worthy to escape the trials of the tribulation by being taken in the rapture. As one partial rapturist wrote, "Only a prepared and expectant section of believers will then be translated."[2]

An interesting feature of partial rapturism is that it identifies multiple raptures throughout the tribulation period. The first of the raptures will take place before the tribulation, when only mature living saints and mature dead saints will be raised. Then, throughout the seven years of the tribulation period, saints who were initially unprepared for the rapture will be raptured at various intervals (see Revelation 7:9,14; 11:12; 12:5). This includes watching believers who will be raptured before the war of Armageddon (16:16) and another rapture at the end of the tribulation.

Partial rapturists cite a number of Scriptures to support their view. For example, Hebrews 9:28 states, "Christ, having been offered once to bear the sins of many, will appear a second time, not to deal with sin but to save those who are eagerly waiting for him." This allegedly refers to Christ delivering (by means of the rapture) those who are waiting for Him. Those not waiting for him will simply be left behind. In this line of thought, unsanctified believers who are left behind on earth will experience a time of purging as they experience the trials of the tribulation period. Their sin makes them unfit to be caught up into the direct presence of Jesus Christ.

Partial rapturists believe the parable of the ten virgins supports this view. In it, five virgins are prepared, and five are unprepared (Matthew 25:1-13). This is interpreted to mean that only faithful and watchful Christians will be raptured. Unfaithful Christians will be left behind to be purged during the tribulation.

In Matthew 24:40-42 Jesus tells His followers, "Then two men will be in the field; one will be taken and one left. Two women will be grinding at the mill; one will be taken and one left. Therefore, stay awake, for you do not know on what day your Lord is coming." This allegedly indicates that the rapture is a reward that not all will experience. Only those who "stay awake" and watch for it will participate in it.

In 1 Corinthians 9:27 Paul said, "I discipline my body and keep it under control, lest after preaching to others I myself should be disqualified." Paul was allegedly aware that some Christians would be disqualified from participating in the rapture.

In Titus 2:11-13 Paul writes that the grace of God is training us to be "waiting for our blessed hope, the appearing of the glory of our great God and Savior Jesus Christ." Only those who are waiting will participate in the blessed hope of the rapture.

In Revelation 3:10 Jesus tells the church at Philadelphia, "Because you have kept my word about patient endurance, I will keep you from the hour of trial that is coming on the whole world, to try those who dwell on the earth." Apparently those who have not kept Christ's word will be disqualified from participating in the rapture.

According to partial rapturists, Scripture reveals that some Christians are less faithful than others and will be excluded from the initial rapture before the tribulation period. Though the following verses do not bear directly on the rapture, they allegedly show that some Christians are more faithful or less faithful than other Christians.

- "Truly, I say to you, in the new world, when the Son of Man will sit on his glorious throne, you who have followed me will also sit on twelve thrones, judging the twelve tribes of Israel. And everyone who has left houses or brothers or sisters or father or mother or children or lands, for my name's sake, will receive a hundredfold and will inherit eternal life. But many who are first will be last, and the last first" (Matthew 19:28-30).

- "No one who puts his hand to the plow and looks back is fit for the kingdom of God" (Luke 9:62).

- "For his sake I have suffered the loss of all things…that I may gain Christ…that I may know him and the power of his resurrection, and may share in his sufferings, becoming like him in his death, that by any means possible I may attain the resurrection from the dead.

  "Not that I have already obtained this or am already perfect, but I press on to make it my own, because Christ Jesus has made me his own. Brothers, I do not consider that I have made it my own. But one thing I do: forgetting what lies behind and straining forward to what lies ahead, I press on toward the goal for the prize of the upward call of God in Christ Jesus" (Philippians 3:8-14).

- "He who has an ear, let him hear what the Spirit says to the churches. The one who conquers will not be hurt by the second death" (Revelation 2:11).

- "The one who conquers will be clothed thus in white garments, and I will never blot his name out of the book of life. I will confess his name before my Father and before his angels" (Revelation 3:5).

In view of such verses, partial rapturists reason that those Christians who are not as committed as others will lose the privilege of participating in the initial rapture prior to the tribulation period. This will be the consequence they pay.

My Assessment

In my thinking, partial rapturists can come to this theological paradigm only by ignoring key passages of Scripture that clearly stand against the idea.[3] Here are some of the more significant problems prophecy scholars have with this view.

All the Saved Participate in the Rapture

Scripture reveals that all who are saved—that is, all who have placed faith in Jesus Christ for salvation (John 3:16-17; Acts 16:31)—will participate in the rapture. As Paul writes in 1 Corinthians 15:51-52, "Behold! I tell you a mystery. We shall not all sleep, but we shall all be changed, in a moment, in the twinkling of an eye, at the last trumpet. For the trumpet will sound, and the dead will be raised imperishable, and we shall be changed." Paul could not have put it any clearer. "We shall *all* be changed"—not "some of us" or "the most holy among us."

The Entire Body of Christ

Scripture reveals that "in one Spirit we were all baptized into one body" (1 Corinthians 12:13). No believers are exempt from being baptized into the body of Christ, which is the church (see Romans 12:5; 1 Corinthians 10:17; 12:27; Ephesians 4:12; 5:23; Colossians 1:24; Hebrews 13:3). There is a perfect unity in the body of Christ (see Ephesians 4:3-4). It therefore stands to reason that all believers will be raptured (1 Thessalonians 4:16-17). Put another way, all of Christ's body—not just pieces of it, such as a finger or an ear—will participate in the rapture.

The Entire Bride of Christ

Likewise, the church is the bride of Christ (2 Corinthians 11:2-3; Ephesians 5:25-27,32), so clearly, the entire bride of Christ and not just part of her will be caught up at the rapture. The entire church will be caught up to meet Christ in the air. If partial rapturism is correct, the marriage motif falls apart when related to the rapture.

The Parable of the Ten Virgins

Pretribulationists grant that in the parable of the ten virgins (Matthew 25:1-13), five virgins are prepared and five are unprepared. But this parable does not refer to the rapture of the church. The virgins who were unprepared represent people (apparently unbelieving Jews) living during the tribulation period who are unprepared for Christ's second coming—seven years after the rapture. After all, Christ's entire Olivet Discourse in Matthew 24–25 speaks specifically of the tribulation period. The parable offers no support for the partial rapture theory.

Israel and the Church

The tribulation period deals not with the church but rather with Israel. Just as Daniel's first 69 weeks of years dealt with Israel, so his seventieth week (the tribulation) will deal with Israel. This is why the tribulation period is referred to as "a time of distress for Jacob" (Jeremiah 30:7). (Jacob is another name for Israel.) And because the tribulation period is intended to deal with Israel, no part of the redeemed church—which Christ purchased with His own blood (Acts 20:28)—could possibly be there.

A Partial Resurrection

The rapture is both a resurrection of dead Christians and a translation of living Christians, so it would seem that to be consistent, partial rapturism would require the resurrection of only faithful dead Christians, just as only faithful living Christians will be translated. In other words, a partial rapture includes a partial resurrection. But this is nowhere taught in the pages of Scripture. In fact, in 1 Thessalonians 4:13-17, the participants in the rapture are "the dead in Christ" and "we who are alive." The text does not say, "some of the dead in Christ" or "some who are alive." It does not say, "the holiest of the dead" or "the holiest of those who are alive."

A Works-Oriented Rapture

The partial rapture theory ultimately bases the rapture on good works. Only the qualified get raptured. Only the worthy are taken.

But how does one know whether one has passed the test? How does one know if one is worthy? How does one know if one has done enough good works? In this line of thinking, the rapture no longer seems to be a blessed hope (Titus 2:13), for no one can know for sure whether or not one will participate in the event. It's more of a "blessed perhaps." Scripture teaches that all of salvation is by grace through faith (see Ephesians 2:8-9). Prophecy expert Herman Hoyt notes, "To insist that a worthy life is the procuring cause of experience in the translation [of our physical bodies into resurrection bodies] is a subtle attack upon the whole doctrine of grace."[4]

One Salvation in Three Stages

Scripture alludes to three stages of salvation—justification, sanctification, and glorification. The first stage, justification, involves salvation from the penalty of sin (see Romans 3:20,28; 5:1). The second stage, sanctification, involves salvation from the power of sin (see 2 Thessalonians 2:13; 1 Peter 1:2; see also Romans 8:13). The third stage, glorification, involves salvation from the presence of sin (see Romans 8:22-23; 1 Corinthians 15:24-26,51-55; Philippians 3:21; Hebrews 2:14; 1 John 3:2; Revelation 21:4).

Glorification, which takes place for church-age saints at the rapture, is a part of God's complete package of salvation. It is never presented in Scripture as a reward for good works. It is based entirely on the sacrifice of Jesus Christ on the cross. There is nothing we can do to merit any of the three stages of salvation.

A Devaluation of the Death of Christ

Partial rapturism devalues the death of Jesus Christ on the cross of Calvary. After all, the view assumes that good works improve a believer's standing with God, making him or her worthy for the rapture. However, Scripture reveals that Christ paid the complete price for our redemption. He paid for every single sin. Christ has taken the penalty for every sin, so God will not punish sinning Christians again by preventing their participation in the rapture. Because of Christ's complete work of redemption on the cross, every believer is rendered worthy to participate in the rapture (see Isaiah 53:4-5; Romans 5:10; 2 Corinthians 5:18-19; Galatians 3:13,26; 1 Peter 1:18-19; 1 John 2:2; Revelation 5:9).

A Type of Purgatory?

If Christians who are left behind are intended to be purged through the trials of the tribulation period, does this not constitute a form of purgatory for less-than-worthy Christians? Such an idea is entirely foreign to the pages of Scripture. Our sins are purged through Christ alone (Hebrews 10:14), so they cannot be purged by the tribulation period. No wonder Romans 8:1 categorically states, "There is therefore now no condemnation for those who are in Christ Jesus."

Rewards at the Judgment Seat of Christ

Scripture never once portrays the rapture as a reward for godly living. Rather, following the rapture, Christians will participate in the judgment seat of Christ, where He will examine the deeds they did while in their bodies. He will also weigh the personal motives and intents of the heart (see Romans 14:8-10; 1 Corinthians 3:11-15; 9:24-27).

Exhortations to Await the Rapture

References to "eagerly waiting for him" (Hebrews 9:28) and "waiting for our blessed hope" (Titus 2:13) do not describe a requirement for participation in the rapture. Rather, they point to a mindset—the anticipation of all the redeemed, who will assuredly participate in the rapture. Partial rapturists are reading their eschatology into these passages.

Conclusion

I do not doubt the sincerity of partial rapturists, but I believe they ignore a great many Bible verses in their presentation. Taking into consideration the whole counsel of God on the matter of the rapture, I find that partial rapturism falls far short of the biblical testimony.

DEBATE 5

How Are We to Understand the Book of Revelation?

13

Which Interpretive Model Is Correct—Historicism, Idealism, Preterism, or Futurism?

There has been much debate regarding how the book of Revelation should be interpreted. I will briefly address each of the four primary approaches.

The Historicist View

In the historicist approach, the book of Revelation provides a prophetic overview of the entire panorama of church history from the first century to the second coming of Christ. This approach emerged in the fourth century when some interpreters saw parallels between current events and the prophecies in the book of Revelation. Later, Joachim of Fiore (1135–1202) developed the approach by dividing history into three primary ages. Still later, the Reformers were attracted to this model, viewing the pope as the antichrist of Revelation 13.

This is a fascinating theory, but it is not without problems. A comparison of the prophecies in the book of Revelation with other prophetic Scriptures—such as Daniel 9:25-27; Matthew 24–25; 1 Thessalonians 4:13–5:11; 2 Thessalonians 2:1-12; and Titus 2:13-14—reveals that these prophecies point to the future tribulation period, antichrist, second coming, millennial kingdom, great white throne judgment, and eternal state.

A fundamental hermeneutical principle affirms that Scripture interprets Scripture. As Bernard Ramm put it so well, "The entire Holy Scripture is the context and guide for understanding the particular passages of Scripture."[1] Ramm's point is that the interpretation of a specific passage must not contradict the total teaching of Scripture. Individual verses do not exist as isolated fragments, but as parts of a whole. The exposition of these verses, therefore, must exhibit them in right relation both to the whole and to each other. As J.I. Packer put it, "If we would understand the parts, our wisest course is to get to know the whole."[2]

As we compare what Revelation says about the tribulation period (Revelation 4–18) with other passages about the tribulation (for example, Jeremiah 30:7; Daniel 9:27; 2 Thessalonians 2:4), and as we compare what Revelation says about the second coming (Revelation 19) with other passages about the second coming (for example, Zechariah 12:10; Matthew 24:42-51; Luke 21:25-27; Acts 1:9-11), and as we compare what Revelation says about the millennium (Revelation 20) with other passages about the millennium (for example, Isaiah 11:4,9; 19:24-25; 35:1-10), we see that all such passages are pointing to the end times. Conversely, historicism applies certain passages to certain seasons of church history.

Historicism has led to endless speculation and subjectivity in dealing with the specific details in the book of Revelation. It is difficult if not impossible to arrive at a consensus in the identification of people and events in the text of Revelation. Historicist interpreters tend to view the events of their own day as relating to prophecies in the book of Revelation. Indeed, John F. Walvoord says that the principal problem with historicism is that "seldom do two interpreters interpret a given passage as referring to the same event. Each interpreter tends to find its fulfillment in his generation."[3]

The Idealist View

The idealist approach holds that the book of Revelation is primarily a symbolic description of the ongoing battle between God and the devil, between good and evil, throughout the church age up until the second coming of Christ. In this view, the book of Revelation does not relate to any historical or future events at all.[4]

Like historicism, the idealist approach to Revelation is not without problems. It is hard to see how the idealist approach to Revelation could bring any genuine comfort to the original recipients of the book, who were suffering through great persecution under the Romans. A more literal understanding of Revelation—an understanding that points to God's absolute control of human history—is much more satisfactory in this regard.

Idealism also ignores the specific time markers within the book. For example, John is instructed to "write therefore the things that you have seen, those that are and those that are to take place after this" (Revelation 1:19). Such words indicate a definite sequence of events.

We also read of time-limited events in Revelation. For example, the holy city is to be trampled for forty-two months (11:2). The Jewish remnant is to find refuge in the wilderness for 1260 days (12:6). These Jews will be nourished in the wilderness for "a time, and times, and half a time" (12:14). Each of these verses refers to a period of three and a half years. Idealism ignores such time-delimited events in Revelation.

The idealist may rebut that the book of Revelation includes many symbols. That is true. However, these symbols are often defined in the immediate context. John said the seven stars in Christ's right hand were the seven angels (or messengers) to the seven churches, and the seven lampstands were the seven churches (1:20). The bowls full of incense were the prayers of the saints (5:8), and the many waters were peoples, multitudes, nations, and tongues (17:15). So these symbols typically point to real personalities and real events. The idealist approach ignores this.

Studies in apocalyptic literature indicate that it always deals with actual events in history. The book of Revelation is properly categorized as apocalyptic literature, so we may surmise that the book deals with real events and not just idealized concepts, such as the struggle between good and evil.[5]

Finally, Jesus informed John, "I will show you what must take place after this" (Revelation 4:1). Jesus's statement becomes nonsensical if He were not referring to real events.

The Preterist View

The word *preterism* derives from the Latin *preter*, meaning "past." In this view, the biblical prophecies in the book of Revelation (especially chapters 6–18) and Matthew 24–25 (Christ's Olivet Discourse) have already been fulfilled. Eusebius (AD 263–339) used this approach to interpreting prophecy in his *Ecclesiastical History*. Later writers who incorporated this approach include Hugo Grotius of Holland (ca. 1644), and, in modern times, David Chilton.[6]

There are two forms of preterism. Moderate preterism is represented by modern writers such as R.C. Sproul, Hank Hanegraaff, and Gary DeMar.[7] They believe that the literal resurrection and second coming are yet future but that the other prophecies in Revelation and Matthew 24–25 were fulfilled when Titus and his Roman warriors overran Jerusalem and destroyed the Jewish temple in AD 70. In this view, most of the book of Revelation does not deal with the future.

Extreme or full preterism goes so far as to say that all New Testament predictions were fulfilled in the past, including those of the resurrection and second coming. This latter view is heretical, denying two of the fundamentals of the faith—the physical resurrection and a literal second coming.

Preterists often point to Matthew 24:34, where Jesus asserted, "Truly, I say to you, this generation will not pass away until all these things take place." This verse allegedly proves the prophecies would be fulfilled in the first century.

Contrary to this idea, evangelical Christians have generally held to one of two interpretations of Matthew 24:34. One interpretation is that Christ is simply saying that those people who witness the signs stated earlier in Matthew 24—the abomination of desolation (verse 15), the great tribulation such as has never been seen before (verse 21), and the sign of the Son of Man in heaven (verse 30)—will also see the coming of Jesus Christ in their own generation. It was common knowledge among the Jews that the future tribulation period would last only seven years (Daniel 9:24-27), so those living at the beginning of this time would likely live to see the second coming seven years later (except for those who lose their lives during this tumultuous time).

Other evangelicals hold that the word *generation* is to be taken in its basic usage of "race, kindred, family, stock, or breed." If this is what is meant, then Jesus is here promising that the nation of Israel will be preserved—despite terrible persecution during the tribulation—until the consummation of God's program for Israel at the second coming. Many divine promises have been made to Israel, including land promises (Genesis 12; 14–15; 17) and a future Davidic kingdom (2 Samuel 7). Jesus could thus be referring to God's preservation of Israel in order to fulfill the divine promises to them (see Romans 11:11-26).

Either way, Matthew 24:34 does not support preterism.

Preterists also argue from Matthew 16:28 that Jesus said some of His followers standing there would not taste death until they saw Him coming in His kingdom. These preterists argue that prophecies of the second coming must have been fulfilled during their generation—apparently in AD 70, when Rome overran Jerusalem.

Contrary to this view, many evangelicals believe Jesus was referring to the transfiguration, which happened precisely one week later (Matthew 17:1-13). In this view, the transfiguration served as a preview of the kingdom in which the divine Messiah would appear in glory. Moreover, some of the disciples standing there were no longer alive by AD 70—all but John had been martyred by then. Still further, no astronomical events occurred in AD 70, such as the stars falling from heaven and the heavens being shaken (Matthew 24:29). And Jesus did not return "on the clouds of heaven with power and great glory" (verse 30). The preterist understanding of Matthew 16:28 does not sync with other prophetic Scriptures.

Preterists rebut that some Bible verses indicate that Jesus would come quickly (for example, Revelation 22:12,20) and that the events in the book of Revelation would be fulfilled shortly (1:1; 22:6). Futurists point out, however, that the Greek word for *quickly* often carries the meaning, "swiftly, speedily, at a rapid rate." The term could simply indicate that when the predicted events first start to occur, they will progress swiftly, in rapid succession. Likewise, the word translated *shortly* can simply mean "suddenly," not necessarily soon.

A favorite argument among preterists is that the book of Revelation was written prior to AD 70, so the book must have been fulfilled in AD 70 when Rome overran Jerusalem. Futurists point out, however, that some of the earliest Church Fathers confirmed a late date of Revelation. Irenaeus (AD 130–202) claimed the book was written at the close of the reign of Domitian (which took place from AD 81 to 96). Victorinus (who died in 303) confirmed this date, as did Eusebius (AD 263–340). Since the book was written after AD 70, it could hardly have been referring to events that were fulfilled in AD 70.

All things considered, I remain unconvinced by preterist arguments. Futurism makes much more sense to me.

The Futurist View

The futurist approach to interpreting the book of Revelation holds that most of the events described in the book will take place in the end times, just prior to the second coming of Jesus Christ. This view honors the book's claim to be prophecy (see Revelation 1:3; 22:7,10,18-19). Moreover, as we have seen, Jesus told John, "I will show you what must take place after this" (Revelation 4:1). The events that "take place after this" pertain to futuristic prophecy.

This view recognizes that just as the more than 100 prophecies of the first coming of Christ were fulfilled literally, so the prophecies of the second coming (and the events that precede and follow it) will be fulfilled just as literally.

> The logical way to discover how God will fulfill prophecy in the future is to discover how He fulfilled it in the past. If the prophecies concerning Christ's first coming were fulfilled literally, how can anyone reject the literal fulfillment of the numerous prophecies concerning His second coming and reign on the earth?[8]

Futurists believe, based on a literal interpretation, that there will one day be a literal tribulation period with literal judgments and a literal antichrist. It will be followed by a literal second coming and a literal millennial kingdom. All this is in keeping with one of the most important interpretive principles—when the plain sense makes good sense, seek no other sense lest you end up in nonsense.

I must repeat that a comparison of the prophecies in the book of Revelation with other prophetic Scriptures—such as Daniel 9:25-27; Matthew 24–25; 1 Thessalonians 4:13–5:11; 2 Thessalonians 2:1-12; and Titus 2:13-14—reveals that these prophecies point to a future tribulation period, antichrist, second coming, millennial kingdom, great white throne judgment, and eternal state. Scripture interprets Scripture! This is a fundamental interpretive principle.

We can also observe that the early church took a futurist view of the book inasmuch as it saw the tribulation, second coming, millennium, and eternal state as future events. This understanding of the book of Revelation would have proven a great comfort to the original readers of the book. The last few chapters of Revelation assured them that we win in the end.

Conclusion

Having examined the four primary views, my assessment is that the futurist view of the book of Revelation is correct. Jesus Himself supports this futuristic aspect in Revelation 4:1. We then see a naturally progressing chain of linked events (with time delimiters) throughout the rest of the book:

- the tribulation period, lasting precisely seven years (chapters 4–18), followed by
- the second coming (19), followed by
- the millennial kingdom and final judgment (20), followed by
- the eternal state (21–22).

How Does Daniel's Seventieth Week Relate to the Book of Revelation?

The timing of Daniel's seventieth week has certainly been an object of debate among Christians. Some people place it in the past, but others (myself included) place it in the future. Similarly, some people place the events described in the book of Revelation in the past, and others place the events in the future. I will summarize the key components of the debate.

Viewpoint 1: Daniel's Seventieth Week Already Happened

> Seventy weeks are decreed about your people and your holy city, to finish the transgression, to put an end to sin, and to atone for iniquity, to bring in everlasting righteousness, to seal both vision and prophet, and to anoint a most holy place. Know therefore and understand that from the going out of the word to restore and build Jerusalem to the coming of an anointed one, a prince, there shall be seven weeks. Then for sixty-two weeks it shall be built again with squares and moat, but in a troubled time. And after the sixty-two weeks, an anointed one shall be cut off and shall have nothing. And the people of the prince who is to come shall

destroy the city and the sanctuary. Its end shall come with a flood, and to the end there shall be war. Desolations are decreed. And he shall make a strong covenant with many for one week, and for half of the week he shall put an end to sacrifice and offering. And on the wing of abominations shall come one who makes desolate, until the decreed end is poured out on the desolator (Daniel 9:24-27).

Futurists apply the last part of this passage—dealing with the signing of the covenant and the ending of sacrifices—to the antichrist, who will come into power during the tribulation period. Others, however, have claimed that the entire passage is actually referring to Jesus Christ, with his covenant of salvation and His ultimate sacrifice on the cross (thereby annulling all temple sacrifices). For example, according to Jamieson, Fausset, and Brown, "The confirmation of the covenant is assigned to Him [Christ]."[1] Bible commentator Matthew Henry wrote, "By offering himself a sacrifice once and for all, he [Jesus] shall put an end to all the Levitical sacrifices."[2] In this view, the antichrist is nowhere to be seen in this passage.

These and other writers offer a variety of proofs against the idea that this passage refers to a future tribulation period and in favor of the idea that the passage was fulfilled 2000 years ago. For example, they argue that no gap is indicated between the sixty-ninth and seventieth weeks. The seventieth week must follow immediately after the sixty-ninth week, we are told. The weeks are sequential.

Further, the passage says nothing about a tribulation period, a rebuilt Jewish temple, or the emergence of an antichrist. Some writers claim that futurists are simply reading these ideas into the biblical text.

These interpreters concede that "the people of the prince who is to come" who destroys "the city and the sanctuary" is a reference to the destruction of Jerusalem and its temple in AD 70. However, they say the reference to confirming a covenant relates to Jesus Christ, not to the antichrist. They appeal to Galatians 3:17, where we read of "a covenant previously ratified by God," and Romans 15:8, which mentions "the promises given to the patriarchs." Christ is thus viewed as the one who ratifies the covenant. Indeed, when Daniel affirms that "he shall make a strong covenant with many," this should allegedly be tied to Matthew 26:28, where Jesus says, "This is my blood of the covenant, which is poured out for many for the forgiveness of sins."

The clause "for half of the week he shall put an end to sacrifice and offering" allegedly points to Jesus's three-and-a-half-year ministry, after which His death on the cross put an end to all sacrifices in the temple.

The words "on the wing of abominations shall come one who makes desolate" allegedly mean that it was a desolate thing for the Jewish leaders to put Jesus to death. This act yielded the ultimate consequence of their own temple being destroyed (or made desolate).

In this view, the seventieth week (which lasts seven years) applies only to the Jewish people, as did the first sixty-nine weeks. We are told that Jesus's public ministry to the Jews lasted three and a half years, and once He died and was resurrected, His disciples allegedly continued to preach to Jewish people for another three and a half years. The gospel then shifted to the Gentiles. These interpretations lead to the claim that the Bible nowhere teaches the idea of a future seven-year tribulation period.

Viewpoint 2: Daniel's Seventieth Week Is Yet Future

Those who claim there is no future tribulation period say futurists are reading their theology into the text of Daniel 9:24-27, and futurists say the opposite is true. Accusations of eisegesis fly both ways.

Futurists believe that in Daniel 9, God provides a prophetic time-table for the nation of Israel. The prophetic clock began ticking when the command went out to restore and rebuild Jerusalem following its destruction by Babylon (verse 25). According to this verse, Israel's timetable was divided into 70 groups of seven years—a total of 490 years.

The first 69 groups of seven years, or 483 years, included the years from the issuing of the decree to restore and rebuild Jerusalem until "an anointed one" comes. This anointed one is obviously the divine Messiah, Jesus Christ. (The Old Testament word translated *Messiah* literally means "anointed one.") The day Jesus rode into Jerusalem to proclaim

Himself Israel's Messiah was 483 years to the day after the command to restore and rebuild Jerusalem had been given.

At that point God's prophetic clock stopped. Contrary to those who see no gap between the sixty-ninth and seventieth weeks, Daniel most certainly describes a gap between the first 483 years and the final 7 years of Israel's prophetic timetable. Daniel 9:26 describes events that take place after the sixty-ninth week but before the beginning of the seventieth week. More precisely, in verse 26 Daniel speaks of seven weeks and then sixty-two weeks (totaling sixty-nine weeks). Then our text says that "after the sixty-two weeks," certain events would transpire:

- the Messiah will be killed,
- the city of Jerusalem and its temple will be destroyed (which occurred in AD 70), and
- the Jews will encounter difficulty and hardship from that time on.

Daniel 9:27 then indicates that the seventieth and final week of seven years will begin for Israel when a covenant is confirmed with Israel. But who signs or initiates this covenant? Proponents of viewpoint 1 believe it is Jesus Christ. Futurists believe it is the antichrist.

One thing is certain. The covenant referenced in Daniel 9 must be confirmed after AD 70—long after Christ's work of salvation at the cross, His resurrection, and His ascension into heaven. A natural reading of the text indicates that the covenant is initiated sometime after "the city and the sanctuary" are destroyed. The blood Christ shed on the cross around AD 33 is definitely related to the new covenant (Luke 22:20). But in Daniel 9, we are dealing with a later covenant, one that occurs after AD 70. So contrary to viewpoint 1 proponents, this passage seems to bear no relation to Galatians 3:17, where we read of "a covenant previously ratified by God," or Romans 15:8, where we read of the confirmation of "the promises given to the patriarchs."

All in all, I believe that a plain reading of Daniel 9, compared with what we read in the book of Revelation, yields a sensible and cohesive chain of events in the end times. Here is an abbreviated summary of these events.

The Signing of the Covenant

Futurists believe that the signing of this covenant with Israel will signal the beginning of the seventieth week, the tribulation period. That signature initiates the seven-year countdown to the second coming of Christ, which follows the tribulation period.

This covenant may have some connection to the invasion in which Russia and a group of Muslim nations—including Iran, Sudan, Turkey, Libya, Kazakhstan, Kyrgyzstan, Uzbekistan, Turkmenistan, Tajikistan, Armenia, and possibly northern Afghanistan—invade Israel in the end times (Ezekiel 38:1-6). After all, Ezekiel's prophecy indicates that the invasion will take place when Israel is living in security and is at rest (verse 11). Israel will not have this strong sense of security and rest until the leader of the revived Roman Empire—the antichrist—signs a peace pact, guaranteeing Israel's protection (Daniel 9:27). Until the signing of this covenant, Israel will remain as she presently is—always on high alert because of the possibility of attack.

The Jewish Temple Will Be Rebuilt

Futurists also believe that Daniel 9:27 indicates that the Jewish temple will be rebuilt. We are told that the antichrist "shall make a strong covenant with many for one week, and for half of the week he shall put an end to sacrifice and offering. And on the wing of abominations shall come one who makes desolate, until the decreed end is poured out on the desolator."

How do we know that the abomination of desolation refers to a future temple and not the temple of Jesus's day? Jesus answers this for us in the Olivet Discourse. Early in the discourse, Jesus speaks of the destruction of the temple of His day.

> Jesus left the temple and was going away, when his disciples came to point out to him the buildings of the temple. But he answered them, "You see all these, do you not? Truly,

I say to you, there will not be left here one stone upon
another that will not be thrown down" (Matthew 24:1-2).

Clearly, then, the temple of Jesus's day was to be utterly and completely destroyed. Then the disciples asked him, "What will be the sign
of your coming and of the end of the age?" So Jesus starts describing
what will occur in the end times. In this context of the end times, Jesus
refers to the desecration of a future temple: "When you see the abomination of desolation spoken of by the prophet Daniel, standing in the
holy place (let the reader understand), then let those who are in Judea
flee to the mountains" (verse 15).

So that my point is not missed, the temple of Jesus's day was soon
to be destroyed. The abomination of desolation refers to another temple—a temple that would exist "at the end of the age." The chronology of those who hold to viewpoint 1—who say that both Daniel 9
and Matthew 24 are referring to the temple of Jesus's day—is in error.
Jesus and Daniel are referring to the desecration of a future temple in
the end times.

An End of Sacrifices

The indication in Daniel 9 that the antichrist will put an end to
sacrifice and offering in the middle of the week (after three and a half
years) and will desolate the Jewish temple presupposes that the Jewish
temple will have already been constructed by this time. Bible prophecy expert John F. Walvoord offers this explanation:

> This expression ["for half of the week he shall put an end
> to sacrifice and offering"] refers to the entire Levitical sys-
> tem, which suggests that Israel will have restored that sys-
> tem in the first half of the 70th seven. After this ruler gains
> worldwide political power, he will assume power in the reli-
> gious realm as well and will cause the world to worship him
> (2 Thess. 2:4; Rev. 13:8). To receive such worship, he will
> terminate all organized religions. Posing as the world's right-
> ful king and god and as Israel's prince of peace, he will then
> turn against Israel and become her destroyer and defiler.[3]

From a prophetic standpoint, all this is highly significant.

- A key chronological prerequisite to the rebuilding of the temple—Israel back in her homeland as a nation—has been a reality since 1948. Moreover, the Jews have been streaming back to the Holy Land from around the world ever since (as prophesied in Ezekiel 36–37).

- The temple must be rebuilt at least by the middle of the seven-year tribulation because Jesus warned of a catastrophic event that assumes the existence of the temple: "When you see the abomination of desolation spoken of by the prophet Daniel, standing in the holy place (let the reader understand), then let those who are in Judea flee to the mountains" (Matthew 24:15-16). This "abomination of desolation" refers to a desecration of the Jewish temple by the antichrist, who will set up an image of himself within the temple (see Daniel 9:27; see also 2 Thessalonians 2:4). The antichrist will actually set himself up as God.

- Even today various individuals and groups are working behind the scenes to prepare various materials for the future temple: the menorah of pure gold, the pure gold crown worn by the high priest, fire pans and shovels, the mitzraq (a vessel used to transport the blood of sacrificial offerings), the copper laver, linen garments of the priests, stone vessels to store the ashes of the red heifer, and the like. These items are being prefabricated by the Temple Institute in Jerusalem so that when the temple is finally rebuilt, everything will be ready for it.

The Antichrist's Double Cross

The covenant the antichrist signs with Israel is supposed to remain in effect for the full seven-year period (the seventieth week of Daniel). But the antichrist will double-cross Israel, for we are told that "for half of the week he shall put an end to sacrifice and offering." In other words, after the covenant has been in effect for three and a half years, he will renege on the covenant and stop Israel's temple sacrifices.

Why stop the sacrifices? Near the midpoint of the tribulation period, the antichrist—having already attained political power—will assume power in the religious realm as well. Setting up an image of himself in the temple amounts to enthroning himself in the place of deity, displaying himself as God (compare with Isaiah 14:13-14 and Ezekiel 28:2-9). This blasphemous act will utterly desecrate the temple, making it abominable and therefore desolate. The antichrist will entice the world to worship him (see 2 Thessalonians 2:4; Revelation 13:8), so he must necessarily destroy all competing religious systems—including the Jewish religion with its Levitical sacrifices and offerings.

This means that the antichrist, who was once Israel's protector, now becomes Israel's persecutor. He was once Israel's defender, but he becomes Israel's defiler by setting up an image of himself in the Jewish temple.

Understandably, all this is utterly detestable to the Jews. The word *abomination* comes from a root term that means "to make foul" or "to stink." Thus it refers to something that makes one feel nauseous, and by implication, something morally abhorrent and detestable.

An abomination took place on a lesser scale in 168 BC. At that time, Antiochus Epiphanes erected an altar to Zeus in the temple at Jerusalem and sacrificed a pig (an unclean animal) on it. Antiochus was thus a prototype of the future antichrist.

Scripture reveals that things get much worse after the abomination of desolation takes place halfway through the tribulation period. The events of the second half of the seven-year tribulation period are properly called "the great tribulation" (Revelation 7:14). As Matthew 24:21 puts it, "There will be great tribulation, such as has not been from the beginning of the world until now, no, and never will be." Daniel 12:1 likewise comments, "There shall be a time of trouble, such as never has been since there was a nation till that time." This time period largely deals with Israel, so Jeremiah 30:7 calls this period "a time of distress for Jacob" (Jacob is another name for Israel).

This means that in the middle of the tribulation period, things become traumatic for the Jewish people in Jerusalem. The antichrist will not only assume global political power but also declare himself to be God and exalt himself in the Jewish temple. To make matters worse, the antichrist will be afire with passion in persecuting the Jewish people.

In the Olivet Discourse, Jesus points to how bad things will be and how Jews living in Jerusalem will need to flee for their lives.

> When you see the abomination of desolation spoken of by the prophet Daniel, standing in the holy place (let the reader understand), then let those who are in Judea flee to the mountains. Let the one who is on the housetop not go down to take what is in his house, and let the one who is in the field not turn back to take his cloak. And alas for women who are pregnant and for those who are nursing infants in those days! Pray that your flight may not be in winter or on a Sabbath. For then there will be great tribulation, such as has not been from the beginning of the world until now, no, and never will be (Matthew 24:15-21).

When these horrific circumstances unfold in Jerusalem, Jesus urges that the Jews living there should have no concern for personal belongings, but rather they should get out of town as quickly as possible. Time spent gathering personal belongings might mean the difference between life and death. Jesus indicates that the distress will escalate dramatically and rapidly.

Conclusion

As I compare Daniel 9 with the book of Revelation, Jesus's Olivet Discourse (Matthew 24–25), and Paul's prophetic writings in 1 and 2 Thessalonians, I am convinced that all of them are describing future, end-times events. This view makes the best sense of the biblical data. Taken together, these passages yield a sensible and cohesive eschatology.

Can We Identify Babylon?

Babylon lay in the land of Shinar (Genesis 10:10). This influential civilization, ruled by kings and priests, was situated on the banks of the Euphrates River, a little more than 50 miles south of modern Baghdad. Because of its ideal location, Babylon was an important commercial and trade center in the ancient world. It became a powerful kingdom under the leadership of Hammurabi (1792–1750 BC).

Like other pagan peoples of the Ancient Near East, the Babylonians believed in many false gods and goddesses. These gods were thought to control the entire world of nature, so to be successful in life, one would do well to placate the gods.

Each city in Babylon had a patron god with an accompanying temple. A number of small shrines were also scattered about each city, and people often met in these to worship various other deities. The chief of the Babylonian gods was Anu, considered the king of heaven. The patron god of Babylon was Marduk.

The Babylonians were well known for their practice of divination. Astrology can trace its roots back to Babylon around 3000 BC. The ancient Babylonians observed how orderly and rhythmically the planets moved across the sky, and they concluded that the planets were gods of the night. The people assigned godlike powers and characteristics to the planets and worshipped them. These gods were believed to control the fate of human beings on earth in a broad sense—that is, they controlled the destiny of nations (see Daniel 1:20; 2:2,10,27; 4:7; 5:7,11,15). The priests of Babylon tried to understand and predict the movements of these planets so that perhaps they could use this knowledge to benefit their nation. To study and worship these deities, the Babylonians built towers called ziggurats. The Tower of Babel was apparently such a ziggurat.

Babylon is often represented in Scripture as being arrayed against God and His people (2 Kings 24:10). In 597 BC, for example, King Nebuchadnezzar took some 3000 Jews into exile in Babylon. Jerusalem and the temple were obliterated (Lamentations 1:1-7). Though God sovereignly used Babylon as His powerful whipping rod to chasten Israel, Babylon was to be utterly destroyed by God's hand of judgment for continually standing against His people (Isaiah 13:1-16).

Because of the historical background of Babylon, we should not be surprised that the city surfaces in the book of Revelation in connection with the antichrist. After all, the antichrist will be anti-God just as ancient Babylon was anti-God. The question is, does the term as used in the book of Revelation refer to the literal Babylon in Iraq along the Euphrates River, or does it metaphorically refer to another geographical location? Let's consider this highly debated issue.

Scriptural Parameters for Interpreting Babylon

In this chapter I will examine a number of interpretations offered for Babylon in the book of Revelation. First, however, let's briefly outline what Revelation 17–18 tells us about this Babylon of the end times.

1. Babylon is a city (Revelation 17:18).
2. It has global importance (17:15,18).
3. It is closely connected with the antichrist (17:3).
4. It is a bastion of false religion (17:4-5; 18:1-2).
5. It is the global commerce center of the end times (18:9-19).
6. It persecutes believers in the end times (17:6; 18:20,24).

7. It will be annihilated at the end of the tribulation period (18:8-10,21-24).[1]

Our interpretation of the end-times Babylon must satisfy all the above data.

Viewpoint 1: Babylon Should Not Be Interpreted Literally

The first viewpoint held by some Christians is that Babylon should not be interpreted literally. Preterists, such as Gary DeMar, reject any idea of a literal future rebuilt city of Babylon. "Should we expect a reconstituted Babylon in the future based upon events described in the Book of Revelation? Is Revelation's Babylon the same as the Babylon of the Old Testament?...Not at all."[2]

Christians have come up with all kinds of different suggestions for what a symbolic Babylon might represent. I will limit my focus to some of the more popular theories. Some say Babylon refers to the Roman Catholic Church and the Vatican. Others say it refers to apostate Christianity. Others say it refers to Rome. Still others say it refers to the evil world system. And still others claim it refers to the Jerusalem of the end times. Let's look at some of the supporting evidence for each view.

The Roman Catholic Church

This view became popular during and following the days of the Reformation. Proponents include such notables as Jonathan Edwards, Adam Clarke, and E.B. Elliott.[3] This theory is typically built on the harlot motif (see Revelation 17:1). The very idea of a harlot implies unfaithfulness. Proponents of this view allege that just as a harlot is sexually unfaithful, so the Roman Catholic Church is unfaithful and has fallen away from the truth of Christianity. Roman Catholicism is viewed as a corruption of Christianity.

Consider how the adulterous woman (religious Babylon) is adorned: "The woman was arrayed in purple and scarlet, and adorned with gold and jewels and pearls" (Revelation 17:4). Some suggest this fits the colors of the robes of both popes and cardinals. As well, the affirmation that the woman was drunk from the saints' blood may point to the Roman Catholic persecution of Protestants.

As convincing as this view may initially appear, it has notable problems. Many of those who hold that the harlot is Roman Catholicism also say that the beast of Revelation is Roman Catholicism. This is problematic because the harlot and the beast are distinct from each other in Revelation. By the end of Revelation 17, we find the beast actually destroying the harlot.

Further, this seems to be a case of commentators reading their own experiences into the text of Scripture. This view emerged and became prominent during the Reformation, when men like John Calvin and Martin Luther were taking a stand against Roman Catholicism. In such a context, Roman Catholicism could easily be read into the harlot or beast of Revelation.

Moreover, one must wonder how a theory involving an ecclesiastical institution centuries after Revelation was written could have had any immediate relevance to the original readers of the book of Revelation. Would they have understood the text this way? Many expositors think not. Such a view would seemingly bring more comfort to sixteenth-century persecuted Protestants than to first-century persecuted Christians.

Apostate Christianity

Like the Roman Catholic theory, this next theory relies heavily on the harlot motif (Revelation 17:1). Again, proponents allege that just as a harlot is sexually unfaithful, so apostate Christianity is unfaithful and has fallen away from the truth of Christianity. Some describe it in terms of adultery. Adultery implies that faithfulness has been replaced with infidelity. Apostate Christianity was once not apostate but has since become apostate. In this theory, many of those left behind after the rapture will be included in this apostate Christianity.

If there is a bone to pick with this view, it involves the question of relevance to the original readers of the book of Revelation. Would they have understood the text this way? Perhaps or perhaps not. In terms of the religious aspect of Babylon, many today consider this a viable option.

Rome

A popular view is that the Babylonian harlot points to first-century Rome. This view is held by many modern commentators. Jewish literature toward the latter part of the first century used the term Babylon as a metaphor for Rome. Also, Rome was engulfed in paganism, and it relentlessly persecuted the early believers. And certainly Rome was a "great city" (Revelation 17:18).

However, this view is not without problems, the most significant of which pertains to the relationship between this harlot and the beast. Many draw a connection between Rome and the beast, so how can the harlot also be Rome if the book of Revelation clearly distinguishes the two? The harlot sits on the beast, so they are clearly distinct from each other (Revelation 17:3). As well, in verse 16 the beast actually destroys the harlot. This, too, shows that the harlot and the beast are distinct and cannot both refer to Rome. So the suggestion of some that the harlot is a recapitulation of the image of the beast has insurmountable problems.

One must also wonder how the Rome view can be made to fit with the theme of the harlot, or adultery, or prostitution (verses 1-5). Rome was never faithful to Christianity to begin with, so how can it now be considered unfaithful, like a harlot?

The Evil World System

Still other Christians have viewed Babylon as a generalized evil world system. Taken in this light, the text refers not to a specific period of time (such as the tribulation period) but could refer to any time in church history in which the evil world system stood against God. This view has been held by some who hold to the idealist interpretation of the book of Revelation (viewing Revelation as a general description of the struggle between good and evil, between God and the devil).

Those who take a futurist approach to the book of Revelation are not satisfied with this viewpoint. Revelation 17 seems to describe something more specific than a generalized evil world system. Remember, Babylon is a city (verse 18) with global importance (verses 15,18) and is closely connected with the antichrist (verse 3). The city is a bastion of false religion (17:4-5; 18:1-2), a global commerce center of the end times (18:9-19), and a persecutor of end-time believers (17:6; 18:20,24).

Jerusalem

Finally, some interpreters hold that the term Babylon perhaps refers to the city of Jerusalem in the first century.[4] Seen in this light, Jerusalem as Babylon was destroyed by God using the whipping rod of the Roman Empire. This view is obviously popular among preterists and partial preterists, who argue that most of the prophecies in the book of Revelation were fulfilled when Rome overran Jerusalem in AD 70.

This view is not satisfactory for futurists. After all, there is a strong case that the book of Revelation was written in the 90s, long after Rome destroyed Jerusalem in AD 70. That being so, the prophetic description of Babylon is hardly applicable to the Jerusalem of earlier decades.

How do we know Revelation was written in the 90s? As we have seen, in the second century, Irenaeus declared that Revelation had been written toward the end of the reign of Domitian (AD 81–96). Later writers, such as Clement of Alexandria, Origen, Victorinus, Eusebius, and Jerome affirm the Domitian date. The book of Revelation must therefore refer to events that are yet future from the vantage point of AD 95.

Viewpoint 2: Babylon Should Be Interpreted Literally

An increasing number of Christians interested in Bible prophecy believe the term Babylon in Revelation 17–18 refers both to a literal city along the Euphrates River and a religious-commercial system. It is similar to the term Wall Street, which refers both to a literal street as well as a commercial system.

Why does Babylon represent false religion? In ancient times, the Babylonians believed in many false gods and goddesses and were deeply entrenched in paganism, idolatry, and divination. With such a history, it is not surprising that the false religious system of the tribulation period is identified with Babylon.

Revelation 17:1 refers to a great prostitute. Prostitution is commonly a graphic scriptural metaphor of unfaithfulness to God (see Jeremiah 3:6-9; Ezekiel 20:30; Hosea 4:15; 5:3; 6:10; 9:1). The great prostitute here symbolizes the apostate religious system of Babylon—probably apostate Christendom, embracing all those who were left behind following the rapture (regarding the pretribulation rapture, see Romans 5:9; 1 Thessalonians 1:9-10; 5:9; Revelation 3:10).

Revelation 17:1 tells us that this prostitute is "seated on many waters." This symbolizes the control false religion exercises over various peoples, multitudes, nations, and languages. As well, the kings of the earth commit "sexual immorality" with her (Revelation 14:8). The fornication described here refers not to actual sexual sin but rather to idolatry, which is unfaithfulness to the true God.

Just as wine can intoxicate people, so people around the globe will become intoxicated by this false religion (Revelation 17:2). Just as wine has a controlling influence on people, so this false religion will have a controlling influence on people worldwide.

This false religious system apparently emerges into prominence during the first half of the tribulation period. But by the midpoint of the tribulation period, this religious system comes under judgment. The antichrist himself destroys this false religion so he can become the sole object of worship. This self-inflated leader will now rule from a literal Babylon, a city along the Euphrates.

This literal city will apparently be rebuilt by the antichrist. It will be a worldwide economic center. This brings to mind how the late Saddam Hussein spent more than a billion dollars of oil money to enhance the city, essentially as a monument to himself. Hussein's renovations will seem insignificant compared to what the antichrist will do with the city.

The antichrist apparently establishes his headquarters in Jerusalem at the midpoint of the tribulation period. This is when he claims to be God and sets up an image of himself in the Jewish temple. Sometime in the latter half of the tribulation period—we are not told precisely when—the antichrist will apparently shift his headquarters to Babylon, which will become a global commercial center. Babylon at this time will likely be in control of the Middle Eastern oil fields (and the money they generate).

The imagery in the book of Revelation seems to indicate that the anti-God political, economic, and commercial system of Babylon will influence everyone on earth—"all nations" and "the kings of the earth." Political-economic Babylon will have universal influence that reaches like an octopus around the world. Because of the commercial success of this city, merchants around the world will become wealthy. Anti-God materialism will run rampant. The city and all it represents will be ripe for judgment.

This Babylonian commercial center is destroyed during Armageddon at the end of the tribulation period. Several key passages describe the utter destruction of Babylon in association with Armageddon.

> Because of the wrath of the LORD she shall not be inhabited but shall be an utter desolation; everyone who passes by Babylon shall be appalled, and hiss because of all her wounds. Set yourselves in array against Babylon all around, all you who bend the bow; shoot at her, spare no arrows, for she has sinned against the LORD...
>
> How Babylon has become a horror among the nations! I set a snare for you and you were taken, O Babylon, and you did not know it; you were found and caught, because you opposed the LORD. The LORD has opened his armory and brought out the weapons of his wrath (Jeremiah 50:13-14,23-25).

Babylon's destruction "will be like Sodom and Gomorrah when God overthrew them" (Isaiah 13:19). "As when God overthrew Sodom and Gomorrah and their neighboring cities, declares the LORD, so no man shall dwell there, and no son of man shall sojourn in her" (Jeremiah 50:40). The book of Revelation graphically describes commercial Babylon's destruction.

> Then a mighty angel took up a stone like a great millstone and threw it into the sea, saying, "So will Babylon the great

city be thrown down with violence, and will be found no more; and the sound of harpists and musicians, of flute players and trumpeters, will be heard in you no more, and a craftsman of any craft will be found in you no more, and the sound of the mill will be heard in you no more, and the light of a lamp will shine in you no more, and the voice of bridegroom and bride will be heard in you no more, for your merchants were the great ones of the earth, and all nations were deceived by your sorcery. And in her was found the blood of prophets and of saints, and of all who have been slain on earth" (Revelation 18:21-24).

Who will attack Babylon and the antichrist? The attack will come from a military coalition from the north.

> For behold, I am stirring up and bringing against Babylon a gathering of great nations, from the north country. And they shall array themselves against her...Behold, a people comes from the north; a mighty nation and many kings are stirring from the farthest parts of the earth. They lay hold of bow and spear; they are cruel and have no mercy. The sound of them is like the roaring of the sea; they ride on horses, arrayed as a man for battle against you, O daughter of Babylon! (Jeremiah 50:9,41-42)

Just as the Babylonians were used in Old Testament times as God's whipping rod of judgment against Israel, so now God uses a northern coalition as His whipping rod against Babylon. Babylon showed no mercy in its oppression of Israel, and now God shows no mercy to Babylon.

When Babylon is destroyed at the end of the tribulation period, the antichrist will not be present in the city. He will be told of its destruction by messengers (see Jeremiah 50:43; 51:31-32). He understandably becomes enraged.

The rulers of the world will grieve when Babylon falls. They have a vested interest in the economic growth of their respective countries, and they will lament when they witness the collapse of the economic system that had enabled them to live so luxuriously (Revelation 18:9-20). The collapse of Babylon will indicate to the rulers of the world that the luxurious empire of the antichrist is utterly doomed. This is devastating news for them, for the antichrist is the source of their own power and wealth.

Evidence for a Literal City

How do we know Babylon refers to a literal city in Iraq in the end times? We find some clues in the text of Scripture. First, other locations listed in the book of Revelation are literal locations (such as the cities of the seven churches in Revelation 2–3). There is no indication in the immediate context that the term Babylon is being used metaphorically, so it makes good sense to take it literally as well. The only time in Revelation where a city is not literal, the text actually tells us so. I am referring to Revelation 11:8, where Jerusalem is called "the great city that symbolically is called Sodom and Egypt." This is the only symbolic reference to a city in Revelation, so it is reasonable to assume that references to other cities are to be taken literally.

Further, references to Babylon throughout the rest of the Bible always point to a godless, sinful, and pagan literal city. This city has stood against God throughout its history, so it is fitting that God destroys it as human history on earth is drawing to a close.

Still further, Babylon is mentioned in the context of the Euphrates River, which indicates that a literal city is meant. One ought never ignore geographical markers in the context.

Also, the descriptions of the end-time destruction of Babylon in the Old Testament Scriptures portray the destruction of a literal city. These Old Testament verses sync well with a literal interpretation of the city in the book of Revelation.

Conclusion

Though metaphorical theories about Babylon's identity are often interesting, my assessment is that the term should be interpreted in terms of a literal city in Iraq along the Euphrates River. Both the immediate context of Revelation and the broader context of all of Scripture supports this view. I find myself in agreement with Thomas Ice: "I believe that just like Israel always refers to Israel in the Bible, so also Babylon always refers to Babylon."[5]

Having said this, I also think that a strong case can be made that the religious aspect of Babylon—the great prostitute—may refer to some form of apostate Christianity. But we cannot be dogmatic about this.

Who Are the 144,000, and What Is Their Ministry?

Two debates are related to the 144,000 mentioned in Revelation 7 and 14. First, who are these 144,000? Second, what is their goal? I will summarize the main viewpoints on both debates.

Debate 1: Who Are the 144,000?

In Revelation 7:3-4 we read the following proclamation from the voice of an angel: "'Do not harm the earth or the sea or the trees, until we have sealed the servants of our God on their foreheads.' And I heard the number of the sealed, 144,000, sealed from every tribe of the sons of Israel." Then in Revelation 14:1-5, we read this:

> Then I looked, and behold, on Mount Zion stood the Lamb, and with him 144,000 who had his name and his Father's name written on their foreheads. And I heard a voice from heaven like the roar of many waters and like the sound of loud thunder. The voice I heard was like the sound of harpists playing on their harps, and they were singing a new song before the throne and before the four living creatures and before the elders. No one could learn that song except the 144,000 who had been redeemed

from the earth. It is these who have not defiled themselves with women, for they are virgins. It is these who follow the Lamb wherever he goes. These have been redeemed from mankind as firstfruits for God and the Lamb, and in their mouth no lie was found, for they are blameless.

Viewpoint 1: The 144,000 Are the Church

Some Bible expositors believe these 144,000 symbolically describe the church. According to this view, "John uses the language of the new Israel and thus refers the 144,000 to the completed church composed of Jew and Gentile."[1] Matthew Henry held to this view.

> The number of those who were sealed, may be understood to stand for the remnant of people which God reserved. Though the church of God is but a little flock, in comparison with the wicked world, yet it is a society really large, and to be still more enlarged. Here the universal church is figured under the type of Israel.[2]

The *ESV Study Bible* makes a similar claim.

> The 144,000, sealed from every tribe of the sons of Israel, have symbolic significance, representing the church...These are not Jacob's sons, for Dan is omitted and Manasseh included. They are not the tribes that inherited land in Canaan, for Dan is omitted, Levi (the priestly tribe) is included, and Joseph is listed instead of his son Ephraim.[3]

Further support for this view is drawn from other New Testament books. For example, Galatians 3:29 tells us, "If you are Christ's, then you are Abraham's offspring, heirs according to promise." Followers of Christ are called "the circumcision" (Philippians 3:3) and "the Israel of God" (Galatians 6:16). Therefore, the church fulfills the role as the true Israel. This means that the 144,000 in Revelation 7 and 14 represent the church and not Israel.

Viewpoint 2: The 144,000 are Ethnic Jews

The second primary viewpoint is that the 144,000 of Revelation 7 and 14 are ethnic Jews, with 12,000 from each of the 12 tribes of Israel. The very fact that specific tribes are mentioned in this context, along with specific numbers for those tribes, removes all possibility that this is a figure of speech. Nowhere else in the Bible does a reference to 12 tribes of Israel mean anything but 12 tribes of Israel. Indeed, the word *tribe* is never used of anything but a literal ethnic group in Scripture.

Why are the Old Testament tribes of Dan and Ephraim omitted from this list of Jewish tribes? First, we should remember that the Old Testament has some 20 variant lists of tribes. No two lists of the 12 tribes of Israel must be identical. Most scholars today agree Dan's tribe was omitted because that tribe committed idolatry on many occasions and was largely obliterated as a result (Leviticus 24:11; Judges 18:1,30; see also 1 Kings 12:28-29). To engage in unrepentant idolatry is to be cut off from God's blessing. The tribe of Ephraim, like the tribe of Dan, was also involved in idolatry and pagan worship (Judges 17; Hosea 4:17). Consequently, both tribes were omitted from Revelation 7.

There is also a good reason why the tribe of Levi was included in the list of Jewish tribes in Revelation rather than maintaining its special status as a priestly tribe under the Mosaic law. The tribe of Levi is probably included here because the priestly functions of the tribe of Levi ceased with the coming of Christ, the ultimate high priest. Indeed, the Levitical priesthood was fulfilled in the person of Christ (see Hebrews 7–10). There was no further need for the services of the tribe of Levi as priests, so there was no further reason for keeping this tribe distinct and separate from the others. That is why they were properly included in the tribal listing in the book of Revelation.

What about the verses that seem to indicate that the church is the new Israel? I dealt with these verses in chapters 3 and 4 and will just provide a brief summary here.

- Galatians 3:29 does tell us, "If you are Christ's, then you are Abraham's offspring, heirs according to promise." However, this does not mean that distinctions between the church and Israel are obliterated. It does not mean that Christians become Jews. Believers are simply spiritual descendants of Abraham.[4]

- Followers of Christ are called "the circumcision" in Philippians 3:3. However, Paul was simply referring to the circumcision of the heart that occurs when a person trusts in Christ for salvation.[5]

- Paul also refers to "the Israel of God" in Galatians 6:16. But Paul is here simply referring to saved Jews—that is, Jews who have trusted in Jesus Christ for salvation. Never forget that the church and Israel always remain distinct in Paul's writings (see Romans 9–11).

Debate 2: What Is the Goal of the 144,000?

Viewpoint 1: The Church Will Seek to Survive and Minister

If the 144,000 are interpreted to be the church, then one obvious goal is to make it through the tribulation period relatively unscathed. This is wishful thinking, however, because the book of Revelation is clear that there will be many martyrs during the tribulation period (Revelation 6:9). Further, it seems fair to say that anyone who lives on the earth during the tribulation period will experience significant suffering. After all, Revelation 3:10 describes the tribulation period as "the hour of trial that is coming on the whole world." No one seems to be exempt. Isaiah likewise speaks of the tribulation as being global: "Behold, the LORD will empty the earth and make it desolate, and he will twist its surface and scatter its inhabitants" (Isaiah 24:1). "Terror and the pit and the snare are upon you, O inhabitant of the earth!" (verse 17). So apparently, no one in the tribulation period will be unscathed.

Another goal of the church during the tribulation period will be to do what the church normally does—that is, to evangelize, comfort, and engage in discipleship. Seen in this way, the church will be a light in the midst of the darkness.

Viewpoint 2: The Jews Will Be a Light to the Gentiles

Here is the backdrop to a proper understanding of the 144,000 Jews during the tribulation period. God had originally chosen the Jews to be His witnesses. Their appointed task was to share the good news of God with all the other people around the world (see Isaiah 42:6; 43:10). The Jews were to be God's representatives to the Gentiles. Biblical history reveals that the Jews failed at this task, especially when they did not recognize Jesus as the divine Messiah, but this was nevertheless their calling.

During the future tribulation, 144,000 Jews who become believers in Jesus the divine Messiah sometime following the rapture will finally fulfill this mandate from God as His witnesses all around the world. Their work will yield a mighty harvest of souls (see Revelation 7:9-14).

God will protectively seal these witnesses—God's faithful remnant.[6] Seals in Bible times were signs of ownership and protection. These Jewish believers are owned by God, and He sovereignly protects them during their time of service during the tribulation period (Revelation 14:1-4; see also 2 Corinthians 1:22; Ephesians 1:13; 4:30).

These Jews probably become believers in Jesus in a way similar to that of the apostle Paul, himself a Jew, who had a Damascus-road encounter with the risen Christ (Acts 9:1-9). In 1 Corinthians 15:8, the apostle Paul refers to himself in his conversion to Christ as "one untimely born." Some Bible expositors, such as J. Dwight Pentecost, believe Paul may have been alluding to his 144,000 Jewish tribulation brethren who would experience a similar spiritual birth much later.[7]

These sealed servants of God will apparently be preachers. They will fulfill Matthew 24:14: "This gospel of the kingdom will be proclaimed throughout the whole world as a testimony to all nations, and then the end will come."

Many believe these 144,000 have a connection to the judgment of the nations (Matthew 25:31-46), which takes place following the second coming of Christ. The nations are comprised of the sheep and the goats, representing the saved and the lost among the Gentiles. According to verse 32, they are intermingled and require separation by a special judgment. They are judged based on how they treat Christ's brothers. Who are these brothers? They are likely the 144,000 Jews mentioned in Revelation 7, Christ's Jewish brothers who bear witness of Him during the tribulation.

These Jewish witnesses will struggle to buy food because they will refuse to receive the mark of the beast (Revelation 13:16-17). Only true believers in the Lord will be willing to jeopardize their lives by extending hospitality to the messengers. These sheep (believers), who treat the brothers (the 144,000) well, will enter into Christ's millennial kingdom. The goats (unbelievers) will go into eternal punishment.

Conclusion

Having examined all of the biblical data, it seems clear to me that the 144,000 are indeed ethnic Jews—12,000 from each tribe. Their goal will be to function as a light to the Gentiles during the tribulation period. They will be supernaturally sealed by God to this end. Their work will result in many conversions.

Who Are the Two Witnesses?

The identity and ministry of the two witnesses of Revelation 11 have long been debated among Christians. Some believe the two witnesses represent the church. Others believe they are literal persons who will be God's end-time prophets. Among those who believe they will be prophets, some believe their actual identity is Moses and Elijah. Others suggest that perhaps they will be Enoch and Elijah. Still others believe they will be two entirely new prophets whom God raises up. Let's look at the differing views on these issues.

Debate 1: The Church or Literal Prophets?

I will grant authority to my two witnesses, and they will prophesy for 1,260 days, clothed in sackcloth.

These are the two olive trees and the two lampstands that stand before the Lord of the earth. And if anyone would harm them, fire pours from their mouth and consumes their foes. If anyone would harm them, this is how he is doomed to be killed. They have the power to shut the sky, that no rain may fall during the days of their prophesying, and they have power over the waters to turn them into blood and to strike the earth with every kind of plague, as often as they desire. And when they have finished their testimony, the beast that rises from the bottomless pit will make war on them and conquer them and kill them, and their dead bodies will lie in the street of the great city that symbolically is called Sodom and Egypt, where their Lord was crucified. For three and a half days some from the peoples and tribes and languages and nations will gaze at their dead bodies and refuse to let them be placed in a tomb, and those who dwell on the earth will rejoice over them and make merry and exchange presents, because these two prophets had been a torment to those who dwell on the earth. But after the three and a half days a breath of life from God entered them, and they stood up on their feet, and great fear fell on those who saw them. Then they heard a loud voice from heaven saying to them, "Come up here!" And they went up to heaven in a cloud, and their enemies watched them (Revelation 11:3-12).

Viewpoint 1: The Two Witnesses Represent the Church

The first major viewpoint, held by many expositors both ancient and modern, is that the two witnesses of Revelation 11 are representative of the church. For example, John Gill (1697–1771) said the two witnesses represent the true church as opposed to the antichrist system of Roman Catholicism.[1] More recently the *Tyndale Commentary* notes, "We should take the witnesses as symbolizing the witnessing church (or part of it)…It is tempting to think of the two witnesses as standing for that part of the church which is faithful."[2] *The Expositor's Bible Commentary* states, "It is better to understand John as referring in chapter 11 to the whole Christian community."[3] The *ESV Study Bible* likewise states, "The witnesses of Revelation 11:3 aptly represent all whom the Lamb has redeemed…The witnesses especially fulfill the church's prophetic role, pouring God's word as fiery judgment from their mouth (cf. 2 Kings 1:10-12), announcing drought like Elijah (1 Kings 17:1), and turning waters…into blood like Moses (Ex. 7:14-25)."[4]

Interpreters defend this position by arguing that the book of

Revelation is highly symbolic. Therefore, the reference to the two witnesses should surely not be taken literally.

Further, it has been suggested that the two witnesses are symbolic of the witnessing church, for Jesus sent out the disciples two by two. "He called the twelve and began to send them out two by two, and gave them authority over the unclean spirits" (Mark 6:7).

In Revelation 11:7, the antichrist makes war on the two witnesses, and in Revelation 13:7, the antichrist makes war on the saints. Some expositors suggest that the two witnesses and the saints must therefore be one and the same people.

Viewpoint 2: The Two Witnesses Are God's End-Time Prophets

The second major viewpoint held by many is that the two witnesses will be God's end-time prophets who minister for three and a half years in the tribulation period. The details of their life and ministry give the distinct impression that the text is a narrative and speaks of two real people. What we read in the text makes perfect sense when taken in a literal, straightforward sense.

If the two witnesses represent the church, we must assume that all members of the church will be executed, lay dead for three days, be resurrected, and then ascend into heaven. But other biblical texts reveal that there will be believers still on earth at the second coming of Christ and that they will enter into Christ's millennial kingdom in their mortal bodies (see Matthew 25:31-46). The only way around this is to claim that the two witnesses represent only a portion of the church. But that seems like an exegesis of convenience—a forced exegesis.

It makes much better sense to say that during the tribulation period, God will raise up two mighty witnesses who will testify to the true God with astounding power. The power of these witnesses brings to mind Elijah (1 Kings 17; Malachi 4:5) and Moses (Exodus 7–11). The Old Testament required that two witnesses confirm testimony (see Deuteronomy 17:6; 19:15; Matthew 18:16; John 8:17; Hebrews 10:28). Their testimony about the Lord will be undeniable.

These witnesses will wear clothing made of goat or camel hair. These garments symbolically express mourning—in this case, mourning over the wretched condition of the world and its lack of repentance.

These prophets are referred to as two olive trees and two lampstands (Revelation 11:4). The imagery here is taken from Zechariah 3–4. Bible expositors offer several interpretations. One understanding is that lamps in biblical days were typically fueled by olive oil. The olive trees and lampstands therefore symbolize the light of spiritual revival. The preaching of the two witnesses will bring this light of revival during the dark days of the tribulation.

Other Bible expositors relate this imagery to the Holy Spirit. In Zechariah 4:2-14, the focus is on Joshua the high priest and Zerubbabel the governor. Both these individuals were empowered by the Holy Spirit, something symbolized by the olive oil. Thus the two witnesses of Revelation 11 will likewise be empowered by the Holy Spirit during their ministry and will shine as lights, just like a lamp.

The time frame of these two witness—1260 days—measures out to precisely three and a half years. This same period is elsewhere defined as 42 months (Revelation 11:2) and "a time, and times, and half a time" (12:14).

It is not clear from Revelation 11 whether this is the first or last three and a half years of the tribulation. It may be best to conclude that the two witnesses do their miraculous work during the first three and a half years, for the antichrist's execution of them seems to fit best with other events that will transpire at the midpoint of the tribulation, such as the antichrist's exaltation of himself to godhood. Moreover, the two witnesses' resurrection after being dead for three days would make a bigger impact on the world at the midpoint of the tribulation than at the end, just prior to the glorious second coming of Christ.

Before the antichrist executes the two witnesses, God supernaturally protects them during the years of their ministry. This is similar to how Jesus was providentially protected during the years of His ministry. Once Jesus's ministry was over, He was put to death on the cross. Until that time, Jesus continually affirmed that His time had not yet come (see, for example, John 7:6,8). Likewise, the 144,000 will be supernaturally preserved until their ministry is complete.

Anyone who tries to harm either of the two prophetic witnesses will come to a fiery end. The ministry of the two witnesses is unstoppable for three and a half years—until "they have finished their testimony" (Revelation 11:7).

The two witnesses have power to shut the sky, power over the waters, and power to strike the earth with every kind of plague (verse 6). In both the Old and New Testaments, God often used miracles to authenticate His messengers (Acts 2:43; Romans 15:18-19; 2 Corinthians 12:12). In the tribulation period, when the world is overrun by supernatural demonic activity, false religion, murder, sexual perversion, and unrestrained wickedness, the supernatural signs performed by these two witnesses will mark them as true prophets of God.

Once the two witnesses complete their ministry, God withdraws His providential protection from them. The antichrist will succeed in killing them, something that many had already lost their lives attempting to do. The witnesses will not die prematurely. All goes according to God's divine timing.

The bodies of the witnesses lie lifeless in Jerusalem (Revelation 11:8). It is apparently by television and the Internet that "the peoples and tribes and languages and nations" will gaze at the dead witnesses for three and a half days (verse 9). The news feeds will be instantaneous.

The refusal to bury a corpse is a way of showing contempt (see Acts 14:19). The Old Testament prohibits this practice (Deuteronomy 21:22-23). By leaving the dead bodies in the street, the people of the world render the greatest possible insult to God's spokesmen. This was considered among the greatest indignities someone could perpetrate on another person (see Psalm 79:2-3). It is equivalent to spitting on the corpses.

People on earth essentially have a satanic Christmas celebration when the witnesses are put to death. They exchange presents, apparently in relief that the witnesses are finally silenced.

The Christmas celebration quickly gives way to fear, however, as people witness a mighty act of God. The lifeless corpses suddenly stand up in full view of television and Internet feeds. Clips of this event will no doubt be replayed over and over again through various media. They will no doubt go viral on the Internet. The resurrection and ascension of God's two witnesses serves as a huge exclamation point to their prophetic words throughout their three-and-a-half-year ministry. (In my mind's eye, I can picture the two resurrected witnesses turning to the stunned crowd and asking, "Any questions?")

Debate 2: Who Are the Witnesses of Revelation 11?

If we accept that the two witnesses are end-time prophets and not symbolic representatives of the church, the question remains, who are these prophets?

Viewpoint 1: Moses and Elijah

A number of Bible expositors believe the two witnesses will actually be Moses and Elijah. These are some of their reasons.

1. In the tribulation, God deals with the Jews—just as He did in the first 69 weeks of Daniel's prophecy. Moses and Elijah are two of the most influential figures in Jewish history. Their presence during the tribulation period would thus make good sense.

2. Both the Old Testament and Jewish tradition expected Moses (Deuteronomy 18:15,18) and Elijah (Malachi 4:5) to return in the future.

3. Moses and Elijah appeared on the mount of transfiguration with Jesus. This shows their centrality. This, too, would make their presence on the scene during the future tribulation period seem appropriate.

4. The miracles portrayed in Revelation 11 are similar to those Moses and Elijah performed (see Exodus 7–11; 1 Kings 17).

5. Moses and Elijah each left the earth in unusual ways. Elijah never died but rather was transported to heaven in a fiery chariot (2 Kings 2:11-12). God supernaturally buried Moses's body in an unknown location (Deuteronomy 34:5-6).

So in the tribulation period, God may send two of His mightiest servants—Moses, the great deliverer and spiritual legislator of Israel, and Elijah, a prince among Old Testament prophets. During Old Testament times, these individuals rescued Israel from bondage and idolatry. They may appear again during the tribulation period to warn Israel against succumbing to the false religion of the antichrist and the false prophet.

Against this view, some scholars suggest that the ancient Jewish expectation of the return of Elijah seems to have been fulfilled in the ministry of John the Baptist. Luke 1:17 states that John was to go forth "in the spirit and power of Elijah" (see also Matthew 3:3; 11:14; 17:10-13; Mark 1:2-3). In view of this, the identification of one of the two end-time witnesses as Elijah must rest its case on factors other than the Jewish expectation of a future coming of Elijah.

Viewpoint 2: Enoch and Elijah

Other Bible expositors suggest that perhaps the two witnesses will be Enoch and Elijah. After all, both Enoch and Elijah were upright men who were raptured to heaven. Neither one experienced death. Both were prophets—one a Gentile (Enoch) and the other a Jew (Elijah). The Church Fathers unanimously held to this view during the first 300 years of church history. Perhaps God will ordain one witness to speak to the Jews and the other witness to speak to the Gentiles during the tribulation.

But again, some scholars suggest that Elijah's expected return seems to have been fulfilled in the ministry of John the Baptist.

Viewpoint 3: New Prophets

Still other expositors say that these two witnesses will not be biblical personalities of the past. They reason that the text would surely identify famous Old Testament personalities if they were indeed coming back. Therefore, the two witnesses will likely be new prophets that God specially raises up for ministry during the tribulation.

In this view, God will raise up two men in the spirit and power of their Old Testament counterparts. They are similar to Moses and Elijah from the standpoint of their ministries, but similarity does not mean identity. Their ministries are similar only because they are ministering to Israel, just as Moses and Elijah did. But they will be two totally new and unique prophets of God.

Other Viewpoints

A variety of other suggestions as to the identity of the two witnesses have been offered throughout church history. Some suggest the apostles Peter and Paul. Others suggest that the two witnesses are representative of Christian martyrs. Still others suggest that the two witnesses are representative of all the prophets. Still others say the witnesses represent both Jewish and Gentile believers in the church. The debate continues.

Conclusion

To interpret these two prophets as literal prophets that God raises up in the future tribulation period makes the best sense to me. It also makes sense to me that they will be two new and unique prophets and not Elijah and Moses or Elijah and Enoch. I am convinced that many will come to the Lord during the tribulation as a result of their ministry (see Revelation 7:9-17).

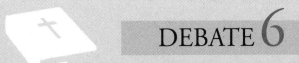

DEBATE 6

How Are We to Understand the Antichrist?

Who Restrains the Antichrist?

The identity of the restrainer of the antichrist has been debated substantially throughout church history. In 2 Thessalonians 2:7-8 we are told that "the mystery of lawlessness is already at work. Only he who now restrains it will do so until he is out of the way. And then the lawless one will be revealed." So the antichrist cannot be revealed until the one who restrains him is taken out of the way.

What, however, is the "mystery of lawlessness"? A mystery in the biblical sense is typically something that was previously unknown (such as in Old Testament times) but that God has now revealed. In 2 Thessalonians 2:7-8, the mystery involves divine revelation of a future climax of global lawlessness. As *The Bible Knowledge Commentary* puts it, "Then and now a movement against divine law directed by Satan was and is operative. But it is being restrained somewhat, and this restraining will continue until the time appointed for revealing the man of sin and the climax of lawlessness."[1]

The antichrist is the "man of sin" (2 Thessalonians 2:3 NKJV). He will embody sin and promote it as it has never been promoted before. Everything about him will be rooted in sin. He will be the definitive man of sin. Sin will be the natural outflow of his sinful character.

The question is, who or what can restrain the antichrist? Some say it is Rome. Others say it is human government. Still others say it is the

Holy Spirit, who indwells the church. Let's briefly consider each view below.

Viewpoint 1: Rome

Some Church Fathers believed the restrainer was the Roman Empire, or more specifically, the Roman emperor himself. In this viewpoint, the early centuries of Christianity witnessed Roman civil authorities increasingly clashing with the Roman Catholic Church. It is therefore understandable that some living at that time interpreted 2 Thessalonians 2:7-8 to mean that Rome's government would restrain the Roman Catholic papacy until the Lord came, after which the papacy would be destroyed.

In this view, the apostle Paul was purposefully vague about the identity of the restrainer. If Paul had explicitly identified the restrainer as Rome, his statement about the restrainer being removed might be considered seditious, as if Paul himself were involved in some movement to overthrow the Roman government.

It is easy to see why this view would have been popular among people living at that time. Today, however, we detect multiple problems with this interpretation. The Roman Empire fell from power in the fifth century, and the antichrist is yet to be revealed. So whoever the restrainer of 2 Thessalonians 2:7-8 is, it is surely not the Roman Empire.

Moreover, Paul may have been vague simply because he had already spoken to the Thessalonians face-to-face about the restrainer. They would have readily understood Paul's brief allusion to the restrainer in 2 Thessalonians 2 without further explanation.

There is another problem with this view. The antichrist not only will be a powerful figure himself but also will be empowered by Satan. This means that whoever the restrainer is, he must be powerful enough to stand against Satan. No human being or human government has the power to restrain Satan, so Rome is not a good candidate for being the restrainer.

Moreover, Daniel 2 and 7 reveal that the antichrist will rule over a revived Roman Empire. It therefore makes no sense to say that the Roman Empire—itself a bastion of false religion over which the antichrist will one day rule—is the restrainer of the antichrist.

Viewpoint 2: Human Government

According to a similar view, human government in general is the restrainer of the antichrist. Theologian Paul Feinberg explains that the idea here is that "restraint through the rule of law (by the government) is the opposite of the man of sin and the mystery of lawlessness."[2] In other words, lawlessness is presently restrained by the enforcement of law by the government. But one day, the antichrist will overthrow human government so he can work his lawless will in the world.

The best argument for this viewpoint comes from the pen of prophecy scholar Arnold G. Fruchtenbaum in his excellent book *The Footsteps of the Messiah*.

> The task of restraining evil was given to human government under the Noahic Covenant in Genesis 9:1-17, and this basic doctrinal truth was reiterated by Paul in Romans 13:1-7. On one hand, human government is even now restraining lawlessness. On the other hand, the government of the last of the three kings will restrain the Antichrist, the lawless one, until the middle of the Tribulation.[3]

Fruchtenbaum has in mind Daniel 7:7-8, which speaks of the rise of the antichrist.

> Behold, a fourth beast, terrifying and dreadful and exceedingly strong. It had great iron teeth; it devoured and broke in pieces and stamped what was left with its feet. It was different from all the beasts that were before it, and it had ten horns. I considered the horns, and behold, there came up among them another horn, a little one, before which three of the first horns were plucked up by the roots. And behold, in this horn were eyes like the eyes of a man, and a mouth speaking great things.

Daniel is here describing the Roman Empire. The backdrop is that Rome already existed in ancient days, but it fell apart in the fifth century AD. It will be revived, however, in the end times, apparently comprised of ten nations ruled by ten kings (ten horns). An eleventh horn—a little horn (the antichrist)—starts out apparently in an insignificant way but grows powerful enough to uproot three of the existing horns (kings), who apparently resist the rise of the antichrist. He eventually comes into absolute power and dominance over this revived Roman Empire.

With that backdrop in mind, Fruchtenbaum says, "It is only when the last of these three kings has been killed, leading to complete submission by the other seven kings, that the Antichrist will be free to take over full global dictatorship...Consequently, the last restrainer of the Antichrist will be the last of the three kings and the government which he represents."[4]

Fruchtenbaum makes a strong case for his view. If there is a weakness, it relates to whether human government is strong enough to stand against the antichrist, who will be energized by Satan. Satan is more powerful than humans by a large measure, so some Bible interpreters reject the possibility of any form of human government restraining him. One scholar notes, "It would seem that a person is required to restrain a person, and a supernatural one to restrain this man of lawlessness who is motivated by Satan himself."[5] For this reason, I personally reject this theory, though it was well argued by Fruchtenbaum.

We might also note that both Scripture and modern empirical evidence reveal that not all human governments restrain sin. Some governments actually encourage sin. Thus it may be unrealistic to say that the restrainer is human government. Nevertheless, we cannot be dogmatic. This view remains at least a possibility.

Viewpoint 3: The Holy Spirit

The most convincing view to me is that the restrainer is the Holy Spirit, who indwells the church. This view was held by many in the early church, including Theodoret, Theodore of Mopsuestia, and Chrysostom.[6]

Only God the Holy Spirit has sufficient power to restrain a person who is energized by the *un*holy spirit, Satan. As Bible expositor Thomas Constable put it, "The Holy Spirit of God is the only Person with sufficient (supernatural) power to do this restraining…The removal of the Restrainer at the time of the Rapture must obviously precede the day of the Lord."[7]

The Popular Bible Prophecy Commentary offers some key grammatical insights on 2 Thessalonians 2:6-7 that support the identity of the restrainer as the Holy Spirit.

> The word "restrain" (Greek, *katecho*, "to hold down") in both verses 6 and 7 is a present active participle, but in verse 6 it appears in the neuter gender ("what restrains") while in verse 7 it is in the masculine ("he who restrains, holds down"). Such usage also occurs in reference to the Spirit of God. The Greek word for "spirit," *pneuma*, is a neuter gender word, but the masculine pronoun is used when referring to the person of the Holy Spirit.[8]

The word *restrain* carries the idea, "to hold back from action, to keep under control, to deprive of physical liberty, as by shackling."[9] This is what the Holy Spirit does in our day in preventing the antichrist from arising.

Mark Hitchcock notes that "the Holy Spirit is spoken of in Scripture as restraining sin and evil in the world (see Genesis 6:3) and in the heart of the believer (see Galatians 5:16-17)."[10] Mal Couch likewise tells us, "By divine providence, and by all the evidence of the Scriptures, the Holy Spirit characteristically restrains and strives against sin (Genesis 6:3). The Spirit presently abides in the world in a special way in this age through the church."[11] Once this special abiding is removed, the antichrist will be manifest.

In keeping with this interpretation, 1 John 4:4 tells us, "He who is in you is greater than he who is in the world." "He who is in" Christians is the Holy Spirit. "He who is in the world" is Satan. This means the Holy Spirit is greater than Satan. Satan is the one who energizes the antichrist, so only the Holy Spirit can restrain him.

Taken Out of the Way at the Rapture

If the Holy Spirit is indeed the restrainer, and if His being taken out of the way is necessary prior to the emergence of the antichrist, then clearly this is a strong support for a pretribulational rapture (see 1 Corinthians 15:50-52; 1 Thessalonians 1:10; 4:13-17; 5:9). The antichrist's signing of a covenant with Israel marks the beginning of the seven-year tribulation period (Daniel 9:26-27), so the rapture of the church must take place prior to the signing of this covenant. Sometime prior to this signing, the Holy Spirit—who indwells the church—will be taken out of the way (by means of the rapture) so the antichrist can be revealed.

The theological backdrop to all this is that Christians and the church are indwelt by the Holy Spirit. First Corinthians tells us, "Do you not know that you are God's temple and that God's Spirit dwells in you?" (3:16). "Do you not know that your body is a temple of the Holy Spirit within you, whom you have from God?" (6:19). "In one Spirit we were all baptized into one body—Jews or Greeks, slaves or free—and all were made to drink of one Spirit" (12:13; see also 1 John 3:24).

This means that if the church is taken off the earth at the rapture, the Holy Spirit will be taken out of the way. This removal of the Holy Spirit's restraint allows the antichrist, energized by Satan, to come into power during the tribulation period.

This may help explain the massive and sudden apostasy (falling away from truth) during the first part of the tribulation period. At the rapture, the Holy Spirit—the Spirit of truth (John 14:17; 16:13)—is removed from earth, thereby allowing the rapid emergence of *un*truth (or apostasy).

A Qualification: The Holy Spirit During the Tribulation

Bible expositor John Phillips makes an important point regarding the continued ministry of the Holy Spirit during the tribulation period.

> What is to be removed is the Holy Spirit's mighty working through the church. Until that happens, Satan cannot bring his plans to a head...After the rapture of the church, the Holy Spirit will continue His work in bringing people

to salvation, but He will no longer baptize them into the mystical body of Christ, the church, nor will He actively hinder Satan from bringing his schemes to fruition.[12]

So even though the Holy Spirit will be removed at the rapture of the church, He will nevertheless continue to visit the earth with His mighty power, bringing many to salvation during the horrific years of the tribulation period. Revelation 7:9-17 reveals that there will be many conversions.

Conclusion

I am convinced that the Holy Spirit is the restrainer of the antichrist. My fundamental reason is that only the Holy Spirit can restrain the *un*holy spirit (Satan), who energizes the antichrist. Only the Spirit of truth can restrain the spirit of *un*truth.

Is the Antichrist a Muslim?

This debate has been catapulted into the forefront during the past decade and has been the focus of books, articles, radio shows, television shows, and Internet discussions. I've personally interacted with people on both sides of the issue and will examine the pros and cons of the theory.[1]

Islamic Eschatology

Before considering the Muslim-antichrist debate, let's touch on a few basics of Islamic eschatology—particularly the Muslim concepts of the antichrist, the Messiah, and Jesus. Once we do this, we can more easily weigh the pros and cons in the debate.

In Muslim eschatology, the antichrist is called the *dajjal*. Muslim literature reveals many interesting ideas about this future ruler. He will allegedly be a Jew, he will be born in Iran to parents who've been childless for 30 years, and he will have only one eye. He will claim to be a prophet, claim to be divine, seek to be worshipped, and deceive people with seemingly miraculous acts. He will also conquer the world (except the cities of Mecca and Medina) with a large army and reign for 40 days, each day seeming like a year.

As for the Islamic messiah, he is called the *Mahdi*. He will reportedly be a descendent of Muhammad, ride on a white horse, and bring global deliverance from the reign of the dajjal. He will conquer and slaughter the Jews, establish his headquarters in Jerusalem, and reign for seven years or more.

Jesus is *not* the messiah of Islam. The Jesus of Islam is obviously quite different from the Jesus of biblical Christianity. According to Muslim theology, Jesus was a sinless messenger of God and one of the foremost prophets of Allah, but he was a lesser prophet than Muhammad. He was not the Son of God, was not God in human flesh, and was not crucified or resurrected from the dead. He did not die as a sacrifice to atone for the sins of humankind. At some point, he was directly raised up to heaven by Allah. He will one day come back to earth to the Mount of Olives, meet up with the Mahdi, and submit himself to him. He will slay all who do not accept Islam as the one true religion, kill the dajjal, and see to the annihilation of the Jews. He will reign for 40 years after the death of the Mahdi, assume control of the Islamic global kingdom, bring global blessing and peace on earth, and marry and have children. He will die and be buried next to Muhammad in Medina and will then be resurrected with all other men and women on the last day.

Having examined the two primary characters of Islamic eschatology, let's now look at the way these relate to the primary characters in Christian eschatology.

Viewpoint 1: The Antichrist Is a Muslim

Christians who subscribe to the Muslim-antichrist theory suggest that the Islamic Mahdi (the Islamic messiah) will actually be the antichrist described in the Bible.[2] It is also suggested that the person Muslims believe to be Jesus will in reality be the false prophet introduced in the book of Revelation. This false prophet (whom Muslims will mistake for Jesus) will render service to the antichrist (whom Muslims will mistake for their Mahdi, or messiah). Both of these individuals will ultimately be destroyed when the true, biblical Jesus returns at the end of the tribulation period.

Christian proponents of this view draw support for it by noting significant similarities between the biblical antichrist and the Muslim Mahdi. Joel Richardson, the author of *The Islamic Antichrist*, summarizes these similarities.

- The Mahdi, like the antichrist, will emerge in the last days as an unparalleled political, military, and religious leader.

- In Muslim eschatology, the Muslim Jesus will emerge to support the Mahdi. The Bible reveals that the false prophet will emerge to support the antichrist.

- In Muslim eschatology, the Mahdi and the Muslim Jesus will seek to subdue the earth by a powerful army. The Bible reveals that the antichrist and the false prophet will seek to do the same.

- In Muslim eschatology, the Mahdi and the Muslim Jesus will establish a new (Islamic) world order. The Bible reveals that the antichrist and the false prophet will do the same.

- Muslim eschatology teaches that the Mahdi and the Muslim Jesus will institute sharia law all over the earth.[3] The Bible reveals that the antichrist and the false prophet will also institute new global laws.

- Muslim eschatology teaches that after the Mahdi conquers the globe for Islam, he will try to change Christianity's rest days of Saturday and Sunday to Friday, the holy day of Islam. The Bible reveals that the antichrist "shall think to change the times" (Daniel 7:25).

- In Muslim eschatology, the Mahdi and the Muslim Jesus will institute a world religion—that is, Islam. The Bible reveals that the antichrist and the false prophet will also institute a world religion.

- In Muslim eschatology, the Mahdi and the Muslim Jesus will execute anyone who does not submit to Islam. The Bible reveals that the antichrist and the false prophet will execute anyone who does not submit to their world religion.

- In Muslim eschatology, the Mahdi and the Muslim Jesus will behead those who refuse to submit to Islam. The Bible reveals that the antichrist and the false prophet will behead those who refuse to submit to them (Revelation 20:4).

- Muslim eschatology teaches that the Mahdi and the Muslim Jesus will seek to kill Jews. The biblical antichrist and false prophet will do the same.

- Muslim eschatology teaches that the Mahdi and the Muslim Jesus will attack Jerusalem and seize it for Islam. The Bible reveals that the antichrist and the false prophet will do this as well.

- In Muslim eschatology, the Mahdi and the Muslim Jesus will establish the Islamic caliphate from Jerusalem. The Bible reveals that the antichrist (with the help of the false prophet) will set himself up in the Jewish temple in a position of authority.

- In Muslim eschatology, the Mahdi will ride on a white horse. The biblical antichrist will as well.

- In Muslim eschatology, the Mahdi and the Muslim Jesus will make a peace treaty through a Jew (specifically a Levite) for seven years. The Bible reveals that the antichrist will make a peace treaty with Israel for seven years.

- Islam denies key doctrines of Christianity (including the Incarnation). The Bible says the spirit of antichrist denies key doctrines of Christianity (such as the Incarnation).[4]

Richardson makes this conclusion.

> We see that several of the most unique and distinguishing aspects of the biblical Antichrist's person, mission, and actions are matched to quite an amazing degree by the descriptions of the Mahdi as found in the Islamic traditions. And now, even further, we see that Muslim scholars actually apply Bible verses about the Antichrist to their

awaited savior, the Mahdi. This must be seen as quite ironic, if not entirely prophetic.[5]

These similarities have led many to believe that the antichrist will be a Muslim. Given the present Islamic antagonism toward Christianity, and considering the incredible present growth of Islam, it is easy for many to believe that a Muslim antichrist could emerge into power in the end times.

Viewpoint 2: The Antichrist Will Not Be a Muslim

Some of the arguments for an Islamic antichrist seem compelling. Yet many Christians find themselves in disagreement with this theory. Solomon, the wisest man who ever lived, once said, "The one who states his case first seems right, until the other comes and examines him" (Proverbs 18:17). When one examines the Muslim-antichrist hypothesis in the light of Scripture, it doesn't quite measure up. Following are some of the key components in the case against the antichrist being a Muslim.

Islamic Eschatology Is Contradictory

Islamic tradition, known as the *Hadith*, forms the basis of Islamic eschatology. But many of the passages in the Hadith that deal with the end times contradict each other. This makes it difficult to construct a detailed Muslim eschatology that most Muslims would agree with. As Bible prophecy expert David Reagan put it, "It is extremely difficult to piece together the Islamic concept of the end times. The information is greatly disjointed, being spread throughout the Hadith."[6] Books and articles written by proponents of the Muslim-antichrist hypothesis rarely mention this, but this factor alone greatly weakens their case.

Muslims Have a Dependent Eschatology

Muhammad, before taking on his role as a prophet, was apprenticed as a camel boy to a rich widow named Khadija. He eventually rose to become the manager of all her trading interests, overseeing caravans on her behalf. As a merchant, Muhammad often went on lengthy caravan journeys, sometimes going as far as Syria and possibly Egypt. These journeys enabled Muhammad to encounter people of different religions and nationalities.[7] He met Christians, Jews, and perhaps Zoroastrians on the trade routes he traveled for the next 15 years.

Historians tell us that Muhammad picked up most of his ideas about the end times from his discussions with Christians and Jews while he was a businessman. Sometime later, his ideas were embellished by his followers, who also knew of biblical prophecies of the end times.[8] Dr. Samuel Shahid, the director of Islamic studies at Southwestern Baptist Theological Seminary in Fort Worth, Texas, agrees, noting that the major concepts of Islamic eschatology were borrowed from the Hebrew Scriptures, the Christian New Testament, and various concepts of Zoroastrianism.[9]

Many of the teachings recorded in the Hadith were also heavily influenced by Christian sources. Academics who study Islam have often noted such theological dependency. For example, some of the Islamic signs of the end times include an increase in false prophets, apostasy, an increase in natural calamities, and an increase in wars—events all found in the Christian Scriptures, which predate Muhammad by far (see, for example, Matthew 24).

Many Christians see Satan's fingerprints all over the emergence of the Islamic religion. Satan is the Father of lies (John 8:44). Scripture is clear that Satan has the ability to inspire false religions and cults (1 Timothy 4:1; 1 John 4:1). Further, Satan's temptation of Christ (Matthew 4:1-11) shows that he has knowledge of Scripture, for he quotes from Scripture when tempting Christ. Thus Satan—who knows biblical prophecy—may have sought to give credence to the false religion of Islam by inspiring similar prophecies (a one-world religion, riding on a white horse, a false prophet, and the like) in that religion. Never forget that Satan is a great deceiver.

Muslims Disagree on the Mahdi

Muslim-antichrist proponents gloss over the fact that Muslims have different views on the Mahdi. This is a primary area of doctrinal conflict between Shi'ite and Sunni Muslims. Shi'ite Muslims believe the Mahdi is now in hiding on earth and will soon emerge. Sunni Muslims, by contrast, believe that the Mahdi has yet to emerge in history. To put it another way, Shi'ite Muslims believe in a "coming out" of the Mahdi, whereas Sunni Muslims believe in a "coming back" of the Mahdi. Clearly, Muslims do not have a unified eschatology.

Islam's Denials of Christian Teachings

Islam's denials of key Christian doctrines, such as the Incarnation and Christ's substitutionary death on the cross, are rooted in the spirit of antichrist (1 John 4:3). But Islam is not unique in this regard. Many false religions and cults deny the Incarnation and other key Christian doctrines. Therefore the "spirit of antichrist" argument lends no real support to the Muslim-antichrist hypothesis.

A Roman Antichrist

Daniel 9:26, addressing the 70 weeks of Daniel, reveals that the antichrist will be a Roman.

> After the sixty-two weeks, an anointed one shall be cut off
> and shall have nothing. And the people of the prince who
> is to come shall destroy the city and the sanctuary. Its end
> shall come with a flood, and to the end there shall be war.
> Desolations are decreed.

This verse prophesies that "the city and the sanctuary" (Jerusalem and its temple) will be destroyed by the "people of the prince who is to come." Who destroyed Jerusalem and its temple in AD 70? Titus and his Roman army. The Roman people are the people of the coming prince, the antichrist. The antichrist will therefore be a Roman.

A Covenant Between the Antichrist and Israel

The tribulation period begins the moment the antichrist signs a covenant with Israel. In Daniel 9:27 we read that the antichrist "shall make a strong covenant with many for one week"—that is, one week of years, or seven years.

Why would a Muslim leader sign a covenant guaranteeing the

protection of Israel? Most Muslims today are not favorably disposed toward the nation of Israel—particularly Palestinian Muslims, who oppose what they consider Israeli expansionism. Extreme Muslims want the Jews out of Israel altogether and do not want to protect the Jewish people in Israel at all.

This covenant may be what allows Israel to live in peace and safety (Ezekiel 28:25-26) so she can rebuild the Jewish temple in the first part of the tribulation period. It seems hard to believe that a Muslim leader would protect Israel in this regard and allow her to build what the Muslims would consider to be a pagan temple in the holy city of Jerusalem.

Moreover, it is positively inconceivable that Israel would actually trust its security to a Muslim leader. How could Israel possibly enjoy a sense of security under a covenant with a Muslim leader?[10] Still further, it seems implausible that the general Muslim population in various Muslim countries around the world would go along with such a covenant with Israel.

Muslim eschatology actually portrays the covenant being made with the Romans, not the Jews. This cannot be reconciled with Daniel 9:27.

End-Time Beheadings

Muslim-antichrist proponents often assume that beheading is an automatic indicator of Islam. Such is not the case. We read about beheadings in both the Old Testament (2 Samuel 4:7) and the New Testament (Matthew 14:10). These beheadings predate the emergence of Islam by many centuries. Beheadings initiated by the antichrist cannot be taken as a proof of a Muslim antichrist.

The Self-Proclaimed Deity of the Antichrist

One of the more heinous aspects of the antichrist is that he "shall exalt himself and magnify himself above every god" (Daniel 11:36). He "opposes and exalts himself against every so-called god or object of worship, so that he takes his seat in the temple of God, proclaiming himself to be God" (2 Thessalonians 2:4).

A Muslim antichrist claiming to be God would be trashing the

Muslim creed—"There is no God but Allah, and Muhammad is his prophet." I cannot imagine a true Muslim claiming he was God. Just as Muslims would never call Jesus God incarnate or the Son of God, so no Muslim would claim he was God. Muslims are radical monotheists. A Muslim antichrist claiming to be God would be an infidel among Quran-believing Muslims.

Islam teaches that God can have no partners. Muslims generally make this assertion when arguing against the doctrines of the Trinity and Jesus's deity. But it would also apply to a human end-time leader claiming to be God.

Traditional Muslims believe that Allah is so radically unlike any earthly reality—so utterly transcendent and beyond anything in the finite realm—that he can scarcely be described in earthly terms. How then could a Muslim claim to be God—a God described in earthly terms?

Muslim-antichrist proponents respond that in the middle of the tribulation period, the antichrist will become self-absorbed and claim to be God. Joel Richardson asserts, "The Mahdi throws the ultimate curve ball. In the same way that Christians view Jesus to be the incarnation of God, so the Mahdi now declares himself an incarnation of Allah, and as such, he demands worship."[11]

What happens next? We are told that some Muslims may be too embarrassed to admit that they have been duped. They will not want to admit they were wrong all along. Richardson suggests, "For many... an utter determination to believe in the legitimacy of the Mahdi and Islam will overwhelm them. These would rather be swept up into a great deception with an Islamic nature than acknowledge having been wrong all along."[12]

I find this scenario very difficult to believe. If true Muslims—firmly committed to Muhammad, the Quran, the Muslim creed, and Allah (who alone grants or withholds eternal salvation)—discovered another Muslim who claimed to be God, they would want to behead that infidel. No true Quran-believing Muslim would allow such a claim to go unanswered.

Richardson suggests another possible scenario. When the antichrist claims to be God, "it is quite likely that at this time multitudes of Muslims will see the evil person that the Antichrist really is and will turn to the true Jesus for salvation. Who knows?"[13] This scenario sounds inviting. After all, Christians want people to be saved—including Muslims. But this is ultimately a moot point since there is so much substantive evidence against the Muslim-antichrist theory.

Conclusion

I could include other arguments in favor of the Muslim-antichrist hypothesis and against it. The above is sufficient to illustrate the primary components of the debate. My assessment is that the antichrist will not be a Muslim but will rather be a Roman Gentile who will rise to power in a revived Roman Empire.

Is the Antichrist a Jew or a Gentile?

For many centuries, Bible readers have debated whether the antichrist will be a Jew or a Gentile. Both views have had famous supporters. I will briefly address both sides of the debate.

Viewpoint 1: The Antichrist Will Be a Jew

Most people who hold that the antichrist will be a Jew base their views on theological issues, but sometimes charges of racism enter into the picture. The late Jerry Falwell claimed at a pastor's conference in 1999 that the antichrist would be a Jew. His reasoning? "Since Jesus came to earth the first time 2,000 years ago as a Jewish male, most evangelicals believe the antichrist will, by necessity, be a Jewish male."[1]

Falwell meant no offense. But the uproar in the Jewish community was nearly immediate. Abraham H. Foxman, director of the Anti-Defamation League, responded, "In identifying the Antichrist as a living Jewish man, Reverend Falwell draws from an especially vicious tradition of Christian theological anti-Judaism…It appears clear that after years of Christian–Jewish dialogue, Reverend Falwell hasn't learned a thing."[2] Foxman claimed that Falwell's comments give "license to bigots and anti-Semites" to continue in their prejudices and feelings of superiority.[3]

Rabbi James Rudin, director of interreligious affairs for the American Jewish Committee in New York, said he was surprised by the comment because he was aware of Falwell's strong support of Israel. He then added this:

> To single out any one man and particularly to identify him as Jewish plays into some latent and historical anti-Semitism from the past...This is very, very radioactive material. I think Christian leaders have to exercise great care because this can produce negative responses among people who are not educated in the New Testament.[4]

Not intending to create a firestorm of controversy, Falwell quickly issued a public apology.

The Jewish Tribe of Dan

An early tradition held that the antichrist would come from Dan, one of the 12 tribes of Israel. Some relate this to the fact that the Danites fell into deep apostasy and idolatry, setting up for themselves a graven image (Judges 18:30). The Testament of Dan (5:6) names Satan as the prince of the tribe. Irenaeus, writing in the latter part of the second century, noted that Dan was omitted from the list of tribes in the book of Revelation because of a tradition that the antichrist was to come from that tribe (*Against Heresies* V.30.2).

Genesis 49:17 is occasionally cited in support of this idea: "Dan shall be a serpent in the way, a viper by the path, that bites the horse's heels so that his rider falls backward." The mention of a serpent and viper naturally brings to mind Satan and the antichrist.

A Common View Among the Church Fathers

A number of the early Church Fathers believed the antichrist would be a Jew. This includes not only Irenaeus but also Hippolytus, a disciple of Irenaeus who wrote that the "antichrist is a Jewish false messiah whose coming is still some time in the future."[5] Origen, Chrysostom, Jerome, and Augustine also believed the antichrist would be a Jew.

Acceptance of a Non-Jewish Leader

Jesus said, "If another comes in his own name, you will receive him"

(John 5:43). Some people argue that the Jews would never receive anyone as a leader who himself was not a Jew.[6] Reformed theologian A.W. Pink says, "He will ape Christ. He will pose as the real Messiah of Israel. In such case he must be a Jew."[7] More recently, the late Grant Jeffery made this suggestion:

> The Jews would one day accept for a time the false claims of the Antichrist as their promised Messiah...Since the prophecies tell us that the Antichrist will present himself to Israel as the Messiah many scholars have concluded that he must be Jewish. Certainly no religious Jew would dream of accepting a Gentile as the Messiah of Israel.[8]

The Antichrist and "the Little Horn"

Daniel 7:7 pictures the antichrist as "the little horn." A horn is a symbol of power and might, an emblem of dominion, representing kingdoms and kings (see Daniel 7–8; Revelation 12:3; 13:1,11; 17:3-6). The reference to a Jewish antichrist as the little horn is appropriate because the Jews are a comparatively small nation. Even so, he will subdue one nation after another until he attains global dominion.

The God of His Fathers

According to Daniel 11:37, the antichrist will not "regard the God of his fathers" (KJV). The term *fathers* is interpreted to be Jewish fathers, which means the antichrist must be a Jew. A.W. Pink comments, "This passage, it is evident, refers to and describes none other than the coming Antichrist...What are we to understand by this expression? Why, surely, that he is a Jew, an Israelite, and that his fathers after the flesh were Abraham, Isaac and Jacob."[9]

The Antichrist Reigns from Jerusalem

Revelation 11:8 tells us that the seat of the antichrist's dominion will be the "great city...where their Lord was crucified." This great city is Jerusalem. This means the antichrist must be a Jew, for only a Jew would reign from Jerusalem.[10]

Viewpoint 2: The Antichrist Will Not Be a Jew

Some of the above arguments may seem convincing, but other Christians have presented arguments against the idea that the antichrist will be a Jew. Here are the ones I find most convincing.

No Explicit Statement

Neither the Old Testament nor the New Testament provides a single explicit statement that the antichrist will be a Jew. This should at least give one pause in subscribing to this theory.

The Gentile Sea

Revelation 13:1 speaks of "a beast rising out of the sea." We are later told what the sea represents—"The waters that you saw...are peoples and multitudes and nations and languages" (17:15). The antichrist rises up out of this sea—the Gentile nations around the earth—so it seems clear that the antichrist will be a Gentile and not a Jew.

A Roman Antichrist

Scripture reveals that the antichrist will be of Roman descent (see Revelation 17:9-12). Daniel 9:26 warns us that "the people of the ruler who will come will destroy the city and the sanctuary." "The city and the sanctuary" are Jerusalem and its temple. The Romans, under Titus, destroyed the city of Jerusalem and its temple in AD 70. The antichrist will be of this same people, so he will be a Roman Gentile.

Jewish Persecution

Prophetic Scripture reveals that the antichrist will be a powerful and cruel persecutor of the Jews (Matthew 24:16-21). This is why "the woman [Israel] fled into the wilderness, where she has a place prepared by God, in which she is to be nourished for 1,260 days" (Revelation 12:6). The antichrist will trample on Jewish laws and traditions and desolate the Jewish temple (Daniel 9:27; 11:31; 12:11). Why would a Jew crush the Jews and their traditions? It hardly seems viable to say that the antichrist will himself be a Jew.

Antiochus Epiphanes

A number of biblical scholars believe that Antiochus Epiphanes was a *type* of the antichrist (see Daniel 11). A type is a historical institution, event, person, object, or ceremony that foreshadows something yet to be revealed. Antiochus Epiphanes foreshadows the antichrist. He was a Gentile who persecuted the Jews and desolated the Jewish temple. The antichrist will follow suit.

An Anti-Jewish Messiah?

Some prophetic interpreters infer that the antichrist will be an "anti" Jewish Messiah. As an antichrist, he will "oppose the very concept of a promised *Jewish* Messiah."[11] This is compatible with the idea that the antichrist will hate the Jews and will seek to persecute and even destroy them during the tribulation period.

Exaltation in Jerusalem

The antichrist will reign in Jerusalem, but that does not necessarily demand that he be a Jew. Scripture reveals that at the midpoint of the tribulation period, the antichrist will become the great persecutor of the Jews, and the Jews will flee out of Jerusalem as quickly as possible (see Matthew 24:16-21; Revelation 12:6). The antichrist will overturn Jewish traditions and sacrifices and desolate the Jewish temple by setting up an image of himself in it (Daniel 9:27; 11:31; 12:11). His strong stand against the Jews allows him to take over and forcibly gain a seat of power in Jerusalem.[12] The antichrist becomes elevated in Jerusalem not because he is Jewish but because of his cruel persecution of the Jews.

Jewish Acceptance

The argument that the antichrist must be Jewish because the Jews would not accept anyone other than a Jewish leader (John 5:43) is logically flawed. The Jewish people sign a covenant with the antichrist (Daniel 9:26), but that does not in any way mean they accept him as their Messiah. The Jews will accept the antichrist not as their Messiah but rather as a political leader and diplomat. They will accept him as a guarantor of peace in the Middle East, nothing more.[13] John 5:43 does not support the idea of a Jewish antichrist.

The Tribe of Dan

Dan's tribe became guilty of idolatry and for this reason was largely obliterated (Leviticus 24:11; Judges 18:1,30; 1 Kings 12:28-29). Bible scholar Robert H. Mounce explains that "when the tribe of Dan migrated to the north and settled at Laish, they set up for themselves the graven image (Judg. 18:30). Later Dan became one of the two great shrines in the northern kingdom (1 Kings 12:29)."[14] To engage in unrepentant idolatry is to be cut off from God's blessing.

However, the fact that Dan's tribe succumbed to idolatry does not constitute a proof that the antichrist would come from that tribe. This is an unjustified assumption, a leap in logic without real evidence. And the assertion that an early Church Father, such as Irenaeus, held to this view doesn't prove the view is correct. The fact that the Church Fathers often held different opinions on different matters proves that they were not infallible interpreters of the biblical text.

The Times of the Gentiles

Scripture reveals that the "times of the Gentiles" (Luke 21:24) refers to the time of Gentile domination of Jerusalem. This period began with the Babylonian captivity that started in 606 BC. The times of the Gentiles were well entrenched by AD 70, when Titus and his Roman warriors overran Jerusalem and destroyed the Jewish temple. These times will not end until the end of the great tribulation and the second coming of Jesus Christ.

This does not rule out the possibility of temporary Jewish control over most of Jerusalem, but such Jewish control will be temporary until the second coming of Jesus Christ. The times of the Gentiles have not yet ended.

Many prophecy scholars believe that the nature of the times of the Gentiles supports a Gentile antichrist. Prophecy expert Arnold Fruchtenbaum puts it this way:

It is agreed by all premillennialists that the period known as the Times of the Gentiles does not end until the second coming of Christ. It is further agreed that the Antichrist is the final ruler of the Times of the Gentiles…If this is so, how then can a Jew be the last ruler at a time when only Gentiles can have the preeminence? To say the Antichrist is to be a Jew would contradict the very nature of the Times of the Gentiles.[15]

The God of His Fathers

Appeal is sometimes made to Daniel 11:37 (KJV), which says the antichrist will not "regard the God of his fathers." This allegedly indicates a Jewish antichrist who will have no regard for the God of the Jewish fathers—Abraham, Isaac, and Jacob.

This argument evaporates when the King James Version mistranslation of this verse is revealed. Most English translations render it as does the English Standard Version: "He shall pay no attention to the gods of his fathers." This is referring not to the one true God of Abraham, Isaac, and Jacob, but to false pagan deities. The verse offers no support for the idea of a Jewish antichrist who has abandoned the Jewish God.

Conclusion

The debate is an interesting one, and I'm sure it will continue for a long time. Having considered all the evidence, my assessment is that the antichrist will not be a Jew but rather a Roman Gentile. This view makes the best sense of the biblical data.

Will the Antichrist Be Killed and Resurrected?

W ill the antichrist be killed and then supernaturally resurrected from the dead? Some prophecy scholars say yes. Others say no. The mortal wound of the antichrist is described for us in Revelation 13:1-3.

> I saw a beast rising out of the sea, with ten horns and seven heads, with ten diadems on its horns and blasphemous names on its heads. And the beast that I saw was like a leopard; its feet were like a bear's, and its mouth was like a lion's mouth. And to it the dragon gave his power and his throne and great authority. One of its heads seemed to have a mortal wound, but its mortal wound was healed, and the whole earth marveled as they followed the beast.

Debate 1: Who or What Gets Wounded and Then Healed?

Viewpoint 1: The Roman Empire

Some have concluded that what gets wounded and then healed is the Roman Empire. Those who hold to this view say the Roman Empire died in the fifth century but will be revived in the end times.

This issue certainly has room for debate, but I believe that Revelation 13:3 is referring not to the revived Roman Empire but to a person—the antichrist. I say this because Revelation 13:12 specifically refers to "the first beast, whose mortal wound was healed." Contextually, the first beast is the person of the antichrist. He is mentioned alongside "another beast," who is the false prophet. Then verse 14 refers to "the beast that was wounded by the sword and yet lived." This is most naturally interpreted as referring to a person.

Viewpoint 2: A Historical Character

Some interpreters say a historical character will come back to life and fulfill the role of the antichrist in the end times. Common suggestions include Nero, Judas Iscariot, Mussolini, Hitler, and Stalin.

This is a fascinating hypothesis, but I find it unconvincing. It seems based more on eisegesis than exegesis. Moreover, it is highly speculative. In my thinking, a novel view on a doctrine requires some good scriptural proof to back it up. In this case, the proof is lacking.

Viewpoint 3: A New and Unique Person

The Bible, as I understand it, points to a new and unique person who will emerge as the antichrist in the end times. He is ultimately unlike any other person who has ever lived. There have been many antichrists (plural) in the past, but none of them compare to the one antichrist who will be revealed during the future tribulation period (see 1 John 2:18-29). This unique and sinister individual will be energized by Satan (2 Thessalonians 2:9).

Debate 2: Will the Antichrist Be Killed and Resurrected?

Viewpoint 1: The Antichrist Will Be Killed and Resurrected

A widely held view is that the antichrist will in fact be killed and then resurrected back to life. For example, Tim LaHaye and Jerry Jenkins, in their book *Are We Living in the End Times?*, assert that the antichrist will not just be wounded but rather will actually die. "We believe that the Beast really is killed, for John twice says that he 'ascends out of the bottomless pit' (11:7; 17:8); we believe this means that the Beast is killed, descends to the pit, and ascends from there to the earth when he is resurrected."[1]

Viewpoint 2: The Antichrist Will Only Appear to be Killed and Resurrected

Other Christians have concluded that the antichrist appears to be killed though he really is not. Through satanic supernaturalism and trickery, he will appear to have been resurrected from the dead. This is my personal view. Let's consider some supportive evidence.

Satan Cannot Resurrect Humans

Satan is extremely powerful and influential in the world.

- He is called the "ruler of this world" (John 12:31), "the god of this world" (2 Corinthians 4:4), and the "prince of the power of the air" (Ephesians 2:2).
- He deceives the whole world (Revelation 12:9; 20:3).
- He has power in the governmental realm (Matthew 4:8-9), the physical realm (Luke 13:11,16; Acts 10:38), the angelic realm (Ephesians 6:11-12; Jude 9), and the ecclesiastical (church) realm (Revelation 2:9; 3:9).

So yes, Satan certainly has supernatural abilities, but he is nevertheless a creature with creaturely limitations. He is not powerful enough to actually resurrect people from the dead. If he had such power, surely he'd resurrect evil people from the dead to carry out his evil ends. But he doesn't do it because he doesn't have that power.

Satan may have some supernatural power, but he cannot be compared to God. Satan does not possess attributes that belong to God alone. Only God is omnipresent (everywhere-present), omnipotent (all-powerful), and omniscient (all-knowing).

Satan is a creature, and as a creature he is less than the Creator. For example, Satan can only be in one place at one time. His strength and knowledge, though great, are limited. God is infinite in power, whereas the devil is finite and limited.

Here's my point—only God can create life (Genesis 1:1,21; Deuteronomy 32:39); the devil cannot (see Exodus 8:19). So we can logically infer that only God can raise the dead (John 10:18; Revelation 1:18).

Certainly the devil has great power to deceive people (Revelation 12:9), to oppress those who yield to him, and even to possess them (Acts 16:16). He is a master magician and a superscientist. With his vast knowledge of God, humankind, and the universe, he is able to perform false signs and wonders (2 Thessalonians 2:9; see also Revelation 13:13-14).

For example, in the city of Samaria, Simon the sorcerer amazed people with his Satan-inspired magic (Acts 8:9-11). But the miracles accomplished through Philip were much greater (Acts 8:13). The devil's counterfeit miracles do not compete with God's major-league miracles.

The Exodus account probably provides the best illustration of Satan's counterfeit wonders. In Exodus 7:10, we read that God turned Moses's rod into a snake. Then Pharaoh "summoned the wise men and the sorcerers, and they, the magicians of Egypt, also did the same by their secret arts" (verse 11). The purpose of these acts, of course, was to convince Pharaoh that his magicians possessed as much power as Moses and Aaron, and Pharaoh did not need to yield to their request to let Israel go. It worked—at least for the first three encounters (Aaron's rod, the plague of blood, and the plague of frogs).

However, when Moses and Aaron brought forth gnats from the sand by the power of God, the magicians were not able to counterfeit this miracle. They could only exclaim, "This is the finger of God" (Exodus 8:19). Satan and his magicians cannot create life.

Biblical scholars differ as to whether Satan just does convincing tricks or genuine (albeit limited) miraculous works. Some scholars assert that Satan inspired Egypt's magicians to perform their feats by sleight of hand. Perhaps the magicians had enchanted the snakes so that they became stiff and appeared to be rods. When thrown down on the floor, they came out of their trance and began to move as snakes. Satan is the father of lies (John 8:44), so he very well may have been pulling some kind of trick instead of performing a true miracle.

Other scholars say these were supernatural and miraculous acts of Satan, who actually turned the magicians' rods into snakes. Dr. Henry Morris, for example, believes the devil and demons may be able to perform some Grade B miracles. They may be capable of "great juggling of the world's natural processes."[2]

Still others, such as theologian John Witmer, believe Satan sometimes does tricks and sometimes does supernatural (albeit limited) miraculous works.

> Some of these spectacles are mere trickery, spurious miracles. Others of them are truly supernatural events, but Satanic in origin and power, not divine. Remember that the devil showed the Lord Jesus "all the kingdoms of the world in a moment of time" (Luke 4:5) and is able to transform himself "into an angel of light" (2 Corinthians 11:14).[3]

Regardless of whether Satan has the ability to perform Grade B miracles or just stage impressive tricks, the scriptural evidence is undeniably clear that only God can perform Grade A miracles. Only God can fully control and supersede the natural laws He Himself created, though on one occasion He did grant Satan the power to bring a whirlwind on Job's family (Job 1:19). As the account of Job illustrates, all the power the devil has is granted him by God and is carefully limited and monitored (see Job 1:10-12). In other words, Satan is on a leash. His finite power is under the control of God's infinite power.

In view of this scriptural evidence, we can reasonably conclude that Satan will either perform a limited Grade B miracle and heal the wounded antichrist (that is, wounded but not really dead) or he will engage in some kind of masterful deception—or perhaps a combination of both. In any event, the world will be amazed.

Satan's Vast Experience

Satan certainly has vast experience in observing and dealing with human beings. His experience is far greater than that of any human being. By his very longevity, Satan has acquired a breadth of experience that easily eclipses the limited knowledge of man. He has observed people firsthand in every conceivable situation, so he can predict with accuracy how they will respond to various circumstances.[4] So even though Satan is not omniscient like God is, his wide experience gives him knowledge that is far superior to anything any man could have.

Here then is an important consideration. Because Satan has vast experience, he has learned many wiles and tricks regarding how to deceive human beings. He is the father of lies (John 8:44). Therefore, much of what he does is rooted in lies and trickery. This is one reason Christians are urged to beware (2 Corinthians 2:11; 1 Peter 5:8).

Perhaps Satan will pull off a masterful trick, making it appear that the antichrist has been resurrected from the dead. Perhaps he will heal a nonfatal wound or simply engage in supernatural trickery. In any event, if this scenario is correct, Satan's vast experience in tricking and influencing human beings will be his major asset in pulling this off.

If talented Las Vegas magicians can deceive large crowds by sleight of hand, how much more so will Satan—the master trickster, who has thousands of years of experience—be able to deceive multitudes about the antichrist's apparent resurrection. These will be times of deception (1 Timothy 4:1; 2 Timothy 4:3-4).

Satan Is the Ape of God

Augustine once called the devil *Simius Dei*—"the ape of God." Satan is the great counterfeiter.[5] He mimics God in many ways. A primary tactic Satan uses to attack God and His program in general is to offer a counterfeit kingdom and program.[6] This is hinted at in 2 Corinthians 11:14, which refers to Satan masquerading as an angel of light.

How does Satan act as the ape of God? Here are some ways.

- Satan has his own church—the "synagogue of Satan" (Revelation 2:9).

- He has his own false apostles and ministers (2 Corinthians 11:13-15).

- Satan has formulated his own system of theology—called "doctrines of demons" (1 Timothy 4:1; Revelation 2:24).

- Satan's ministers proclaim a counterfeit gospel, which Paul referred to as "a gospel contrary to the one we preached to you" (Galatians 1:7-8).

- Satan has his own throne and his own worshippers (Revelation 13:2,4).

- Satan inspires false christs and self-constituted messiahs (Matthew 24:4-5).

- Satan employs false teachers who promote destructive heresies (2 Peter 2:1).

- Satan sends out false prophets (Matthew 24:11).

One theologian has concluded that "Satan's plan and purposes have been, are, and always will be to seek to establish a rival rule to God's kingdom. He is promoting a system of which he is the head and which stands in opposition to God and His rule in the universe."[7]

Scripture reveals that Satan performs counterfeit signs and wonders. Indeed, 2 Thessalonians 2:9 tells us, "The coming of the lawless one is by the activity of Satan with all power and false signs and wonders."

As related to the antichrist, an apparent resurrection would be in perfect keeping with Satan's character as the ape of God. This contrived resurrection will mimic the genuine resurrection of Jesus Christ (the slain Lamb—Revelation 5:6). Many will marvel at it.

Satan Blinds Minds

Second Corinthians 4:4 reveals that "the god of this world [Satan] has blinded the minds of the unbelievers, to keep them from seeing the light of the gospel of the glory of Christ, who is the image of God." This passage indicates that Satan inhibits the unbeliever's ability to think or reason properly in regard to spiritual matters.[8] Might we infer from this that if Satan pulls off some kind of counterfeit resurrection, he will be able to blind people's minds, and they will accept this as an indication of the antichrist's power and deity and subsequently worship him? There is good reason to think so.

Emerging out of the Abyss

How then can we explain the antichrist emerging out of the abyss? There is a viable explanation that is compatible with the idea that he will be severely wounded but not killed. Bible scholar Walter Price explains it this way.

> The apostle Paul…was stoned in Lystra, and the citizens "dragged him out of the city, supposing that he was dead" (Acts 14:19). While in an unconscious state, Paul "was caught up into Paradise, and heard unspeakable words, which it is not lawful for a man to utter" (2 Cor. 12:4). Paul had received, as it were, what seemed like a death stroke. At the same time he was thought to be dead, his spirit was caught up into the third heaven and there received a profound revelation from God. This same thing, in reverse, will happen to the Antichrist. The Antichrist, sometime during his career as Caesar, will receive a death stroke. He will be no more dead than was the apostle Paul. But just as the citizens of Lystra thought Paul was dead, so the Antichrist will be thought dead.[9]

Price raises the possibility that just as Paul's spirit departed from his body and was taken up to God's domain, where he received further revelations, so the antichrist's spirit may depart from his body (appearing to be dead) and be taken into the abyss by Satan, where Satan will offer the world's kingdoms to him.

> Just as Satan took Jesus up into a high mountain and showed him all the kingdoms of the world, and offered them to him, if he would fall down and worship him; so Satan will take the Antichrist into the depths of the Abyss and show him all the kingdoms of the world…Jesus refused to bow down to Satan. The Antichrist will not refuse.[10]

Price suggests that the antichrist's spirit will then return from the abyss (Revelation 11:7), reenter what appears to be a dead body, thereby giving the appearance of a resurrection from the dead, and continue on his satanically inspired mission. Prophecy expert Mark Hitchcock suggests that while in the abyss, the "Antichrist probably receives his orders and strategy from Satan, literally selling his soul to the devil, and then comes back to earth with hellish ferocity to establish his world domination over a completely awestruck earth."[11]

Conclusion

My assessment is that only God can do Grade A miracles, such as resurrecting people from the dead. However, I also believe that Satan has supernatural abilities and can perform what might be called Grade B miracles. He is a superscientist and a master trickster, and he has thousands of years of experience in duping human beings. All of this will likely come into play in the future tribulation period when Satan pulls off one of the greatest hoaxes of all time—making it appear that the antichrist has actually risen from the dead just as Jesus did.

22

What Is the Mark of the Beast?

The nature of the mark of the beast is among the most-debated issues in prophetic circles. There are several components of the debate: What is the significance of the mark? What is the meaning of the number 666? Is the mark high technology? Let's consider the various answers Christians have offered for these questions.

The Prophetic Backdrop

According to Revelation 13, the diabolical duo of the antichrist and the false prophet will subjugate the entire world so that no one can buy or sell who does not receive the mark of the beast. This will apparently take place at the midpoint of the tribulation period.

> [The false prophet] causes all, both small and great, both rich and poor, both free and slave, to be marked on the right hand or the forehead, so that no one can buy or sell unless he has the mark, that is, the name of the beast or the number of its name. This calls for wisdom: let the one who has understanding calculate the number of the beast, for it is the number of a man, and his number is 666 (verses 16-18).

It is interesting to observe that followers of both the antichrist and Jesus Christ will have identifying marks during the tribulation period. Revelation 14:1 tells us, "Then I looked, and behold, on Mount Zion stood the Lamb, and with him 144,000 who had his [the Lamb, Jesus Christ's] name and his Father's name written on their foreheads."

Some Bible expositors suggest that the antichrist's mark may be a parody of God's sealing of the 144,000 witnesses of Revelation 7 and 14. Thomas Ice and Timothy Demy offer this suggestion:

> God's seal of His witnesses most likely is invisible and for the purpose of protection from the antichrist. On the other hand, antichrist offers protection from the wrath of God—a promise he cannot deliver—and his mark is visible and external...For the only time in history, an outward indication will identify those who reject Christ and His gospel of forgiveness of sins.[1]

Receiving the mark of the beast has fatal consequences.

> If anyone worships the beast and its image and receives a mark on his forehead or on his hand, he also will drink the wine of God's wrath, poured full strength into the cup of his anger, and he will be tormented with fire and sulfur in the presence of the holy angels and in the presence of the Lamb (Revelation 14:9-10).

Likewise, we read in Revelation 16:2, "The first angel went and poured out his bowl on the earth, and harmful and painful sores came upon the people who bore the mark of the beast and worshiped its image."

This means that any who express loyalty to the antichrist and his cause will suffer the wrath of our holy and just God. There is no way to undo receiving the mark of the beast. How awful it will be for these to experience the full force of God's divine anger and unmitigated vengeance (see Psalm 75:8; Isaiah 51:17; Jeremiah 25:15-16). Believers in the Lord Jesus Christ, by contrast, refuse the mark of the beast, choosing death instead.

> I saw the souls of those who had been beheaded for the testimony of Jesus and for the word of God, and those

who had not worshiped the beast or its image and had not received its mark on their foreheads or their hands. They came to life and reigned with Christ for a thousand years (Revelation 20:4).

Debate 1: What Is the Significance of the Mark of the Beast?

Many suggestions have been made through the centuries as to the significance of the mark of the beast. As we will see below, most are quite similar.

Viewpoint 1: A Mark of Ownership and Submission

Humans will somehow be branded during the future seven-year tribulation period, just as animals are branded today. This is similar to the way slaves were once branded by their slaveholders. The branding indicates one's agreement to submit to the antichrist, even agreeing to worship him. Without this mark, one cannot buy or sell anything, including food.

Viewpoint 2: A Mark of Preservation

Ezekiel 9:4 provides us with an ancient historical precedent for marking human beings. "The LORD said to him, 'Pass through the city, through Jerusalem, and put a mark on the foreheads of the men who sigh and groan over all the abominations that are committed in it.'" In this context, the mark on the forehead was one of preservation, just as blood on the doorposts spared the Israelites from death during the tenth Egyptian plague (see Exodus 12:21-29). The antichrist apparently perverts this idea, giving a mark of preservation to those who submit to him. People are preserved only in the sense that they are able to buy and sell.

Viewpoint 3: A Mark of Religious Loyalty

Marks on the body were sometimes used in connection with pagans and false deities in ancient times. Bible scholar Robert Thomas offers this insight:

The mark must be some sort of branding similar to that given soldiers, slaves, and temple devotees in John's day. In Asia Minor, devotees of pagan religions delighted in the display of such a tattoo as an emblem of ownership by a certain god. In Egypt, Ptolemy Philopator I branded Jews, who submitted to registration, with an ivy leaf in recognition of their Dionysian worship (cf. 3 Macc. 2:29). This meaning resembles the longtime practice of carrying signs to advertise religious loyalties (cf. Isa. 44:5) and follows the habit of branding slaves with the name or special mark of their owners (cf. Gal. 6:17). *Charagma* ("mark") was a [Greek] term for the images or names of emperors on Roman coins, so it fittingly could apply to the beast's emblem put on people.[2]

John MacArthur offers a similar comment.

In the Roman Empire, this was a normal identifying symbol, or brand, that slaves and soldiers bore on their bodies. Some of the ancient mystical cults delighted in such tattoos, which identified members with a form of worship. Antichrist will have a similar requirement, one that will need to be visible on the hand or forehead.[3]

Viewpoint 4: A Sign of Orthodoxy

The mark of the beast may also be a symbol indicating that one is religiously orthodox—that is, orthodox as defined by the antichrist and the false prophet.

The mark will allow the Antichrist's followers to buy and sell because it identifies them as religiously orthodox—submissive followers of the Beast and worshipers of his image. Those without the mark are forbidden to buy because they are identified as traitors.[4]

Though receiving the mark is essentially a spiritual decision, this spiritual decision will have life-and-death consequences.

Even though the mark of the beast is described in slightly different terms in each of these viewpoints, these may be viewed as variations of a theme. They are quite similar. In a capsule, the mark of the beast may indicate ownership and submission, religious commitment, and one's religiously orthodoxy.

Debate 2: The Meaning of 666

Not surprisingly, there has also been endless debate as to the significance of the number 666 (Revelation 13:18). (Googling the numeral 666 yields more than 100 million results.) Here are just a few of the more interesting suggestions as to the meaning of the number.

Viewpoint 1: The Mark of a Nero-Like Man

Some have suggested that perhaps the number 666 refers to a specific man—such as the Roman emperor Nero. If Nero's name is translated into the Hebrew language, the numerical value of its letters is 666. Or perhaps the antichrist will be a different man who will be like the evil and ruthless Nero of old.

Viewpoint 2: The Mark of an Imperfect Human

Some have suggested that inasmuch as 7 is the number of perfection and 6 is the number of man, perhaps 666 points to an imperfect human being. The threefold number may emphasize the antichrist's imperfection as a man.

Viewpoint 3: The Mark of an Unholy Trinity

If 7 is the number of perfection, then the number 777 may reflect the perfect Trinity. If this is correct, perhaps 666 points to an unholy trinity, composed of the antichrist, the false prophet, and Satan. Receiving a mark on the hand or head could indicate submission to this unholy Trinity. *The Bible Knowledge Commentary* suggests that "the number six is one less than the perfect number seven, and the threefold repetition of the six would indicate that for all their pretentions to deity, Satan and the two beasts were just creatures and not the Creator."[5]

Viewpoint 4: The Mark of Evil

Some have suggested that the number 666 represents supernatural evil. If this is correct, the number would point to the intrinsic evil of the antichrist (as energized by Satan) and his program during the tribulation period.

Viewpoint 5: A Mystery

Bible expositor Thomas Constable suggests that perhaps we will not know the meaning of 666 until the antichrist actually emerges in the world.

> This disagreement and confusion [over the number 666] may be due in part to the fact that the meaning of this number may not be evident until the Antichrist appears... I think that neither the identity of the Antichrist nor the number of his name will be evident until he appears and fulfills prophecy. Then wise believers will be able to calculate his number as well as identify his person. Until then both aspects of Antichrist's identity will remain a mystery.[6]

If Constable is correct, then until the antichrist appears, we can only speculate.

One Thing Is Certain

Despite the differences interpreters have on this issue, we can all agree that in some way that is presently unknown to us, the number 666 will be a crucial part of the antichrist's identification. As we have seen, receiving the mark of the beast is apparently an unpardonable sin (Revelation 14:9-10). The decision to receive the mark is irreversible. Once made, there is no turning back.

To receive the mark is to approve of the antichrist as a leader and of his purpose. No one takes this mark accidentally. One must choose to do so with all the facts on the table. It will be a deliberate choice with eternal consequences. Those who choose to receive the mark will do so with the full knowledge of what they have done.

This means that a radical polarization will emerge during the tribulation period. There will be no possible middle ground. One will choose either for or against the antichrist, for or against God. People in our present day think they can avoid God and His demands on their lives by feigning neutrality, but no such neutrality will be possible during the tribulation.

Debate 3: Is the Mark High Technology?

Viewpoint 1: The Mark Is High Technology

Many Christians in recent decades have said that the mark of the beast will likely be a computer chip that will be implanted beneath the skin, perhaps in the fatty tissue of the hand. This microchip will contain not only basic identification information but also bank account numbers and maybe even GPS tracking technology. A mark of this kind would facilitate the antichrist's economic control of the world.

Viewpoint 2: The Mark Is Not High Technology

Other Christians believe that even though modern technology will enable the antichrist and false prophet to bring about a cashless society and then control all commerce on earth, we must differentiate between this technology and the mark of the beast. The technology itself is not the mark.

According to Revelation 13:16, people will be "marked on the right hand or the forehead." This mark will be *on* people, not *in* them (like some kind of microchip). It will be on the right hand or forehead and will be visible to the eye (perhaps like a barcode tattoo), not hidden beneath the skin.

Scripture reveals that the mark itself will identify allegiance to the antichrist, but that is distinct from the technology that enables him to enforce his economic system. My former prophecy mentor, John F. Walvoord, commented on how technology will enable economic control based on whether or not people have received the mark.

> There is no doubt that with today's technology, a world
> ruler, who is in total control, would have the ability to

keep a continually updated census of all living persons and know day-by-day precisely which people had pledged their allegiance to him and received the mark and which had not.[7]

It is highly likely that "chip implants, scan technology, and biometrics will be used as tools to enforce his policy that one cannot buy or sell without the mark."[8]

It has been well said that prophetic events cast their shadows before them. David Jeremiah draws this conclusion:

> We are on the cutting edge of having all the technology that the Antichrist and False Prophet would need to wire this world together for their evil purposes. Right now it is well within the range of possibility for a centralized power to gain worldwide control of all banking and purchasing...As we see things that are prophesied for the tribulation period beginning to take shape right now, we are made aware of the fact that surely the Lord's return is not far off.[9]

Conclusion

My assessment is that the mark of the beast will indicate ownership and submission, religious commitment, and religious orthodoxy in submitting to the antichrist, who positions himself as God. The mark will be visibly apparent on the skin. The enforcement of the antichrist's economic policy will be made possible by modern technology, perhaps even involving implanted microchips.

Which View of the Millennium Is Correct?

23

The Case for Amillennialism

The word *millennium* comes from the Latin *mille*, which means "thousand." The term relates to the statement in Revelation 20:4 that the saints "came to life and reigned with Christ for a thousand years." When prophecy enthusiasts speak of the millennial kingdom, they are primarily referring to this verse.

One of the most consistently debated issues in eschatology relates to the nature of the millennial kingdom. One's hermeneutical approach in interpreting prophecy is closely connected to one's view of the millennial kingdom. Those who take an allegorical approach generally embrace either amillennialism or postmillennialism. Those who take a literal approach embrace premillennialism.

Of course, all three views are within the bounds of orthodoxy. There are good Christians on all sides of the debate. And yet, as we will see in this and the next two chapters, there are far-reaching consequences associated with each of the views.

I will begin our discussion on the millennium by examining the primary tenets of amillennialism.

Primary Tenets of Amillennialism

Amillennialism—espoused by such well-known theologians as Oswald T. Allis, William Hendriksen, and Anthony A. Hoekema—

takes a spiritualized or symbolic approach in interpreting biblical prophecy.[1] Old Testament predictions made to Israel are viewed as being fulfilled in the New Testament church. This is "replacement theology"—that is, the church replaces Israel as the recipient of God's promises.

The term *amillennial* literally means "no millennium." Instead of believing in a literal rule of Christ on earth, amillennialists generally interpret prophetic verses related to the reign of Christ metaphorically and say they refer to Christ's present spiritual rule from heaven. Whatever kingdom there is, is now—it is heaven's rule over the church.[2]

In this view, good and evil will continue to grow until Christ comes again at the close of the church age. But conditions will worsen on earth before the second coming. The return of the Lord is then immediately followed by a general resurrection and general judgment and the commencement of the eternal state. This view teaches that when Christ comes, eternity will begin with no prior literal 1000-year kingdom on earth. Amillennialist J.G. Vos confirms this understanding of amillennialism.

> Amillennialism is that view of the last things which holds the Bible does not predict a "millennium" or a period of worldwide peace and righteousness on this earth before the end of the world. Amillennialism teaches that there will be a parallel and contemporaneous development of good and evil—God's kingdom and Satan's kingdom—in this world, which will continue until the Second Coming of Christ. At the Second Coming of Christ, the resurrection and judgment will take place, followed by the eternal order of things—the absolute, perfect kingdom of God, in which there will be no sin, suffering or death.[3]

Primary Arguments of Amillennialism

These are among the primary arguments offered in support of amillennialism.

1. Many amillennialists believe the Abrahamic and Davidic covenants (involving both throne promises and land promises to Israel) were conditional. There will be no future fulfillment because the conditions were not met. Israel was disobedient and thus sinned away her right to the promises.

2. Other amillennialists claim that the land promises of the covenants were fulfilled in the time of Joshua (Joshua 21:43-45), David (2 Samuel 8:3), or Solomon (1 Kings 4:21).[4]

3. Still other amillennialists claim that the promises to Israel are fulfilled in the church in a nonliteral way. Many believe Christ is symbolically now seated on the throne of David in heaven and is reigning from there. Therefore we should not expect a 1000-year rule on David's throne on earth, as premillennialists hold.

4. Apocalyptic literature ought to be interpreted symbolically, amillennialists say. We should not take the text literally when it says Christ will rule on earth for 1000 years.

5. Israel and the church are not two distinct entities but rather one people of God united by the covenant of grace. (This is a central tenet of covenant theology.)

6. The New Testament demonstrates that Old Testament prophecies are fulfilled in the church (for example, Jeremiah 31:31; Hebrews 8:8-13), so the same must be true of the promises in the biblical covenants.

7. Amillennialism is the view most compatible with the idea that the Old Testament is fulfilled in the New Testament.

8. Amillennialism was held by the later Augustine (AD 354–430) as well as by Reformers Martin Luther (1483–1546) and John Calvin (1509–1564). Most of the Puritans were amillennial, as are most Roman Catholics. Famous proponents of the view in more recent history include J.I. Packer (born 1926) and Louis Berkhof (1873–1957).

9. Amillennialists reject dispensationalism as a recent human invention, holding instead to covenant theology, which interprets the entire Bible in terms of two covenants—the covenant of works and the covenant of grace. The covenant of works was allegedly an agreement between God and Adam in which God promised life for obedience and death for disobedience. (Adam failed.) The covenant of grace is an agreement between the offended God and the offending but elect sinner in which God promises salvation through Christ. A covenant of redemption (a third covenant) is also typically included in the system. This covenant was enacted in eternity past between the Father, Son, and Holy Spirit, defining each person's role in the redemptive plan.

The Problem with Amillennialism

Premillennialists have noted a number of problems with amillennialism. Here are the most substantial among them.

Unconditional Covenants

Premillennialists believe the Old Testament covenants were unconditional. Consider the Abrahamic covenant. God made this covenant with Abraham (Genesis 12:1-3; 15:18- 21) and later reaffirmed it with Isaac (17:21) and Jacob (35:10-12). In this covenant, God promised to make Abraham's descendants His own special people. More specifically, God made these promises to Abraham:

> I will make you a great nation.
> I will bless you.
> I will make your name great.
> You will be a blessing.
> I will bless those who bless you.
> I will curse those who curse you.
> All peoples on earth will be blessed through you.
> I will give you the land of Canaan.

These covenant promises were unconditional. As a backdrop, there were two kinds of covenants in biblical days—conditional and unconditional. A conditional covenant has an *if* attached. This type of covenant demanded that the people meet certain obligations or conditions before God was obligated to fulfill that which He promised. If God's people failed in meeting the conditions, God was not obligated in any way to fulfill the promise.

As opposed to this, an unconditional covenant depended on no such conditions for its fulfillment. There were no *ifs* attached. That which was promised by God was sovereignly given apart from any merit (or lack thereof) on the part of the recipient. Some scholars refer to this type of covenant as a unilateral covenant, one-sided covenant, or divine-commitment covenant.

The important point to observe here is that the covenant God made with Abraham was unconditional. It was characterized by God's "I will," indicating that God was determined to do just as He promised.

How do we know the covenant was unconditional? According to ancient custom, the two parties of a conditional covenant would divide an animal into two equal parts and then walk between the two parts, indicating that each was responsible to fulfill the obligations of the covenant (see Jeremiah 34:18-19). In the case of the Abrahamic covenant, however, God alone passed between the parts after Abraham had been put into a deep sleep (Genesis 15:12,17). This indicates that God made unconditional promises to Abraham in this covenant. Abraham had no obligations to fulfill in order to receive the covenant promises.

God's covenant with David was also an unconditional covenant. Its fulfillment did not depend on David in any way. David realized this when he received the promise from God and responded with an attitude of humility and a recognition of God's sovereignty over the affairs of men.

In this covenant, God promised David that one of his descendants would rule forever (2 Samuel 7:12-13; 22:51). The three key words of this covenant are *kingdom*, *house*, and *throne*. Such words point to the political future of Israel. The word *house* here carries the idea of a royal dynasty.

This covenant finds its ultimate fulfillment in Jesus Christ, who was born from the line of David (Matthew 1:1) and will one day rule on the throne of David in Jerusalem during the future millennial kingdom (Ezekiel 36:1-12; Micah 4:1-5; Zephaniah 3:14-20; Zechariah 14:1-21). The fact that this is an unconditional covenant guarantees its fulfillment.

We find the Davidic covenant still in full force during the time of Jesus in the New Testament. Prior to Jesus's birth, the angel Gabriel appeared to Mary and informed her, "The Lord God will give to him the throne of his father David, and he will reign over the house of Jacob forever, and of his kingdom there will be no end" (Luke 1:32-33). Notice the three significant words in this passage—*throne*, *house*, and *kingdom*. Each of these words is found in the covenant God made with David in which God promised that one from David's line would rule forever (2 Samuel 7:16). Gabriel's words must have immediately brought these Old Testament promises to mind for Mary, a devout young Jew. Indeed, Gabriel's words constituted a clear announcement that the Davidic covenant would be fulfilled by the child within her womb.

One is wise not to spiritualize this covenant as somehow being fulfilled in the church. After all, the precedent has already been set in regard to how we should interpret prophecy. To find out how God will fulfill prophecies in the future, we merely need to look at how He fulfilled them in the past. Just as the prophecies pertaining to the first coming of Christ were fulfilled literally—He was born of a virgin (Isaiah 7:14), born in Bethlehem (Micah 5:2), pierced for our sins (Zechariah 12:10), and so on—so Revelation 20:4, which says Christ will reign for 1000 years on earth, will be fulfilled literally.

Israel and the Church

We have seen that amillennialists teach that Israel and the church are not two distinct entities but rather one people of God united by the covenant of grace. In this book, however, I have argued in chapters 3 and 4 that there is a clear distinction between the church and Israel in prophecy. I will not repeat all that material here but will only briefly note these summary points.

1. Both Israel and the church are in fact part of the people of God, both are part of God's spiritual kingdom, and both participate in the spiritual blessings of both the Abrahamic and new covenants.

2. However, the church came into being on the day of Pentecost (Acts 1:5; 1 Corinthians 12:13).

3. Israel is an earthly political entity (Exodus 19:5-6), but the universal church is the invisible spiritual body of Christ (Ephesians 1:3).

4. Israel was composed of Jews, but the church is composed of both redeemed Jews and redeemed Gentiles (see Ephesians 2:15).

5. One becomes a Jew by physical birth, whereas one becomes a member of the church by a spiritual birth (John 3:3).

6. Israel and the church are viewed as distinct throughout the book of Acts. The word *Israel* is used 20 times, and the word *church* is used 19 times.

7. The apostle Paul clearly distinguishes between the church and Israel in 1 Corinthians 10:32.

8. The apostle Paul was quite clear that national Israel will be restored before Christ returns (Romans 11:1-2,29).

For these and other reasons, premillennialists view the church and Israel as distinct entities. This means, then, that the promises God made to Israel in Old Testament times, including the throne promises of the Davidic covenant and the land promises of the Abrahamic covenant, will be literally fulfilled to Israel.

Reaffirmations of the Land Covenant

We saw that some amillennialists claim that the land promises of the covenants were fulfilled either in the time of Joshua or David or Solomon. The obvious problem with this claim is that neither Joshua, David, or Solomon were in full possession of all the land that was promised by God, nor did the land remain forever in Israel's possession, as God clearly promised. Therefore, the amillennial position is shortsighted. God continued to reaffirm the land promises to Israel throughout the rest of the Old Testament—long after the times of Joshua, David, or Solomon (see Isaiah 60:21; Jeremiah 24:6; 30:18; 32:37-40; 33:6-9; Ezekiel 28:25-26; 34:11-12; 36:24-26; 39:28; Hosea 3:4-5; Amos 9:14-15; Micah 2:12; 4:6-7; Zephaniah 3:20; Zechariah 8:7-8). Every Old Testament prophet except Jonah speaks of a permanent return to the land of Israel by the Jews. Amillennialists must interpret these passages symbolically.

Symbolical Interpretation

Amillennialists often try to justify their interpretations by appealing to a hermeneutic of symbolism, for apocalyptic literature is highly symbolic. Premillennialists respond that even though symbols are often used in apocalyptic literature, the symbols are often defined in many contexts. In the book of Revelation, for example, John said the seven stars in Christ's right hand were the seven angels [messengers] to the seven churches, and the seven lampstands were the seven churches (1:20); the bowls full of incense were the prayers of the saints (5:8); and the many waters were peoples, multitudes, nations, and languages (17:15). We find that each symbol represents something literal. Textual clues often point us to the literal truth found in a symbol—either in the immediate context or in the broader context of the whole of Scripture. The premillennialist is not willing to embrace the amillennialist's symbolic approach to prophecy.

Moreover, the Bible contains many nonsymbolic prophecies. We should read these prophecies according to the normal, everyday, common understanding of the terms. Review my comments in chapter 1 regarding the wisdom of using a literal approach in interpreting Bible prophecy. A consistent literal approach leads effortlessly to premillennialism.

Conclusion

Certainly, much more could be said to describe and critique amillennialism. I believe that the fatal flaw of amillennialism is its spiritualizing or allegorizing of biblical prophecy. I do not see any warrant for this approach. I believe the weight of Scripture is on the side of premillennialism.

The Case for Postmillennialism

Postmillennialism, like amillennialism, takes a spiritualized or allegorical approach in interpreting biblical prophecy. It holds that through the church's progressive influence, the world will become Christianized before Christ returns. The kingdom of God is allegedly now being extended in the world through the preaching of the gospel. Because the gospel of Jesus Christ is the power of God (Romans 1:16), postmillennialists believe the world must be converted.

In this view, the millennium will be an extended period—perhaps much longer than 1000 years—of peace and prosperity that precedes Christ's physical return. Some postmillennialists believe the millennium will begin gradually. Others see a more abrupt beginning to the spread of righteousness throughout the earth.

Postmillennialist Loraine Boettner provides this brief description of postmillennialism.

> [Postmillennialism is] that view of last things which holds that the kingdom of God is now being extended in the world through the preaching of the Gospel and the saving work of the Holy Spirit in the hearts of individuals, that the world is eventually to be Christianized, and that the return of Christ is to occur at the close of a long period of righteousness and peace commonly called the "Millennium"...

> The second coming of Christ will be followed immediately
> by the general resurrection, the general judgment, and the
> introduction of heaven and hell in their fullness.[1]

In postmillennial thinking, the Christianizing of the world will improve every dimension of life—economic, social, cultural, and political. This view sees the church as triumphing over all that stands against it. Evil will one day be reduced to negligible proportions.

Postmillennialists believe that certain Bible verses support the idea that the world will be Christianized. For example, they point to Christ's parable of the leaven, which indicates that the kingdom will become universal (Matthew 13:33). Moreover, Zechariah 9:10 indicates that Christ's kingdom will spread from sea to sea. Numbers 14:21 indicates that the whole earth will be filled with the Lord's glory. Christ died for the sins of the whole world (1 John 2:2), so surely most of the world will eventually be saved.

Revelation 19:11-21 allegedly portrays Christ returning at the second coming to a world where the Great Commission has been fulfilled. This passage is believed to metaphorically picture the entire time period between the first and second comings of Jesus Christ, reflecting Christ's advancing victory over the world.

In support of their view, postmillennialists point out that many things are getting better in our day. Cultural evils like slavery have lessened. Rich nations give foreign aid to impoverished countries. Christians give charitably to their local churches. The Bible is now available to most countries of the world. Christian media has never been larger. Bible colleges and seminaries are training new preachers to evangelize the world. And transportation advances make it easier to reach the lost around the world.[2]

In this view, after the world is completely Christianized, the millennium will emerge, and it could last far longer than 1000 years. In this view, however, Christ will not be on the earth during the millennium. We are told that life in the millennium will be similar to the present age except that sin will be greatly reduced and Christian principles will reign supreme. Premillennial theologian Charles C. Ryrie notes that in postmillennialism "the kingdom will be on earth, but it will be a 'church kingdom' not a Jewish kingdom, and the King, Christ, will be absent from the earth, not present on it. He will rule in the hearts of the people and return to the earth only after the millennium is complete."[3] This view is called postmillennialism precisely because Christ will come after the millennium.

Some of the more notable proponents of this view include A.A. Hodge (1823–1886), Benjamin B. Warfield (1851–1921), Augustus H. Strong (1836–1921), Loraine Boettner (1932–2000), and R.J. Rushdoony (1916–2001).[4]

Arguments for Postmillennialism

Postmillennialists offer the following arguments in favor of their view.

1. A universal proclamation of the gospel is promised in Scripture (Matthew 28:18-20). This implies a Christianizing of the world as time progresses.

2. People from all nations will come to salvation (Revelation 7:9-10). This necessitates a worldwide Christianization.

3. Christ's throne is in heaven, and He will rule from this throne, not a throne on earth (see Psalm 9:4,7; 11:4; 45:6; 47:8, and so on). As He rules from heaven, the world continues to become better.

4. Jesus's parable of the mustard seed indicates there will be a continual advance of Christianity in the world (Matthew 13:31-32). A mustard seed is small, but what grows from this seed is incredibly large.

5. World conditions are supposedly improving morally, socially, and spiritually—all due to the church's influence. This will continue and eventually give way to the emergence of the millennium, after which Christ will come again.

The Problem with Postmillennialism

The World Is Not Getting Better

Premillennialists do not believe the world is improving morally, socially, and spiritually. Certainly there are some notable exceptions. But overall, the world seems to be plummeting ever deeper into sin. Postmillennialism is not nearly as popular as it once was because of the growth of evil in the world. But when postmillennialism was popular in the nineteenth century, hope was high that the world could become better. Theologian Paul Enns reflects on this.

> The occasion for this view is noteworthy, inasmuch as it followed a period of optimism and progress in science, culture, and the standard of living in general. It was also prior to World Wars I and II...Postmillennialism declined considerably following the world wars because the conflagrations militated against the optimism of the doctrine.[5]

Premillennialists believe the Bible teaches that apostasy—not Christianizing—will be predominant in the end times. The word *apostasy* comes from the Greek word *apostasia*, which means "falling away." The word refers to a falling away from the truth. It depicts a determined, willful defection from the faith, an abandonment of the faith.

Scripture tells us that apostasy will increase in the end times. For example, 1 Timothy 4:1-2 warns, "The Spirit expressly says that in later times some will depart from the faith by devoting themselves to deceitful spirits and teachings of demons, through the insincerity of liars whose consciences are seared."

Moreover, 2 Timothy 4:3-4 warns, "The time is coming when people will not endure sound teaching, but having itching ears they will accumulate for themselves teachers to suit their own passions, and will turn away from listening to the truth and wander off into myths." Who can doubt that these words describe the very days in which we live? As one channel surfs on television in the evening, one will come across examples of numerous such false teachers espousing doctrines that appeal to people's passions, such as the health and wealth gospel.

Second Timothy 3:1-5 provides some specifics regarding end-times apostasy.

> Understand this, that in the last days there will come times of difficulty. For people will be lovers of self, lovers of money, proud, arrogant, abusive, disobedient to their parents, ungrateful, unholy, heartless, unappeasable, slanderous, without self-control, brutal, not loving good, treacherous, reckless, swollen with conceit, lovers of pleasure rather than lovers of God, having the appearance of godliness, but denying its power.

Notice that in the last days there will be lovers of self (humanism), lovers of money (materialism), and lovers of pleasure (hedonism). Humanism, materialism, and hedonism are three of the most prominent philosophies in our world today, and they often go together in a complementary fashion. The predominance of such philosophies is incompatible with the claim that the world is getting better and better. Jesus Himself gave this warning:

> Because lawlessness is increased, most people's love will grow cold...For the coming of the Son of Man will be just like the days of Noah. For as in those days before the flood they were eating and drinking, marrying and giving in marriage, until the day that Noah entered the ark, and they did not understand until the flood came and took them all away; so will the coming of the Son of Man be (Matthew 24:12,37-39 NASB).

This passage specifically refers to the future tribulation period, but I cannot help but notice that we see the attitude Jesus described even in our own day. People are merrily going about their way, seemingly with no concern for the things of God, or perhaps they have embraced a false god.

America is undoubtedly engulfed in a moral crisis. The moral fiber of this country is eroding before our very eyes, and if the trend continues, it is only a matter of time before the country capitulates. We see widespread acceptance of homosexuality. Abortion—even the barbaric practice of partial-birth abortion—continues to be widely practiced, with some 50 million unborn babies having been murdered since the enactment of *Roe v. Wade* in 1973. Pornography is pervasive and freely available on the Internet, enslaving millions as sex addicts. Drug abuse and alcoholism are pervasive as well among both teenagers and adults. Promiscuity, fornication, and adultery continue to escalate to ever new heights, bringing about the carnage of sexually transmitted diseases.

Meanwhile, the family unit is disintegrating before our eyes. The divorce rate remains around 50 percent, and many today are living together outside of marriage. Out-of-wedlock births have escalated to new highs, with 40 percent of women not being married when they give birth. As well, gay couples are adopting children and raising them in a homosexual atmosphere.

People today seem to be more interested in happiness than in holiness. They yearn more for pleasure than for praising God. Humanism, materialism, and hedonism continue to reign supreme.

In view of these Bible verses and cultural facts, it seems impossible to claim that the world is getting better and better or that it will be Christianized before the Lord comes back.

Postmillennialism becomes all the more problematic when we consider the seven years that precede Christ's second coming, a period known as the tribulation. Here's what Scripture reveals about this period.

1. Scripture refers to a definite period of time at the end of the age called the tribulation (Matthew 24:29-35).

2. It will be of such severity that no period in history past or future will equal it (verse 21).

3. It will be shortened for the sake of the elect (verse 22), as no flesh could survive it otherwise.

4. It is called the time of Jacob's trouble, for it is a judgment on Messiah-rejecting Israel (Jeremiah 30:7; Daniel 12:1-4).

5. The nations will also be judged for their sin and rejection

of Christ during this tribulation (Isaiah 26:21; Revelation 6:15-17).

6. This tribulation period lasts seven years (Daniel 9:24,27).

7. It will be so bad that people will want to hide and even die (Revelation 6:16).

8. This period is characterized by wrath (Zephaniah 1:15,18), judgment (Revelation 14:7), indignation (Isaiah 26:20-21), trial (Revelation 3:10), destruction (Joel 1:15), darkness (Amos 5:18), desolation (Daniel 9:27), overturning (Isaiah 24:1-4), and punishment (Isaiah 24:20-21). This being so, the postmillennial idea that things will get better and better before Christ returns seems impossible.

Universal Proclamation of the Gospel

There are still further problems with postmillennialism. For example, it requires a leap in logic to claim that the universal proclamation of the gospel prior to the Lord's return (Matthew 28:18-20) will make the world better and better until it is finally Christianized. The truth is that despite this universal proclamation, many will continue to reject the gospel. This is one reason Jesus said, "Enter by the narrow gate. For the gate is wide and the way is easy that leads to destruction, and those who enter by it are many. For the gate is narrow and the way is hard that leads to life, and those who find it are few" (Matthew 7:13-14). Premillennialists praise the Lord for the spread of the gospel, but Scripture never promised that by such efforts the entire world would be Christianized. The devil is fighting back with a vengeance, as evidenced in the current explosive growth of the cults and false religions in our world.

Postmillennialists are correct in claiming that people from all nations will come to salvation (Revelation 7:9-10). But this does not indicate a worldwide Christianization. This is what the text says:

> After this I looked, and behold, a great multitude that
> no one could number, from every nation, from all tribes

> and peoples and languages, standing before the throne
> and before the Lamb, clothed in white robes, with palm
> branches in their hands, and crying out with a loud voice,
> "Salvation belongs to our God who sits on the throne, and
> to the Lamb!"

The problem for the postmillennialist is that this verse has a narrow application to the future seven-year tribulation period (Daniel 9:26-27; Revelation 14–18). And during the tribulation, the world most certainly is not Christianized. After all, the book of Revelation is equally clear that the entire world will then be under the dominance of the antichrist (Revelation 13), hardly a Christianized environment. Further, the book of Revelation speaks of the world during that time as having been deceived by the great prostitute, or false religion—the religious Babylon of the end times. There will also be many Christian martyrs (Revelation 6:9). It therefore hardly seems appropriate to cite Revelation 7:9-10 in favor of postmillennialism.

Christ's Rule

Postmillennialists argue that Christ's throne is in heaven, and that He rules from this throne, not a throne on earth (see Psalm 93:2; 103:19). Premillennialists do not deny that Christ is now reigning spiritually. But this does not nullify the unconditional Davidic covenant, which specifically promises that David's descendent, the divine Messiah, will literally reign on the throne of David in the millennial kingdom. Christ's spiritual rule does not fulfill what God promised to David in 2 Samuel 7:13-16. The Davidic covenant was an unconditional covenant, so God will fulfill the promises of this covenant in the future.

The Parable of the Mustard Seed

Jesus's parable of the mustard seed does picture a continual advance of Christianity in the world (Matthew 13:31-32). But again, it involves an incredible leap in logic to conclude from Jesus's statement that the entire world will get better and better and become Christianized before

He returns again at the second coming. Satan's kingdom will continue to grow as well. This is why the tares will have to be separated from the wheat and the goats separated from the sheep at the end of the age (see Matthew 25:31-46). And, as noted above, Scripture prophesies both doctrinal and moral apostasy in the end times (1 Timothy 4:1-2; 2 Timothy 4:3-4).

Misappropriation of Bible Verses

Postmillennialists misappropriate certain Bible verses in support of their viewpoint. For example, they note that Zechariah 9:10 indicates that Christ's kingdom will spread from sea to sea, and Numbers 14:21 indicates that the whole earth will be filled with the Lord's glory. In context, however, these verses are fulfilled not prior to Christ's coming, but rather after Christ's coming when He sets up His literal 1000-year reign on earth. The whole world will be filled with the glory of the Lord because the Lord of glory will physically reign from the actual throne of David on earth (2 Samuel 7:12-16).

Postmillennialists also misappropriate Revelation 19:11-21. This passage does not picture the entire time period between the first and second comings of Jesus Christ. Rather, it refers to the singular and definitive coming of the Lord Jesus at the height of Armageddon, following seven years of tribulation.

> Then I saw heaven opened, and behold, a white horse! The one sitting on it is called Faithful and True, and in righteousness he judges and makes war. His eyes are like a flame of fire, and on his head are many diadems, and he has a name written that no one knows but himself. He is clothed in a robe dipped in blood, and the name by which he is called is The Word of God. And the armies of heaven, arrayed in fine linen, white and pure, were following him on white horses. From his mouth comes a sharp sword with which to strike down the nations, and he will rule them with a rod of iron. He will tread the winepress of the fury of the wrath of God the Almighty. On his robe

and on his thigh he has a name written, King of kings and Lord of lords.

Then I saw an angel standing in the sun, and with a loud voice he called to all the birds that fly directly overhead, "Come, gather for the great supper of God, to eat the flesh of kings, the flesh of captains, the flesh of mighty men, the flesh of horses and their riders, and the flesh of all men, both free and slave, both small and great." And I saw the beast and the kings of the earth with their armies gathered to make war against him who was sitting on the horse and against his army. And the beast was captured, and with it the false prophet who in its presence had done the signs by which he deceived those who had received the mark of the beast and those who worshiped its image. These two were thrown alive into the lake of fire that burns with sulfur. And the rest were slain by the sword that came from the mouth of him who was sitting on the horse, and all the birds were gorged with their flesh.

One must heap allegory upon allegory to come up with the postmillennial interpretation of this passage.

Conclusion

From a doctrinal perspective, I find little to commend postmillennialism. Scripture portrays the end times prior to Christ's return as being characterized by a massive falling away from the truth. As I examine the world around me, I remain unconvinced that the world is getting better and better. To be sure, the world is making some significant technological advances, and that is good. But with every new technological advance, humankind seems to find new ways to pervert and exploit that technology toward its own sinful ways. More than ever, I am convinced that premillennialism makes the best sense of the whole of Scripture.

The Case for Premillennialism

Premillennialism teaches that Christ will return before the millennial kingdom. More specifically, it teaches that following the second coming, Christ will institute a kingdom of perfect peace and righteousness on earth that will last for 1000 years.

Two forms of premillennialism have emerged. Dispensational premillennialism, championed by John F. Walvoord (1910–2002) among others, distinguishes between the church and Israel and holds that in the millennium, God will fulfill the unconditional promises He made to Israel.[1] Historic premillennialism, espoused by George Eldon Ladd (1911–1982) among others, does not insist on the distinction between the church and Israel (the church is viewed as spiritual Israel), nor does it demand a consistently literal interpretive method.[2]

My discussion will zero in on dispensational premillennialism.

Biblical Arguments for Dispensational Premillennialism

Dispensational premillennialists offer the following arguments in favor of their position.

1. This view naturally emerges from a literal hermeneutic.

2. This view best explains the unconditional land promises made to Abraham and his descendants, which are yet to be fulfilled (Genesis 13:14-18; Deuteronomy 30).

3. This view makes the best sense of the unconditional Davidic covenant in regard to the throne promise (2 Samuel 7:12-16).

4. This view is most compatible with numerous Old Testament predictions about the coming messianic age.

5. This view is consistent with the Old Testament ending with a firm expectation of the messianic kingdom (for example, Isaiah 9:6; 16:5; Malachi 3:1).

6. This view best explains the scriptural teaching that Jesus and the apostles would reign on thrones in Jerusalem (Matthew 19:28; 25:31-34; Acts 1:6-7).

7. This view is most consistent with the apostle Paul's promise that Israel will one day be restored (Romans 9:3-4; 11:1).

The obvious contrast with amillennialism and postmillennialism is that the kingdom Christ establishes will be a literal 1000-year kingdom over which Christ Himself will physically rule. In contrast to postmillennialism in particular, Christ is the one who establishes the kingdom, not the church through the Christianizing of the world. Notice also that in the millennial kingdom, all of the covenant promises to Israel will be fulfilled to Israel (rather than being presently fulfilled in the church). This is based on a literal interpretation of biblical prophecy and the biblical covenants in contrast to the allegorical approach utilized by amillennialists and postmillennialists. The dispensational premillennialist is convinced that in biblical prophecy, *Israel* means Israel (the physical descendants of Abraham) and *church* means the church.

The biblical covenants are particularly important in premillennial thought. Premillennial theologian Paul Enns explains how these covenants find their ultimate fulfillment in the millennial kingdom.

> The unconditional covenants demand a literal, physical return of Christ to establish the kingdom. The Abrahamic covenant promised Israel a land, a posterity and ruler, and a spiritual blessing (Gen. 12:1-3); the Palestinian covenant

promised Israel a restoration to the land and occupation of the land (Deut. 30:1-10); the Davidic covenant promised a ruler for the throne of David (2 Sam. 7:16); the New Covenant promised Israel forgiveness—the means whereby the nation could be blessed (Jer. 31:31-34). At the Second Advent these covenants will be fulfilled as Israel is regathered from the nations (Matt. 24:31), converted (Zech. 12:10-14), and restored to the land under the rulership of her Messiah.[3]

Many throughout church history have held to premillennialism, including Church Fathers Justin Martyr (100–165), Clement of Alexandria (150–215), and Tertullian (155–225). Augustine (354–430) held to this view early in his theological career. Other premillennial luminaries include John Nelson Darby (1800–1882), Griffith Thomas (1861–1924), Lewis Sperry Chafer (1871–1952), and James Montgomery Boice (1938–2000).[4]

Within premillennial theology, there are different views in regard to when the rapture of the church occurs. Pretribulationism is the view that Christ will rapture the entire church before any part of the tribulation begins. Midtribulationism is the view that Christ will rapture the church in the middle of the tribulation period. Posttribulationism is the view that Christ will rapture the church after the tribulation at the second coming of Christ. The pre-wrath view argues that the rapture occurs toward the end of the tribulation before the great wrath of God falls. The partial rapture view argues that only faithful and watchful Christians will be raptured and that unfaithful Christians will be left behind to be purged throughout the tribulation. I believe the pretrib position—the majority view among premillenialists—is most consistent with the biblical testimony (1 Thessalonians 1:9-10; 5:4-9; Revelation 3:10). (I address all these views in detail in chapters 8–12.)

Instead of holding to a general resurrection and a general judgment, as amillennialists and postmillennialists do, premillennialists understand that resurrections and judgments will take place on several occasions. They are not all lumped together in a general fashion.

For example, the righteous are resurrected at the rapture (1 Thessalonians 4:13-17), the two witnesses are resurrected during the tribulation (Revelation 11:3,11-12), tribulation martyrs are resurrected at the end of the tribulation (Revelation 20:4-5), and millennium converts are resurrected at the end of the 1000-year millennial kingdom. In terms of judgments, Christians will be judged at the judgment seat of Christ after the rapture (1 Corinthians 3:1-15; 2 Corinthians 5:10), the Gentile nations will be judged following Christ's second coming (Matthew 25:31-46), and the wicked dead will be judged at the great white throne judgment after the millennial kingdom (Revelation 20:11-15).

Characteristics of the Millennial Kingdom in Premillennialism

Scripture provides some interesting descriptions of life in the millennium. Here are some brief highlights.

Christ Will Govern

Christ's government will be global. "To him was given dominion and glory and a kingdom, that all peoples, nations, and languages should serve him; his dominion is an everlasting dominion, which shall not pass away, and his kingdom one that shall not be destroyed" (Daniel 7:14). Christ will have the nations as His heritage and the ends of the earth as His possession (Psalm 2:6-9).

Christ's government will be centered in Jerusalem. "Out of Zion shall go the law, and the word of the LORD from Jerusalem. He shall judge between the nations" (Isaiah 2:3-4; see also Jeremiah 3:17; Ezekiel 48:30-35; Joel 3:16-17; Micah 4:1,6-8; Zechariah 8:2-3).

Christ will reign on the throne of David. "Behold, the days are coming, declares the LORD, when I will raise up for David a righteous Branch, and he shall reign as king and deal wisely, and shall execute justice and righteousness in the land. In his days Judah will be saved, and Israel will dwell securely" (Jeremiah 23:5-6).

Christ's government will be perfect and effective. "For to us a child is born, to us a son is given; and the government shall be upon his shoulder, and his name shall be called Wonderful Counselor, Mighty God,

Everlasting Father, Prince of Peace. Of the increase of his government and of peace there will be no end, on the throne of David and over his kingdom, to establish it and to uphold it with justice and with righteousness from this time forth and forevermore. The zeal of the LORD of hosts will do this" (Isaiah 9:6-7).

Christ's government will bring lasting global peace. "He shall judge between many peoples, and shall decide for strong nations far away; and they shall beat their swords into plowshares, and their spears into pruning hooks; nation shall not lift up sword against nation, neither shall they learn war anymore; but they shall sit every man under his vine and under his fig tree, and no one shall make them afraid, for the mouth of the LORD of hosts has spoken" (Micah 4:3-4). Christ's government will succeed where all former human governments have failed.

There Will Be Many Physical Blessings

Premillennialists believe, based on a literal interpretation of Scripture, that those who enter into Christ's millennial kingdom will enjoy some unique physical blessings.

People will live in a blessed and enhanced environment. "The wilderness and the dry land shall be glad; the desert shall rejoice and blossom like the crocus; it shall blossom abundantly and rejoice with joy and singing. The glory of Lebanon shall be given to it, the majesty of Carmel and Sharon. They shall see the glory of the LORD, the majesty of our God" (Isaiah 35:1-2).

There will be plenty of rain for the ground and plenty of food for animals. "[God] will give rain for the seed with which you sow the ground, and bread, the produce of the ground, which will be rich and plenteous. In that day your livestock will graze in large pastures, and the oxen and the donkeys that work the ground will eat seasoned fodder, which has been winnowed with shovel and fork" (Isaiah 30:23-24).

All animals will live in harmony with each other and with humans, their predatory and carnivorous natures having been removed. "The wolf shall dwell with the lamb, and the leopard shall lie down with the young goat, and the calf and the lion and the fattened calf together; and a little child shall lead them. The cow and the bear shall graze; their young shall lie down together; and the lion shall eat straw like the ox" (Isaiah 11:6-7).

Longevity will be greatly increased. "No more shall there be in it an infant who lives but a few days, or an old man who does not fill out his days, for the young man shall die a hundred years old" (Isaiah 65:20).

Physical infirmities and illnesses will be removed. "In that day the deaf shall hear the words of a book, and out of their gloom and darkness the eyes of the blind shall see" (Isaiah 29:18).

Prosperity will prevail, resulting in joy and gladness. "They shall come and sing aloud on the height of Zion, and they shall be radiant over the goodness of the LORD, over the grain, the wine, and the oil, and over the young of the flock and the herd; their life shall be like a watered garden, and they shall languish no more. Then shall the young women rejoice in the dance, and the young men and the old shall be merry. I will turn their mourning into joy; I will comfort them, and give them gladness for sorrow. I will feast the soul of the priests with abundance, and my people shall be satisfied with my goodness, declares the LORD" (Jeremiah 31:12-14).

Christ Will Bestow Spiritual Blessing

Christ will also bring great spiritual blessing in His millennial kingdom. All such spiritual blessings relate to the wonderful reality that Jesus Christ Himself will be present with His people on earth. Christ being with His people on earth will affect the spiritual life of humankind like never before.

No wonder Isaiah the prophet tells us that "the earth shall be full of the knowledge of the LORD as the waters cover the sea" (Isaiah 11:9). Satan will be bound during the millennial kingdom (Revelation 20:1-3), so we can scarcely imagine the depth of spiritual blessings that will prevail on earth during this time, blessings based on the new covenant (Jeremiah 31:31-34).

The Holy Spirit will be present and will indwell all believers. "I will put my Spirit within you, and you shall live, and I will place you in your own land. Then you shall know that I am the LORD; I have spoken, and I will do it, declares the LORD" (Ezekiel 37:14).

The Holy Spirit will be "poured upon us from on high" (Isaiah 32:15). "It shall come to pass afterward, that I will pour out my Spirit on all flesh; your sons and your daughters shall prophesy, your old men shall dream dreams, and your young men shall see visions. Even on the male and female servants in those days I will pour out my Spirit" (Joel 2:28-29).

Righteousness will prevail around the world. "Your people shall all be righteous; they shall possess the land forever" (Isaiah 60:21).

Obedience to the Lord will prevail. "All the ends of the earth shall remember and turn to the LORD, and all the families of the nations shall worship before you" (Psalm 22:27).

Holiness will prevail. "A highway shall be there, and it shall be called the Way of Holiness; the unclean shall not pass over it. It shall belong to those who walk on the way…The ransomed of the LORD shall return and come to Zion with singing; everlasting joy shall be upon their heads; they shall obtain gladness and joy, and sorrow and sighing shall flee away" (Isaiah 35:8-10).

Faithfulness will prevail. "Steadfast love and faithfulness meet; righteousness and peace kiss each other. Faithfulness springs up from the ground, and righteousness looks down from the sky" (Psalm 85:10-11).

The world's residents will worship the Messiah. "From the rising of the sun to its setting my name will be great among the nations, and in every place incense will be offered to my name, and a pure offering. For my name will be great among the nations, says the LORD of hosts" (Malachi 1:11).

God's presence will be made manifest. "Sing and rejoice, O daughter of Zion, for behold, I come and I will dwell in your midst, declares the LORD. And many nations shall join themselves to the LORD in that day, and shall be my people. And I will dwell in your midst, and you shall know that the LORD of hosts has sent me to you" (Zechariah 2:10-11).

Arguments against Premillennialism

To be fair, Christians in other eschatological camps have offered these criticisms of premillennialism.

- Biblical prophecy ought to be interpreted allegorically and not literally. (Premillennialists believe prophecy, like the rest of Scripture, ought to be interpreted literally. I address this issue in detail in chapter 1.)

- The biblical covenants were conditional, and Israel did not live up to the covenant stipulations, so Israel forfeited the covenant blessings. (Premillennialists believe the covenants were unconditional. I address this issue in chapter 4.)

- The church is the new Israel and therefore receives God's prophetic blessings. (Dispensational premillennialists believe that the church and Israel remain distinct in biblical prophecy. I address this issue in detail in chapter 4.)

- Prophecies about Christ reigning are fulfilled in His spiritual rule from heaven. (Premillennialists believe Christ will physically rule on the throne of David in a 1000-year kingdom. This is based on a literal interpretation of the Davidic covenant in 2 Samuel 7.)

Conclusion

In my studied opinion, premillennialism makes the best sense of all the scriptural data. It is a natural outgrowth of a literal hermeneutic. As I have previously stated, when the plain sense makes good sense, seek no other sense lest you end up in nonsense. Premillennialism makes good sense!

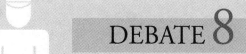

DEBATE 8

Is It Okay to Set Dates on Prophetic Events?

Yes, Set Dates

People have been predicting imminent doom or glorious apocalypse since the Pharaohs ruled Egypt. According to legend, humanity became grievously afflicted with millennial fever near the close of the first millennium. Some accounts indicate that around AD 999, so many people in Christian lands thought the world was coming to an end that they began acting in a truly unaccustomed fashion. They became so brotherly, so charitable, so filled with self-abnegation and love for their neighbor that the true millennium, however briefly, seemed to be at hand.[1]

> Men forgave their neighbors' debts; people confessed their infidelities and wrongdoings. Farm animals were freed as their owners prepared for the final judgment...The churches were besieged by crowds demanding confession and absolution. Commerce was interrupted. Beggars were liberally fed by the more fortunate. Prisoners were freed, yet many remained—wishing to expiate their sins before the end. Pilgrims flocked to Jerusalem from Europe. Class differences were forgotten. Slaves were freed.
>
> Nearing December, groups of flagellants roamed the countryside whipping each other. Christmas passed with a splendid outpouring of love and piety. Food shops gave

away food and merchants refused payment. Of course, when December 31st approached a general frenzy reached new heights. In Rome, Pope Sylvester II held midnight mass in the Basilica of St. Peters to a standing room only audience. But they weren't standing. All lay on their knees praying.

After the mass had been said, a deathly silence fell. The clock kept on ticking away its last minutes as Pope Sylvester raised his hands to the sky. The attendees at this time lay with their faces to the ground listening to the tick tick tick.

Suddenly the clock stopped. Several bodies, stricken by fear, dropped dead as the congregation began screaming in terror. Just as it had suddenly stopped ticking the clock resumed to meet the midnight hour. Deathly silence still reigned until the clock ticked past 12. Bells in the tower began to scream jubilantly. Pope Sylvester stretched out his hands and gave a blessing over his flock. When the *Te Deum* had been sung, men and women fell in each other's arms, laughing and crying and exchanging the kiss of peace.

Not long after the suspense at St. Peter's and elsewhere, life resumed its normal rhythm. Owners captured their once freed animals. Merchants ceased giving away their goods. Prisoners were captured to be placed back in the slammer. Debts were remembered. And life went on as if nothing happened.[2]

Did all of this really occur around AD 1000? One might think so from all the articles and books that have appeared on the subject.[3] However, when one digs deep for hard, indisputable historical evidence, one is less than satisfied.[4] If a widespread panic and hysteria had really occurred, wouldn't we have more than the surviving 12 or 13 accounts of what happened at the turn of the first millennium—only half of which mention apocalyptic panic?[5]

Raoul Glaber, a Burgundian monk born in the late tenth century, wrote *Histories*—considered by many to be a prime source for what went on at the turn of the millennium. His writings indicate a panic concerning the approaching end.[6] A number of historians, however, have disputed Glaber's work.[7]

Moreover, historians interpret Glaber and other available writings of the time (few though they be) in different ways.

> People of the time wrote wills and testaments, clearly indicating an awareness of a future. But, note others, opening clauses of many of the surviving wills begin with some version of "The end of the world being close, I hereby..." or "The world coming to its conclusion, I..."[8]

Who's to say what all this meant? Lines such as these were merely standard, boilerplate openers for legal documents of that day.[9]

Despite all the confusion, I think we can say with a fair degree of certainty that while there probably was no mass hysteria or panic at the close of the first millennium, there was widespread concern that the end of the world may be near. A number of highly respected scholars support this view, noting that people living at the close of the first millennium had a definite case of the pre-apocalyptic shivers. Reformed scholar Louis Berkhof confirms this in *The History of Christian Doctrines*.

> In the tenth century there was a widespread expectation of the approaching end of the world...it was associated with the idea of the speedy coming of Antichrist. Christian art often chose its themes from eschatology. The hymn *Dies Irae* sounded the terrors of the coming judgment, painters depicted the end of the world on the canvas, and Dante gave a vivid description of hell in his *Divina Commedia*.[10]

Philip Schaff, in his highly respected *History of the Christian Church*, gives a flavor of the times. Pope Sylvester II (who lived around AD 1000) gave "the first impulse, though prematurely, to the crusades at a time when hundreds of pilgrims flocked to the Holy Land in expectation of the end of the world after the lapse of the first Christian millennium."[11]

Stanley J. Grenz, in his book *The Millennial Maze*, offers this perspective:

> Repeatedly church history has witnessed times of increased speculation concerning the end and the advent of a golden age on earth. The approach of the year AD 1000, for example, caused a great stir of expectations. When both that year and AD 1033 (a thousand years after Christ's death) passed, interest turned to AD 1065, for in that year Good Friday coincided with the Day of the Annunciation. Multitudes journeyed to Jerusalem to await the Lord's return, some arriving already during the previous year and waiting in the Holy City until after Easter.[12]

Grenz later adds this note.

> Augustine's various statements concerning the meaning of the millennium mentioned in Revelation 20 were not without some ambiguity…They could be (and were) readily understood to indicate that Christ's Second Coming should occur one thousand years after his first advent. This implicit prediction, carrying as it did the authority of the bishop of Hippo coupled both with the theme of the old age of the world and with a rise in political and natural disasters, resulted in a great sense of anticipation in parts of Christendom first as AD 1000 and then as AD 1033 approached.[13]

In his in-depth study, Henri Focillon made this conclusion:

> We have established that in the middle of the tenth century there existed a movement, a groundswell of the belief that the world was drawing to a close…Once the terminal year of the millennium had passed, the belief in the end of the world spread with renewed vigor in the course of the eleventh century.[14]

Though recognizing this groundswell, Focillon is careful to point out that there was no mass hysteria as some of the legendary accounts of the time seem to indicate.

To sum up then, the turn of the first millennium saw no mass hysteria, but many people were definitely concerned that the end of the world was approaching. Now, here's my point—just as many people were concerned about the end of the world around the turn of the first millennium, so many people also became concerned about the approach of the year AD 2000. Some believed that the end of the world was near. Others believed a glorious utopia awaited humanity.

Millennial Madness AD 2000

Regardless of what happened around AD 1000, the approach of the year AD 2000 certainly put the fear of God into a good many people.[15] Some predicted imminent doom, others looked for a glorious utopia, and still others predicted doom followed by utopia. Any way you look at it, millennial madness surfaced with a vengeance as we neared AD 2000. Cultural commentator Christopher Lasch made this observation:

> As the twentieth century approaches its end, the conviction grows that many other things are ending too. Storm warnings, portents, hints of catastrophe haunt our times. The "sense of ending," which has given shape to so much of twentieth century literature, now pervades the popular imagination as well.[16]

Stanley Grenz made a similar comment.

> At the close of the twentieth century the message of the doomsday preachers—once the brunt of jokes and the laughingstock of "enlightened" citizens of the modern world—has become in the minds of many people a serious possibility and a genuine concern in a way unparalleled in prior decades. For the first time in recent history we sense that our civilization is tottering on the edge of a precipice peering into the abyss of self-destruction and chaos.[17]

The Contribution of Nostradamus

Nostradamus (1503–1566) was a French astrologer and occultist who attained notoriety for his prophecies, many of which were vague, allusive, cryptic, enigmatic, and difficult to understand. Were any of them accurate? Many Nostradamus sympathizers say yes—though a great deal of interpretive liberty is involved in how such prophecies are read. Former *Los Angeles Times* religion editor Russell Chandler, in his book *Doomsday: The End of the World*, summarizes the alleged prophetic fulfillments.

> Nostradamus's mystical poems have been used to predict the future history of France (including the rise of Napoleon and the French Revolution); the American Revolution; the era of World War II and Hitler ("Hister"), Mussolini, and Franklin Roosevelt; the assassinations of John and Robert Kennedy; the coming of such inventions as air travel, aerial balloons and air warfare, gas masks, submarines, periscopes, manned space stations, and the atomic bomb; such disasters as the London fire of 1666, the 1986 explosion of the Challenger spacecraft, and the Chernobyl nuclear plant accident; the epidemic of AIDS; the identity of three antichrists; the fall of the Roman Catholic Church and the decline of communism—to name but a few extrapolations.[18]

Chandler notes that "modern-day Nostradamians do a much better job of matching his predictions with historical events after they have happened rather than pinpointing beforehand exactly what the aristocratic astrologer had in mind."[19] This is in noted contrast to the biblical prophets, whose predictions were clearly understood prior to their fulfillment. Israelites clearly understood, for example, that the Messiah would be born in Bethlehem (Micah 5:2) by a virgin (Isaiah 7:14) and would be pierced for the sins of humankind (Isaiah 53:5; Zechariah 12:10).

In any event, a number of people believe that 450 years ago, Nostradamus set the stage for the AD 2000 millennial madness. John Hogue, author of *Nostradamus and the Millennium*, says Nostradamus predicted that humanity had two alternative futures for the period between 1992 and 1999—one involving destruction, the other involving a utopia.

Hogue based his view on Nostradamus's assertion that the most important element for the last seven years of the twentieth century would be fire. Perhaps man would be destroyed by fire (nuclear?), or perhaps a spiritual fire would ignite man's consciousness and lead to a utopian society.[20]

Other interpreters of Nostradamus say he predicted only doom for the decade preceding AD 2000. Rene Noorbergen, a former war correspondent and Nostradamus admirer, says the prophet gave a forecast of World War III. Here's what he interpreted the sage to be saying:

> Sometime before 1995, Russia and the United States will ally themselves against China, the Arab Middle East, and Latin America in the most destructive and terrifying war the world has ever experienced. In what may well become the last great war, conducted by conventional and nuclear weaponry as well as by biological warfare, no continent will escape devastation.[21]

Of course, AD 2000 has long passed, so Nostradamus's predictions—or Noorbergen's interpretation of them—turned out to be much ado about nothing.

Cults, New Agers, and Millennial Madness

Some New Agers were among those who predicted a utopia in the years following 2000. Ken Carey, author of several New Age handbooks, envisioned AD 2000 as a kind of psychic watershed, beyond which lay "a realizable utopian society" in which people will have "a real sense of a new beginning."[22]

David Spangler, another New Ager, agreed and pointed to a Central American prophecy that predicted a great cleansing in our time. Following this, a New Age of harmony and wholeness would emerge. Spangler commented, "The Hopi Indians of the American Southwest have a similar prophecy, also focused on the period from 1980 to 2000 AD as a time of transition into a new cycle of cooperation."[23]

Elizabeth Clare Prophet, controversial New Age leader of the Church Universal and Triumphant (CUT), claimed she had been informed by an Ascended Master that catastrophe awaited the world.[24] She had been saying for years that Russia would invade the United States. Prophet said the period around 1994 would be particularly dangerous. "I believe that anytime between now and 2002 there is a high probability, a likelihood, of a war between the United States and the Soviet Union."[25]

In view of this, Prophet and her followers built large bomb shelters to house the faithful. Church members were able to purchase room in the shelters for a mere $6000 to $10,000 apiece.[26] Mrs. Prophet likened the shelters to Noah's Ark in the earth.[27]

These New Age speculations also turned out to be much ado about nothing.

Edgar C. Whisenant

This background leads us to the sad reality that millennial madness also afflicted Christians. In the years leading up to 2000, more and more Christian date-setters came out of the woodwork to predict the timing of the rapture and other prophetic events. Edgar C. Whisenant wrote a book titled *88 Reasons Why the Rapture Will Be in 1988*. This 58-page book sold a whopping 4.5 million copies and stirred no small controversy in the church. The rapture, Whisenant said, would occur September 11, 12, or 13, 1988.

To calculate when the rapture would occur, Whisenant relied on such unchristian sources as pyramidology, astrology, divination, and numerology.[28] He relied also on the testimony of astrologer-psychic Jeanne Dixon.[29]

In his book *Soothsayers of the Second Advent*, my late friend William Alnor noted that Charles Taylor planned his 1988 tour of Israel to coincide with Whisenant's date, offering the possibility of being raptured from the Holy Land as a sales incentive. "Only $1,975 from Los Angeles or $1,805 from New York (and return if necessary)," said his *Bible Prophecy News*. He later made this pitch for the tour:

> We stay at the Intercontinental Hotel right on the Mount
> of Olives where you can get the beautiful view of the

Eastern Gate and the Temple Mount. And if this is the year of our Lord's return, as we anticipate, you may even ascend to Glory from within a few feet of His ascension.[30]

When Whisenant's date of the rapture did not pan out, he merely adjusted his calculations. He changed the September 11–13 date to October 3, and when that date failed, he affirmed, "It is going to be in a few weeks anyway." Did Whisenant repent when that date failed? No. Instead he claimed his calculations were off by a year and that Christ would return during Rosh Hashanah (September 30) in 1989, or perhaps at the end of the Feast of Tabernacles on October 14–20, 1989.[31]

Harold Camping

In his controversial book *1994?*, Harold Camping of Family Radio predicted that Jesus Christ would return in September of 1994. "No book ever written is as audacious or bold as one that claims to predict the timing of the end of the world, and that is precisely what this book presumes to do."[32]

"If I am correct in this," Camping said deliberately, "and there is every indication that I am, we have a very short time left to get right with God." In his book he warned that "when September 6, 1994 arrives, no one else can become saved. The end has come."[33] Camping boasted that the likelihood of him being wrong on his calculations was "very remote."[34] Camping asserted, "I would be very surprised if the world reached the year 2000."[35]

Of course, Camping's predictions failed spectacularly. But he wasn't finished. Much later he prophesied that Jesus would come for His own on May 21, 2011. After this there were to be five months of planet-wide fire, brimstone, and plagues, with millions of people dying each day. The final destruction of the world was to be on October 21, 2011. Another spectacular failure!

I could cite many other Christian leaders. Two immediately come to mind. Prophecy teacher Mary Stewart Relfe said she received "divine revelations from the Lord" indicating that the second coming of Christ would occur in 1997.[36] Lester Sumrall said in his book *I Predict*

2000 AD, "I predict the absolute fullness of man's operation on planet Earth by the year 2000 AD. Then Jesus Christ shall reign from Jerusalem for 1,000 years."[37]

Conclusion

I myself am a big believer in the rapture. There is not a single prophecy that must be fulfilled before this glorious event occurs. I also believe that Christ calls us to be accurate observers of the times so we can give studied consideration as to whether we may be living in the end times (see Matthew 16:1-3; 24:32-33). However, while we can be excited that we may be drawing near to the rapture, Scripture is absolutely clear that dates are never to be set for prophetic events. Never! I will address this issue in the next chapter.

No, Don't Set Dates

In the previous chapter, I provided a brief survey of some people who have attempted to set dates through the centuries. Space allowed me to only touch on a few examples. I would love to have provided countless other examples, space permitting. I'm sure many others will continue to set dates in the future.

Now I will briefly and concisely offer ten good reasons why Christians should not succumb to setting prophetic dates.

A Dismal Track Record

Over the past 2000 years, those who have predicted or expected the end have been wrong 100 percent of the time. The history of doomsday predictions is little more than a history of dashed expectations. Though I believe there is a strong likelihood that we today are living in the season of the Lord's coming for us at the rapture, it could still be a long way off. Guessing a date for the rapture or any other prophetic event is therefore foolish. Let's resist the temptation.

Harmful Decisions

Christians who succumb to believing in specific dates for prophetic events make harmful decisions. Selling one's possessions and heading for the mountains, joining a survivalist sect, spending a lot of money to purchase a bomb shelter, stopping the educational process, not saving money for retirement, leaving family and friends...these destructive actions can potentially ruin one's life.

Damage to Your Faith

Christians who succumb to believing in specific dates for prophetic events, such as expecting the rapture to occur by a specific date, may damage their faith with failed expectations. These Christians may also find their confidence in the Bible waning because of misplaced and unbiblical hopes. I've read newspaper articles about some disillusioned Christians who accepted Harold Camping's predictions. Some of them donated a large portion of their financial savings to Camping's ministry because they believed the rapture was near. Today, some of them ask God, "Why did You let this happen to me?" Of course, God didn't. God in His Word warned against setting dates (Acts 1:7). Harold Camping is the real culprit.

Motivation to Live in Purity

If one loses confidence in the prophetic portions of Scripture because of a failed prophetic date, biblical prophecy may cease to be a motivation to purity and holiness in daily life.[1] Notice how the apostle Paul ties end-time expectation to holiness in everyday living.

> The grace of God has appeared, bringing salvation for all people, training us to renounce ungodliness and worldly passions, and to live self-controlled, upright, and godly lives in the present age, waiting for our blessed hope, the appearing of the glory of our great God and Savior Jesus Christ, who gave himself for us to redeem us from all lawlessness and to purify for himself a people for his own possession who are zealous for good works (Titus 2:12-14).

Christians who become disillusioned when a date fails to pan out for the rapture (the "blessed hope") may find themselves less motivated to "renounce ungodliness and worldly passions, and to live self-controlled, upright, and godly lives in the present age."

When Peter wrote about the prophetic day of the Lord and God's creation of a new heavens and a new earth, he asked his readers, "What sort of people ought you to be in lives of holiness and godliness?" (2 Peter 3:11). If a rapture date we had high hopes for fails, we could be less motivated to live in holiness and godliness.

John encourages all Christians, "Beloved, we are God's children now, and what we will be has not yet appeared; but we know that when he appears we shall be like him, because we shall see him as he is. And everyone who thus hopes in him purifies himself as he is pure" (1 John 3:2-3). If we've been burned by a failed prophetic date, our motivation to purify our lives could wane. Many pastors are concerned about the possibility. Frankly, this was one of my biggest concerns for those duped by Harold Camping.

Damaging People's Faith

Christians who succumb to believing in specific dates for prophetic events may inadvertently damage the faith of new believers and immature believers when the predicted events fail to materialize. Let's face it. New believers who have not yet been educated and discipled in the Word of God are more spiritually gullible than those who are mature in the Word. A recent convert might fall for a date-setting scheme of a radio preacher and wrongly conclude that the preacher is accurately reflecting the Word of God. Then, when the date fails to materialize, the new believer may become disillusioned, wondering if the Word of God is accurate after all.

Prophetic Agnosticism

Christians who succumb to believing in specific dates for prophetic events may end up as "prophetic agnostics" when dates fail to materialize. The word *agnosticism* comes from two Greek words—*a*, meaning "no" or "without," and *gnosis*, meaning "knowledge." *Agnosticism* literally means "no knowledge" or "without knowledge." Generally speaking, an agnostic is a person who claims he is unsure (having no knowledge) about spiritual matters, especially the existence of God. A prophetic agnostic, as I'm using the term, is a person who is unsure about Bible prophecy. With all of the failed date predictions and dashed hopes, it's a real possibility that people may begin to believe we just can't be sure of what the future holds.

Sensationalism

Christians who succumb to believing in specific dates for prophetic events tend to gravitate toward sensationalism. The truth is, sensationalism of any kind is unbefitting to a follower of the Lord Jesus Christ. Rather, Christ calls His followers to live soberly and alertly as they await His coming. For example, in Mark 13:32-37 Jesus makes this affirmation:

> Concerning that day or that hour, no one knows, not even the angels in heaven, nor the Son, but only the Father. Be on guard, keep awake. For you do not know when the time will come. It is like a man going on a journey, when he leaves home and puts his servants in charge, each with his work, and commands the doorkeeper to stay awake. Therefore stay awake—for you do not know when the master of the house will come, in the evening, or at midnight, or when the rooster crows, or in the morning—lest he come suddenly and find you asleep. And what I say to you I say to all: Stay awake.

As we consider prophetic events, we are to "be on guard," and "keep awake," and "stay awake." Jesus wouldn't have urged His followers to keep awake if it were possible for us to determine exact dates and times of the Lord's coming.

Damage to the Cause of Christ

Christians who succumb to believing in specific dates for prophetic events may ultimately do damage to the cause of Christ. Some unbelievers enjoy scornfully pointing to Christians who put stock in end-time predictions—especially when specific dates have been attached to specific events.[2] They love to write articles about gullible Christians. Why give ammo to those who are antagonistic to Christianity?

Becoming Sidetracked

Christians who succumb to believing in specific dates for prophetic events may get sidetracked from their first priority—living righteous and holy lives as they keep their eyes on Jesus. We ought to continually be about the business of "looking to Jesus, the founder and perfecter of our faith" (Hebrews 12:2). This is in keeping with the words of the psalmist, "My eyes are ever toward the LORD" (Psalm 25:15). "Our eyes look to the LORD our God" (Psalm 123:2).

Only God Knows

The timing of end-time events is completely in God's hands, and He has not given us the exact specifics on timing. Jesus told His followers, "It is not for you to know times or seasons that the Father has fixed by his own authority" (Acts 1:7). The disciples wanted to know when Christ would institute the messianic kingdom. They wanted to know if it would be soon. Jesus told them it was not for them to know the Father's timing on the issue of the messianic kingdom. Following Jesus's ascension into heaven, of course, more prophetic revelation was provided that enabled believers to understand more about the end times (for example, 1 Thessalonians, 2 Thessalonians, 1 Timothy, 2 Timothy, and the book of Revelation). In such passages, God revealed what the religious landscape would look like in the end times.

For example, in 1 Timothy 4:1 Paul said, "The Spirit expressly says that in later times some will depart from the faith by devoting themselves to deceitful spirits and teachings of demons." He also said, "The time is coming when people will not endure sound teaching, but having itching ears they will accumulate for themselves teachers to suit their own passions, and will turn away from listening to the truth and wander off into myths" (2 Timothy 4:3-4). In 2 Timothy 3:1-5 Paul wrote this:

> Understand this, that in the last days there will come times of difficulty. For people will be lovers of self, lovers of money, proud, arrogant, abusive, disobedient to their parents, ungrateful, unholy, heartless, unappeasable,

slanderous, without self-control, brutal, not loving good, treacherous, reckless, swollen with conceit, lovers of plea-sure rather than lovers of God, having the appearance of godliness, but denying its power.

Such verses reveal to us what the end times will look like. And we should not be blind to what Scripture says about it. Remember that Jesus urged His followers to be thoughtful observers of the times (see Matthew 16:1-3). We are to be aware of what biblical prophecy teaches and then keep a close eye on unfolding events in the world so that we become aware of any possible correlation between world events and biblical prophecy.

Even then, however, we are never to set dates (Matthew 24:36). We do not know the specific day or hour of Jesus's coming (Acts 1:7). We don't know God's precise timing. We can only know the general season of the Lord's return by virtue of the signs of the times (Matthew 24:33).

Conclusion

I see nothing wrong with Christians being excited that we are apparently living in the end times. It is good to live righteously, antic-ipating the possibility that the rapture may occur at any moment. At the same time, however, we must never set specific dates on end-time events. Only God knows those dates! Let's live our lives as if the Lord could come for us today but plan our lives as if we'll be here our entire lifetime expectancy. That way we are prepared for time and eternity.

Debate but Don't Divide

We have considered a lot of mini-debates about the end times in this book. You may have been unaware that Christians hold so many opinions on so many issues related to biblical prophecy. I hope this book has given you a better handle on these debates. As well, I hope it has helped you to clarify your own position on these matters.

As I bring this book to a close, my heart's desire is to end on a unifying note. Even though we debate many of the finer issues of Bible prophecy, we agree on the big stuff—Christ is coming again, we will receive incredible body upgrades (resurrection bodies), we will be held accountable for how we lived on earth at a future judgment, we will live forever with God face-to-face, and one day there will be no more sin, suffering, Satan, or death. Is that not good news? So despite all our differences, let's keep the big stuff in the forefront of our thinking.

And when we do debate the finer points of biblical prophecy, we need not have divisive attitudes. When it comes to the issue of prophetic interpretation, we all need a good dose of humility to temper our leanings toward dogmatism.

Given our basic doctrinal commonality on the essential doctrines of Christianity (such as the belief in one triune God, the deity of Christ, salvation by grace through faith, and the like), there is something to be said for allowing diversity within our basic unity (see Paul's comments in Romans 14:2-5). Humans are finite and fallible, so we will always have differences of opinion, especially on nonessential matters (such as the exact timing of the rapture).

We are free to hold our own cherished views on the specific issues of Bible prophecy and even to become fully convinced that we are right. But we should never make these nonessential teachings tests of orthodoxy or Christian fellowship. As a pretrib, I have plenty of posttrib friends, and I'm going to keep it that way.

Regardless of whether all Christians are in full agreement with me on issues related to prophecy, I want to be known as a Christian who loves all other Christians. When I express my differing views to other Christians, I want to do it in a loving way, "speaking the truth in love" (Ephesians 4:15).

It is not simply what we believe but also how we behave that is important. Jesus certainly emphasized the importance of truth. He said, "You will know the truth, and the truth will set you free" (John 8:32). But He also said that love, not simply truth, is the distinguishing mark of a Christian (John 13:35). One can be right in what he says and wrong in the way he says it. The true Christian should strive to be as helpful and loving as he is correct.

I love the writings of J.C. Ryle. In his classic book *Holiness*, he notes how hurtful words can be among Christians who disagree with each other and how such hurtful words are actually self-defeating.

> I must enter my protest against the sneering, taunting, contemptuous language which has been frequently used of late...To say the least, such language is unseemly, and only defeats its own end. A cause which is defended by such language is deservedly suspicious. Truth needs no such weapons. If we cannot agree with men, we need not speak of their views with discourtesy and contempt.[1]

Ryle thus urges, "Let us exercise charity in our judgments of one another," noting that to "exhibit bitterness and coldness" toward those who disagree with us on some matter "is to prove ourselves very ignorant of real holiness."[2]

Theologian J.I. Packer uses a family metaphor to help us understand the importance of charitable behavior in the body of Christ.

> How ought families—siblings, specifically brothers and sisters—to behave? Well, you are not going to deny that siblings ought to act like and look like parts of a family. If brothers and sisters never meet together, never speak to each other, appear to be entirely indifferent to each other—that is an unnatural and scandalous state. That would be true of any human family. I put it to you without fear of contradiction: the same is true of the family of God...divisions in the church which prevent the family from acting like one family and the body from functioning like one body...are unnatural; unnatural to the point of being shameful.[3]

The better way is the way of love and charity.

I think the apostle Paul struck the perfect balance when he exhorted the Ephesians about the importance of "speaking the truth in love" (Ephesians 4:15). As we seek to speak the truth in love, we may eventually discover that our view on a particular matter is wrong after all and that others have been right. Even if we are right, though, we should hold our view in humility (1 Peter 3:15). Certainly we should not sever fellowship or cease cooperation with those holding contrary views on nonessential matters (such as the exact timing of the rapture, the timing of the Ezekiel invasion, or one's view of the particular ministry of the 144,000 Jews in Revelation 7).

I close with a simple but well-known admonition:

> In essentials, unity;
> in non-essentials, liberty;
> and in all things, charity.

Speaking the truth in love may not always be easy, but it's the charitable thing to do!

Bibliography

Alcorn, Randy. *Heaven*. Wheaton: Tyndale House, 2004.

Barnhouse, Donald Grey. *Revelation: An Expository Commentary*. Grand Rapids: Zondervan, 1971.

Boa, Kenneth, and Robert Bowman. *Sense and Nonsense about Heaven and Hell*. Grand Rapids: Zondervan, 2007.

Fruchtenbaum, Arnold. *The Footsteps of the Messiah*. San Antonio: Ariel Ministries, 2004.

Habermas, Gary, and J.P. Moreland. *Immortality: The Other Side of Death*. Nashville: Thomas Nelson, 1992.

Hays, J. Daniel, J. Scott Duvall, and C. Marvin Pate. *Dictionary of Biblical Prophecy and End Times*. Grand Rapids: Zondervan, 2007.

Hindson, Ed. *Revelation: Unlocking the Future*. Chattanooga: AMG, 2002.

Hitchcock, Mark. *Bible Prophecy*. Wheaton: Tyndale House, 1999.

Hoyt, Herman. *The End Times*. Chicago: Moody, 1969.

Ice, Thomas, and Timothy Demy. *Prophecy Watch*. Eugene: Harvest House, 1998.

Jeremiah, David. *Escape the Coming Night: An Electrifying Tour of the World as It Races Toward Its Final Days*. Dallas: Word, 1990.

LaHaye, Tim, and Ed Hindson. *The Popular Bible Prophecy Commentary*. Eugene: Harvest House, 2006.

———. *The Popular Encyclopedia of Bible Prophecy*. Eugene: Harvest House, 2004.

LaHaye, Tim, and Jerry Jenkins. *Are We Living in the End Times?* Wheaton: Tyndale House, 1999.

Newell, William. *Revelation Chapter-by-Chapter*. Grand Rapids: Kregel, 1994.

Pache, Rene. *The Future Life*. Chicago: Moody, 1980.

Pentecost, J. Dwight. *Things to Come*. Grand Rapids: Zondervan, 1964.

Price, Walter K. *The Coming Antichrist*. New Jersey: Loizeaux Brothers, 1985.

Rhodes, Ron. *40 Days Through Revelation: Uncovering the Mystery of the End Times*. Eugene: Harvest House, 2013.

————. *Northern Storm Rising: Russia, Iran, and the Emerging End-Times Military Coalition Against Israel*. Eugene: Harvest House, 2008.

————. *Unmasking the Antichrist*. Eugene: Harvest House, 2012.

Richardson, Joel. *The Islamic Antichrist*. Los Angeles: WND, 2009.

————. *Epicenter: Why Current Rumblings in the Middle East Will Change Your Future*. Carol Stream: Tyndale House, 2006.

Ryrie, Charles C. *Dispensationalism Today*. Chicago: Moody, 1965.

Swindoll, Charles. *Insights on Revelation*. Grand Rapids: Zondervan, 2011.

Thomas, Robert L. *Revelation 1–7: An Exegetical Commentary*. Chicago: Moody, 1992.

————. *Revelation 8–22: An Exegetical Commentary*. Chicago: Moody, 1995.

Walvoord, John F. *Daniel: The Key to Prophetic Revelation*. Chicago: Moody, 1971.

————. *End Times*. Nashville: Word, 1998.

————. *The Millennial Kingdom*. Grand Rapids: Zondervan, 1975.

————. *The Prophecy Knowledge Handbook*. Wheaton: Victor, 1990.

Wood, Leon J. *The Bible and Future Events: An Introductory Summary of Last-Day Events*. Grand Rapids: Zondervan, 1973.

————. *A Commentary on Daniel*. Grand Rapids: Zondervan, 1973.

Notes

Chapter 1: The Hermeneutics of Bible Prophecy: Literal or Allegorical?

1. Charles Swindoll and Roy B. Zuck, eds., *Understanding Christian Theology* (Nashville: Thomas Nelson, 2003), p. 1368.

2. Floyd Hamilton, *The Basis of the Millennial Faith* (Grand Rapids: Eerdmans, 1955), p. 38.

3. Cited in Arnold Fruchtenbaum, *The Footsteps of the Messiah* (San Antonio: Ariel Ministries, 1983), np.

4. Charles C. Ryrie , *The Basis of the Premillennial Faith* (Dubuque, IA: ECS Ministries, 2005), np.

5. Ryrie, *The Basis of the Premillennial Faith.*

6. Charles Feinberg, *Premillennialism or Amillennialism?* (Grand Rapids: Zondervan, 1936), p. 39.

Chapter 2: Covenant Theology Versus Dispensationalism

1. See, for example, Cyrus Ingersol Scofield, *Rightly Dividing the Word of Truth* (Prosser, WA: Classic Christian Reprints, 2008).

2. See John F. Walvoord, *The Millennial Kingdom: A Basic Text in Premillennial Theology* (Grand Rapids: Zondervan, 1983); Charles C. Ryrie, *The Basis of Premillennial Faith* (Dubuque, IA: Loizeaux Brothers, 1981).

3. See Craig A. Blaising and Darrell L. Bock, eds., *Dispensationalism, Israel and the Church: The Search for Definition* (Grand Rapids: Zondervan, 2010).

4. Thomas Ice, "What Is Progressive Dispensationalism?" www.raptureready.com/featured/ice/WhatIsProgressiveDispensationalism.html.

5. Robert Saucy, *The Case for Progressive Dispensationalism* (Grand Rapids: Zondervan, 1993), pp. 69-75.

6. Ice, "What Is Progressive Dispensationalism?"

7. See, for example, Oswald T. Allis, *Prophecy and the Church* (Eugene: Wipf & Stock, 2001).

8. Paul Enns, *The Moody Handbook of Theology,* rev. ed. (Chicago: Moody, 1989), p. 490.

9. Norman Geisler, *Systematic Theology,* vol. 4, *Church, Last Things* (Minneapolis: Bethany House, 2005), np.

10. See, for example, Anthony A. Hoekema, *The Bible and the Future* (Grand Rapids: Eerdmans, 1994).

Chapter 3: The Case for the Church Replacing Israel

1. Cited in Thomas Ice, "What Is Replacement Theology?" www.pre-trib.org/data/pdf/Ice-What isReplacementThe.pdf.

2. Kenneth L. Gentry, "Supersessional Orthodoxy; Zionistic Sadism," *Dispensationalism in Transition,* vol. 6, no. 2 (February 1993), p. 1.

3. Gentry, "Supersessional Orthodoxy; Zionistic Sadism."

4. Cited in Thomas Ice, "What Is Replacement Theology?"

5. Hans LaRondelle, *The Israel of God in Prophecy* (Berrien Springs, MI: Andrews University Press, 1983), p. 108.

6. Justin Martyr, *Dialogue with Trypho* 11, in *Ante-Nicene Fathers,* 1:200.

7. S. Lewis Johnson, "Paul and 'The Israel of God': An Exegetical and Eschatological Case Study," in *Essays in Honor of J. Dwight Pentecost,* ed. Stanley Toussaint and Charles Dyer (Chicago: Moody Press, 1986), p. 183.

8. Cited in Randall Price, *Jerusalem in Prophecy* (Eugene: Harvest House, 1998), p. 234.

9. Russell Jones, *The Latter Days* (Grand Rapids: Baker, 1961), p. 83.

Chapter 4: The Case for the Church and Israel Remaining Distinct

1. Thomas Constable, "Notes on Galatians," *Constable's Expository Notes on the Bible,* www.sonic light.com/constable/notes/pdf/galatians.pdf.

2. F.F. Bruce, *The Epistle to the Galatians* (Grand Rapids: Eerdmans, 1982), p. 275.

3. S. Lewis Johnson, "Paul and 'The Israel of God': An Exegetical and Eschatological Case Study," in *Essays in Honor of J. Dwight Pentecost,* ed. Stanley Toussaint and Charles Dyer (Chicago: Moody Press, 1986), p. 189.

4. Peter Richardson, *Israel in the Apostolic Church* (Cambridge: Cambridge University, 1969), p. 83.

5. Cited in Mark Hitchcock, *The Late Great United States* (Colorado Springs: Multnomah, 2009), pp. 129-30.

Chapter 5: Do Current Signs Point to Prophetic Fulfillment?

1. Mark Hitchcock, *The End: A Complete Overview of Bible Prophecy and the End of Days* (Wheaton: Tyndale House, 2012), p. 107.

2. Arnold Fruchtenbaum, *The Footsteps of the Messiah* (San Antonio: Ariel Ministries, 2004), p. 108.

3. Hitchcock, *The End,* p. 107.

4. Hitchcock, *The End,* p. 107.

Chapter 6: Is America in Bible Prophecy?

1. Excellent information on all this is available in Mark Hitchcock, *The Late Great United States* (Colorado Springs: Multnomah, 2009), p. 93.

2. See Tim LaHaye and Ed Hindson, *Global Warning: Are We on the Brink of World War III?*

(Eugene: Harvest House, 2008), p. 19. See also Ron Rhodes, *Northern Storm Rising* (Eugene: Harvest House, 2008), chapters 1-3.

3. John F. Walvoord and Mark Hitchcock, *Armageddon, Oil, and Terror* (Carol Stream: Tyndale House, 2007), p. 72.

Chapter 7: Can We Know When the Ezekiel Invasion Will Occur?

1. Thomas Ice, "Are We Living in the Last Days?" www.raptureready.com/featured/ice/AreWeLivingintheLastDays.html.

2. Ice, "Are We Living in the Last Days?"

3. J. Dwight Pentecost, "Where Do the Events of Ezekiel 38–39 Fit into the Prophetic Picture?" *Bibliotheca Sacra* (October–December 1957), pp. 334-46.

4. Harold Hoehner, "The Progression of Events in Ezekiel 38–39," in *Integrity of Heart, Skillfulness of Hands*, ed. Charles Dyer and Roy B. Zuck (Grand Rapids: Baker Books, 1994), p. 84.

5. Thomas Ice, "Ezekiel 38 and 39, Part 1," www.pre-trib.org/data/pdf/Ice-(Part1)Ezekiel38&39.pdf.

6. See John F. Walvoord, *End Times* (Nashville: Word, 1998), p. 124.

7. Arnold Fruchtenbaum, *The Footsteps of the Messiah* (San Antonio: Ariel Ministries, 2004), pp. 118-19.

8. Mark Hitchcock, *Iran: The Coming Crisis* (Colorado Springs: Multnomah Books, 2006), pp. 182-84.

9. J. Dwight Pentecost, *Things to Come* (Grand Rapids: Zondervan, 1965), p. 352.

10. Pentecost, "Where Do the Events of Ezekiel 38–39 Fit into the Prophetic Picture?"

11. Ralph H. Alexander, "A Fresh Look at Ezekiel 38 and 39," *Journal of the Evangelical Theological Society* 17 (Summer 1974), pp. 157-69.

12. J. Paul Tanner, "Rethinking Ezekiel's Invasion by Gog," *Journal of the Evangelical Theological Society* 39, no. 1 (March 1996), pp. 29-46, www.etsjets.org/files/JETS-PDFs/39/39-1/39-1-pp029-046_JETS.pdf.

13. Mark Hitchcock, *Bible Prophecy* (Wheaton: Tyndale House, 1999), pp. 214-15.

14. Alexander, "A Fresh Look at Ezekiel 38 and 39."

Chapter 8: The Case for Pretribulationism

1. See John F. Walvoord, *The Rapture Question* (Grand Rapids: Zondervan, 1979); J. Dwight Pentecost, *Things to Come* (Grand Rapids: Zondervan, 1965); Charles C. Ryrie, *The Basis of Premillennial Faith* (Dubuque: Loizeaux Brothers, 1981).

2. Renald Showers, *Maranatha: Our Lord Come!* (Bellmawr: Friends of Israel, 1995), p. 214.

3. Arnold Fruchtenbaum, *The Footsteps of the Messiah* (San Antonio: Ariel Ministries, 2004), np.

4. Cited in Showers, *Maranatha: Our Lord Come!*, p. 197. See also Ron Rhodes, *Five Views on the Rapture: What You Need to Know* (Eugene: Harvest House, 2011).

5. Showers, *Maranatha: Our Lord Come!*, p. 128.

Chapter 9: The Case for Midtribulationism

1. See J. Oliver Buswell, *Systematic Theology of the Christian Religion* (Grand Rapids: Zondervan,

1962); Merrill C. Tenney, *Interpreting Revelation* (Grand Rapids: Eerdmans, 1988); Gleason L. Archer et al., *Three Views on the Rapture* (Grand Rapids: Zondervan, 1966).

2. See Herman Hoyt, *The End Times* (Chicago: Moody Press, 1969), p. 82; Robert Lightner, *The Last Days Handbook* (Nashville: Thomas Nelson, 1990), p. 66.

3. Charles C. Ryrie, *Basic Theology* (Chicago: Moody, 1999), p. 581. See also Ron Rhodes, *Five Views of the Rapture: What You Need to Know* (Eugene: Harvest House, 2011).

4. Hoyt, *The End Times*, p. 83.

Chapter 10: The Case for Posttribulationism

1. See George Eldon Ladd, *The Blessed Hope: A Biblical Study of the Second Advent and the Rapture* (Grand Rapids: Eerdmans, 1955); Robert Gundry, *The Church and the Tribulation: A Biblical Examination of Posttribulationism* (Grand Rapids: Zondervan, 2010); Alexander Reese, *The Approaching Advent of Christ* (Grand Rapids: Grand Rapids International, 1975).

2. Charles C. Ryrie, *Basic Theology* (Chicago: Moody, 1999), np.

3. See Ron Rhodes, *Five Views of the Rapture: What You Need to Know* (Eugene: Harvest House, 2011).

Chapter 11: The Case for the Pre-wrath View

1. Robert Van Kampen, *The Rapture Question Answered* (Grand Rapids: Revell, 1997); Marvin Rosenthal, *Prewrath Rapture of the Church* (Nashville: Thomas Nelson, 1990).

2. See John F. Walvoord, *The Rapture Question* (Grand Rapids: Zondervan, 1979); J. Dwight Pentecost, *Things to Come* (Grand Rapids: Zondervan, 1965); Charles C. Ryrie, *The Basis of Premillennial Faith* (Dubuque: Loizeaux Brothers, 1981).

3. Norman Geisler, *Church / Last Things*, vol. 4 of *Systematic Theology* (Minneapolis: Bethany House, 2005), np.

Chapter 12: The Case for the Partial Rapture View

1. See, for example, Robert Govett, *Robert Govett on Revelation* (Haysville: Schoettle, 2010); Joseph A. Seiss, *The Apocalypse: Lectures on the Book of Revelation* (New York: Cosimo Classics, 2007).

2. Thomas Waugh, *When Jesus Comes* (London: Charles Kelly, 1901), p. 108.

3. See Ron Rhodes, *Fives Views of the Rapture: What You Need to Know* (Eugene: Harvest House, 2011); Ron Rhodes, *Dictionary of Bible Prophecy* (Eugene: Harvest House, 2010), q.v. "Partial Rapture."

4. Herman Hoyt, *The End Times* (Chicago: Moody Press, 1969), p. 91.

Chapter 13: Which Interpretive Model Is Correct?

1. Bernard Ramm, *Protestant Bible Interpretation* (Grand Rapids: Baker, 1978), p. 105.

2. J.I. Packer, *"Fundamentalism" and the Word of God* (Grand Rapids: Eerdmans, 1958), p. 102.

3. John F. Walvoord, "Revelation," in *Bible Knowledge Commentary*, New Testament edition, ed. John F. Walvoord and Roy B. Zuck (Wheaton: Victor Books, 1983), p. 926.

4. Alan Johnson, *Revelation*, vol. 12 of *The Expositor's Bible Commentary*, ed. Frank E. Gaebelein (Grand Rapids: Zondervan, 1981), p. 410.

5. George Eldon Ladd, *A Theology of the New Testament*, ed. Donald A. Hagner (Grand Rapids: Eerdmans, 1993), p. 672.

6. See David Chilton, *The Days of Vengeance: An Exposition of the Book of Revelation* (Waterbury Center: Dominion Press, 2006).

7. See, for example, Hank Hanegraaff, *The Apocalypse Code: Find Out What the Bible REALLY Says About the End Times...and Why It Matters Today* (Nashville: Thomas Nelson, 2010); Gary DeMar, *Last Days Madness: Obsession of the Modern Church* (Atlanta: American Vision, 1999).

8. Charles C. Ryrie, *The Basis of the Premillennial Faith* (Dubuque: ECS Ministries, 2005), np.

Chapter 14: How Does Daniel's Seventieth Week Relate to the Book of Revelation?

1. Robert Jamieson, A.R. Fausset, and David Brown, *Commentary Critical and Explanatory on the Whole Bible* (Hartford: S.S. Scranton, 1871), p. 641.

2. Matthew Henry, *Matthew Henry's Commentary on the Whole Bible*, vol. 4, Isaiah to Malachi (New York: Revell, 1712), pp. 1094-1095.

3. John F. Walvoord and Roy B. Zuck, "Additional Commentary on Daniel 9:25-27," in *The Bible Knowledge Commentary*, Old Testament edition, ed. John F. Walvoord and Roy B. Zuck (Wheaton: Victor Books, 1983), p. 1362.

Chapter 15: Can We Identify Babylon?

1. See Mark Hitchcock, *101 Answers to the Most Asked Questions About the End Times* (Sisters, OR: Multnomah Books, 2001), pp. 58-62.

2. Gary DeMar, *Last Days Madness: Obsession of the Modern Church* (Atlanta: American Vision, 1999), p. 358.

3. See, for example, *Adam Clarke's Commentary on the Bible* (Grand Rapids: Baker, 1983).

4. J. Massyngberde Ford, *Revelation*, vol. 38 of *The Anchor Bible*, ed. William Foxwell Albright and David Noel Freedman (Garden City: Doubleday, 1975), pp. 54-56, 93, 259-307.

5. Thomas Ice, "Babylon in Bible Prophecy," www.raptureready.com/featured/ice/BabylonIn BibleProphecy.html.

Chapter 16: Who Are the 144,000, and What Is Their Ministry?

1. Alan F. Johnson, "Revelation," in *Hebrews Through Revelation*, ed. Frand E. Gaebelein, vol. 12 of *The Expositor's Bible Commentary* (Grand Rapids: Zondervan, 1982), see note at Revelation 7:4.

2. Matthew Henry, *Matthew Henry's Concise Commentary on the Whole Bible* (Nashville: Thomas Nelson, 2003), see note at Revelation 7:4.

3. *The ESV Study Bible* (Wheaton: Crossway, 2008). See note at Revelation 7:4-8.

4. Thomas Constable, "Notes on Galatians," in *Constable's Expository Notes on the Bible*, www.sonic light.com/constable/notes/pdf/galatians.pdf, see notes on Galatians 3:29.

5. Constable, "Notes on Galatians."

6. God has had His faithful remnant in all ages. For example, though the time of Elijah was characterized by great apostasy, 1 Kings 19:18 indicates that God had 7000 people who were yet faithful to Him (see also Isaiah 1:9; 4:3; 11:16; Jeremiah 6:9; Ezekiel 14:22; Micah 2:12; Romans 9:27; 11:5). During the tribulation period, the faithful remnant of Jews will include the 144,000 Jewish witnesses (Revelation 7) as well as God's two prophetic witnesses (Revelation 11).

7. Dr. Pentecost mentioned this during his course on Revelation at Dallas Theological Seminary, 1981.

Chapter 17: Who Are the Two Witnesses?

1. John Gill, "Revelation 11," in *John Gill's Exposition on the Whole Bible*, www.studylight.org/com/geb/view.cgi?bk=65&ch=11. See notes at verse 3.

2. Leon Morris, *Revelation*, vol. 20 of *Tyndale New Testament Commentaries*, ed. Leon Morris (Downers Grove: IVP Academic, 2008). See notes on Revelation 11:3.

3. Kenneth L. Barker et al., eds., *The Expositor's Bible Commentary*, abridged ed., vol. 2 (Grand Rapids: Zondervan, 2004). See notes on Revelation 11:3.

4. *The ESV Study Bible* (Wheaton: Crossway, 2008). See notes at Revelation 11:3.

Chapter 18: Who Restrains the Antichrist?

1. Thomas Constable, "2 Thessalonians," in *The Bible Knowledge Commentary*, New Testament edition, ed. John F. Walvoord and Roy B. Zuck (Wheaton: Victor Books, 1983). See notes at 2 Thessalonians 2:7.

2. Paul Feinberg, "2 Thessalonians 2 and the Rapture," in *When the Trumpet Sounds*, ed. Thomas Ice and Timothy Demy (Eugene: Harvest House, 1995), p. 307.

3. Arnold G. Fruchtenbaum, *The Footsteps of the Messiah* (San Antonio: Ariel Ministries, 2003), np.

4. Fruchtenbaum, *The Footsteps of the Messiah*.

5. Feinberg, "2 Thessalonians 2 and the Rapture," p. 307.

6. Feinberg, "2 Thessalonians 2 and the Rapture," p. 307.

7. Thomas Constable, "2 Thessalonians," in *The Bible Knowledge Commentary*, ed. John F. Walvoord and Roy B. Zuck (Wheaton: SP Publications 1983), p. 719.

8. Tim LaHaye and Ed Hindson, eds., *The Popular Bible Prophecy Commentary* (Eugene: Harvest House, 2006), p. 455.

9. Mal Couch, "Restrainer," in *The Popular Encyclopedia of Bible Prophecy*, ed. Tim LaHaye and Ed Hindson (Eugene: Harvest House, 2004), p. 325.

10. Mark Hitchcock, *Is the Antichrist Alive Today?* (Colorado Springs: Multnomah, 2002), p. 83.

11. Couch, "Restrainer," p. 325.

12. Cited in David Jeremiah, *The Coming Economic Armageddon* (New York: Faith Words, 2010), p. 114.

Chapter 19: Is the Antichrist a Muslim?

1. Joel Richardson and Joseph Farah are two of the proponents of this theory with whom I've communicated.

2. The brief summary that follows is based in part on the research of my friend David R. Reagan, who presented a paper titled "The Muslim Antichrist Theory: An Evaluation" at the annual Pre-Trib Conference in Dallas, Texas, in December 2010. A transcript is available online at lamblion.com/articles/articles_islam6.php.

3. Sharia is the moral code and religious law of Islam.

4. Joel Richardson, *The Islamic Antichrist* (Los Angeles: WND Books, 2009), pp. 171-75.

5. Richardson, *The Islamic Antichrist*, p. 50.

6. Reagan, "The Muslim Antichrist Theory: An Evaluation."

7. Kenneth Boa, *Cults, World Religions, and You* (Wheaton: Victor Books, 1979), p. 49.

8. See Ron Rhodes, *Reasoning from the Scriptures with Muslims* (Eugene: Harvest House, 2002), pp. 36-37.

9. Cited in Reagan, "The Muslim Antichrist Theory: An Evaluation." See also Ron Rhodes, *The 10 Things You Need to Know About Islam* (Eugene: Harvest House, 2007), pp. 43, 106.

10. Consider Iranian president Mahmoud Ahmadinejad's 2006 quote of Khomeini that "the occupation regime over Jerusalem should vanish from the page of time." See "Israel's Deputy Prime Minister Admits Ahmadinejad Never Said Israel Should Be 'Wiped Off the Face of the Map,'" *Common Dreams*, April 18, 2012, www.commondreams.org/headline/2012/04/18-2.

11. Richardson, *The Islamic Antichrist*, pp. 182-83.

12. Richardson, *The Islamic Antichrist*, p. 184.

13. Richardson, *The Islamic Antichrist*, pp. 182-83.

Chapter 20: Is the Antichrist a Jew or a Gentile?

1. Larry Witham, "Falwell Angers Jews with Antichrist Talk," *The Washington Times*, January 20, 1999.

2. Cited in Witham, "Falwell Angers Jews with Antichrist Talk."

3. Chana Shavelson, "Jews, Christians Speak Out After Falwell's Assertion That Antichrist Is Jewish Man," *The Jewish Advocate*, March 25, 2011.

4. Associated Press, "Falwell Says Christ Will Return Soon, Antichrist Is Jewish, May Be Alive Now," *The Virginian-Pilot*, January 16, 1999.

5. Cited in Thomas Ice, "The Ethnicity of the Antichrist," Rapture Ready, www.raptureready.com/featured/ice/TheEthnicityofTheAntichrist.html.

6. Charles Hodge, *Systematic Theology* (Peabody: Hendriksen, 1999), np.

7. Arthur W. Pink, *The Antichrist: A Study of Satan's Christ* (Blacksburg: Wilder, 2008), p. 28.

8. Grant R. Jeffrey, *Prince of Darkness: Antichrist and the New World Order* (Toronto: Frontier Research Publications, 1994), p. 39.

9. Pink, *The Antichrist*, p. 29.

10. Hodge, *Systematic Theology*.

11. David Parsons, "The Antichrist," *The Jerusalem Post*, January 24, 1999.

12. Hodge, *Systematic Theology*.

13. See David Reagan, "The Rise and Fall of the Antichrist," Rapture Ready, www.raptureready.com/featured/reagan/dr33.html.

14. Robert H. Mounce, *The Book of Revelation*, vol. 18 of *The New International Commentary on the New Testament*, ed. Gorden Fee and Joel Green (Grand Rapids: Eerdmans, 1977), pp. 169-70.

15. Arnold Fruchtenbaum, *The Nationality of the Anti-Christ* (Englewood: American Board of Missions to the Jews, n.d.), pp. 24, 26.

Chapter 21: Will the Antichrist Be Killed and Resurrected?

1. Tim LaHaye and Jerry Jenkins, *Are We Living in the End Times?* (Wheaton: Tyndale House, 1999), p. 281.

2. Henry Morris, "Biblical Naturalism and Modern Science," *Bibliotheca Sacra* 125 (July–September 1968), pp. 195-204.

3. John A. Witmer, "The Doctrine of Miracles," *Bibliotheca Sacra* 130 (April 1973), pp. 126-34.

4. Charles C. Ryrie, *Balancing the Christian Life* (Chicago: Moody Press, 1978), p. 124.

5. Charles C. Ryrie, *A Survey of Bible Doctrine* (Chicago: Moody Press, 1980), p. 94.

6. Charles C. Ryrie, *Basic Theology* (Wheaton: Victor Books, 1986), p. 147.

7. Ryrie, *Balancing the Christian Life*, p. 124.

8. Paul Enns, *The Moody Handbook of Theology*, rev. ed. (Chicago: Moody Press, 1989), p. 297.

9. Walter K. Price, *The Coming Antichrist* (Neptune: Loizeaux Brothers, 1985), p. 145.

10. Price, *The Coming Antichrist*, pp. 146-47.

11. Mark Hitchcock, *The Complete Book of Bible Prophecy* (Wheaton: Tyndale House, 1999), pp. 199-200.

Chapter 22: What Is the Mark of the Beast?

1. Thomas Ice and Timothy Demy, *The Coming Cashless Society* (Eugene: Harvest House, 1996), pp. 125-26.

2. Cited in Thomas Ice and Timothy Demy, *Fast Facts on Bible Prophecy from A to Z* (Eugene: Harvest House, 2004), p. 129.

3. John MacArthur, *The MacArthur Study Bible* (Nashville: Thomas Nelson, 2003), np.

4. David Jeremiah, *The Coming Economic Armageddon: What Bible Prophecy Warns About the New Global Economy* (New York: FaithWords, 2010), p. 146.

5. John F. Walvoord, "Revelation," in *The Bible Knowledge Commentary*, New Testament edition, ed. John F. Walvoord and Roy B. Zuck (Wheaton: Victor books, 1983), p. 963.

6. Thomas Constable, "Constable's Notes on Revelation," in *Constable's Expository Notes on the Bible*, soniclight.com/constable/notes/pdf/revelation.pdf.

7. John F. Walvoord, *The Final Drama: Fourteen Keys to Understanding the Prophetic Scriptures* (Grand Rapids: Kregel, 1997), p. 125.

8. Ice and Demy, *The Coming Cashless Society*, p. 132.

9. Jeremiah, *The Coming Economic Armageddon*, pp. 163-64.

Chapter 23: The Case for Amillennialism

1. See Anthony A. Hoekema, *The Bible and the Future* (Grand Rapids: Eerdmans, 1994); Oswald T. Allis, *Prophecy and the Church* (Eugene: Wipf & Stock, 2001).

2. Some amillennialists do not like this label and suggest other terms, such as *realized millennialism*, to indicate that they do not deny a millennium but simply believe it is fulfilled entirely in the present age as Christ rules from heaven.

3. Cited in Robert Lightner, *Handbook of Evangelical Theology: A Historical, Biblical, and Contemporary Survey and Review* (Grand Rapids: Baker, 1995), p. 269.

4. See Charles C. Ryrie, *Basic Theology: A Popular Systematic Guide to Understanding Biblical Truth* (Chicago: Moody Press, 1999), np.

Chapter 24: The Case for Postmillennialism

1. Cited in Charles C. Ryrie, *Basic Theology: A Popular Systematic Guide to Understanding Biblical Truth* (Chicago: Moody Press, 1999), p. 511.

2. See Paul Enns, *The Moody Handbook of Theology*, rev. ed. (Chicago: Moody Press, 1989), p. 408; Ryrie, *Basic Theology*, chapter 78.

3. Charles C. Ryrie, *A Survey of Bible Doctrine* (Chicago: Moody Press, 1972), p. 163.

4. See Loraine Boettner, *Millennium* (Phillipsburg: Presbyterian and Reformed, 1990).

5. Enns, *The Moody Handbook of Theology*, p. 370.

Chapter 25: The Case for Premillennialism

1. See John F. Walvoord, *The Millennial Kingdom* (Grand Rapids: Zondervan, 1975); see also Charles C. Ryrie, *Dispensationalism Today* (Chicago: Moody, 1965).

2. See George Eldon Ladd, *The Blessed Hope: A Biblical Study of the Second Advent and the Rapture* (Grand Rapids: Eerdmans, 1990).

3. Paul Enns, *The Moody Handbook of Theology*, rev. ed. (Chicago: Moody Press, 1989), pp. 418-19.

4. See, for example, John Nelson Darby, *Notes on the Book of Revelation* (Whitefish, MT: Kessinger, 2009); Lewis Sperry Chafer, *Systematic Theology* (Grand Rapids: Kregel, 1993).

Chapter 26: Yes, Set Dates

1. Charles Berlitz, *Doomsday 1999 AD* (New York: Doubleday & Company, 1981), p. 9.

2. Based on Berlitz, *Doomsday 1999 AD*, and Frederick H. Marten, *The Story of Human Life*; cited in *Critique* 31 (June–September 1989), p. 65.

3. For example, see Bill Lawren, "Are You Ready for Millennial Fever?" *Utne Reader 38* (March–April 1990); Stanley Young, "An Overview of the End," *Critique* 31 (June-September 1989), pp. 28-31.

4. Note that most of the accounts of the turbulence and panic that accompanied the arrival of AD 1000 come indirectly from the *Histories of Raoul Glaber*, a Burgundian monk born in the late tenth century.

5. Russell Chandler, *Doomsday: The End of the World* (Ann Arbor: Servant, 1993), p. 54.

6. See Chandler, *Doomsday*, p. 52.

7. Yuri Rubinsky and Ian Wiseman, *A History of the End of the World* (New York: William Morrow, 1982), p. 66.

8. Chandler, *Doomsday*, p. 54.

9. Chandler, *Doomsday*, p. 54.

10. Louis Berkhof, *The History of Christian Doctrines* (Grand Rapids: Baker, 1981), p. 263.

11. Philip Schaff, *History of the Christian Church*, vol. 2 (Grand Rapids: Eerdmans, 1994), p. 348.

12. Stanley J. Grenz, *The Millennial Maze: Sorting Out Evangelical Options* (Downers Grove: InterVarsity, 1992), p. 14.

13. Grenz, *The Millennial Maze*, p. 44.

14. Henri Focillon, *The Year 1000* (New York: Frederick Ungar, 1969), pp. 59-60.

15. See R. Gustav Niebuhr, "Millennium Fever: Prophets Proliferate, The End Is Near," *Wall Street Journal*, December 5, 1989, A5.

16. Cited in Grenz, *The Millennial Maze*, p. 19.

17. Grenz, *The Millennial Maze*, p. 22.

18. Chandler, *Doomsday*, p. 60.

19. Chandler, *Doomsday*, p. 67.

20. John Hogue, "The Millennium: The Last Predictions—Nostradamus and our Future," *Critique* 31, p. 43.

21. Cited in Chandler, *Doomsday*, p. 62.

22. Cited in Lawren, "Are You Ready for Millennial Fever?" p. 96.

23. David Spangler, *Emergence: The Rebirth of the Sacred* (New York: Dell, 1984), p. 19.

24. Ascended Masters are believed to be formerly historical persons who have finished their earthly evolutions by means of reincarnation. As these Ascended Masters continue in their own evolution toward the godhead, they voluntarily help lesser-evolved humans to reach the Masters' present level. These Masters allegedly give revelations to spiritually attuned human beings.

25. Cited in John Dart, "Sect Leader Continues to Spread Word Despite Uproar over Forecasts," *Los Angeles Times*, February 23, 1991, F20.

26. See Ron Rhodes, "What's New in the Headlines?" *Christian Research Newsletter*, vol. 3, no. 3, p. 6.

27. Cited in Timothy Egan, "Guru's Bomb Shelter Hits Legal Snag," *New York Times*, April 24, 1990, A8.

28. William Alnor, *Soothsayers of the Second Advent* (Grand Rapids: Eerdmans, 1989), p. 31.

29. Alnor, *Soothsayers of the Second Advent*, p. 33.

30. Cited in Alnor, *Soothsayers of the Second Advent*, p. 29.

31. Alnor, *Soothsayers of the Second Advent*, p. 31.

32. Cited in Perucci Ferraiuolo, "Could '1994' Be the End of Family Radio?" *Christian Research Journal* (Summer 1993), p. 5.

33. Cited in Ferraiuolo, "Could '1994' Be the End of Family Radio?" p. 5.

34. Harold Camping, *Open Forum* program, September 4, 1992.

35. Harold Camping, *1994?* (Burlington: Vantage Press, 1992), p. xvi.

36. Mary Stewart Relfe, *Economic Advisor*, February 28, 1983.

37. Lester Sumrall, *I Predict 2000 AD* (South Bend: Sumrall, 1987), p. 74.

Chapter 27: No, Don't Set Dates

1. See Ron Rhodes, "How, Then, Should We Live?" in *Northern Storm Rising* (Eugene: Harvest House, 2008).

2. For example, see Gerald A. Larue, "Survival in the Apocalyptic Era: A Humanist Prescription for Countering Biblical Apocalypticism," *The Humanist* (September–October 1987), p. 11.

Postscript: Debate but Don't Divide

1. J.C. Ryle, *Holiness* (Moscow, ID: Charles Nolan, 2001), p. xxiii.

2. Ryle, *Holiness*, p. xv.

3. J.I. Packer, *Serving the People of God* (Great Britain: Paternoster Press, 1998), p. 23.

Other Great Harvest House Books by Ron Rhodes

Books About the Bible

- The Big Book of Bible Answers
- Bite-Size Bible® Answers
- Bite-Size Bible® Charts
- Bite-Size Bible® Definitions
- Bite-Size Bible® Handbook
- Commonly Misunderstood Bible Verses
- The Complete Guide to Bible Translations
- Find It Fast in the Bible
- The Popular Dictionary of Bible Prophecy
- Understanding the Bible from A to Z
- What Does the Bible Say About…?

Books About the End Times

- 40 Days Through Revelation
- Cyber Meltdown
- The End Times in Chronological Order
- Northern Storm Rising
- Unmasking the Antichrist

Books About Other Important Topics

- 5-Minute Apologetics for Today
- 1001 Unforgettable Quotes About God, Faith, and the Bible
- Angels Among Us
- Answering the Objections of Atheists, Agnostics, and Skeptics
- Christianity According to the Bible
- The Complete Guide to Christian Denominations
- Find It Quick Handbook on Cults and New Religions
- The Truth Behind Ghosts, Mediums, and Psychic Phenomena
- What Happens After Life?
- Why Do Bad Things Happen If God Is Good?
- The Wonder of Heaven

The 10 Most Important Things Series

- The 10 Most Important Things You Can Say to a Catholic
- The 10 Most Important Things You Can Say to a Jehovah's Witness
- The 10 Most Important Things You Can Say to a Mason
- The 10 Most Important Things You Can Say to a Mormon
- The 10 Things You Need to Know About Islam
- The 10 Things You Should Know About the Creation vs. Evolution Debate

Quick Reference Guides

- Halloween: What You Need to Know
- Islam: What You Need to Know
- Jehovah's Witnesses: What You Need to Know

The Reasoning from the Scriptures Series

- Reasoning from the Scriptures with Catholics
- Reasoning from the Scriptures with the Jehovah's Witnesses
- Reasoning from the Scriptures with Masons
- Reasoning from the Scriptures with Muslims
- Reasoning from the Scriptures with the Mormons

Little Books

- The Little Book About God
- The Little Book About Heaven
- The Little Book About the Bible

To learn more about Harvest House books and
to read sample chapters, visit our website:

www.harvesthousepublishers.com

HARVEST HOUSE PUBLISHERS
EUGENE, OREGON